STREETWISE

FINANCE &
ACCOUNTING

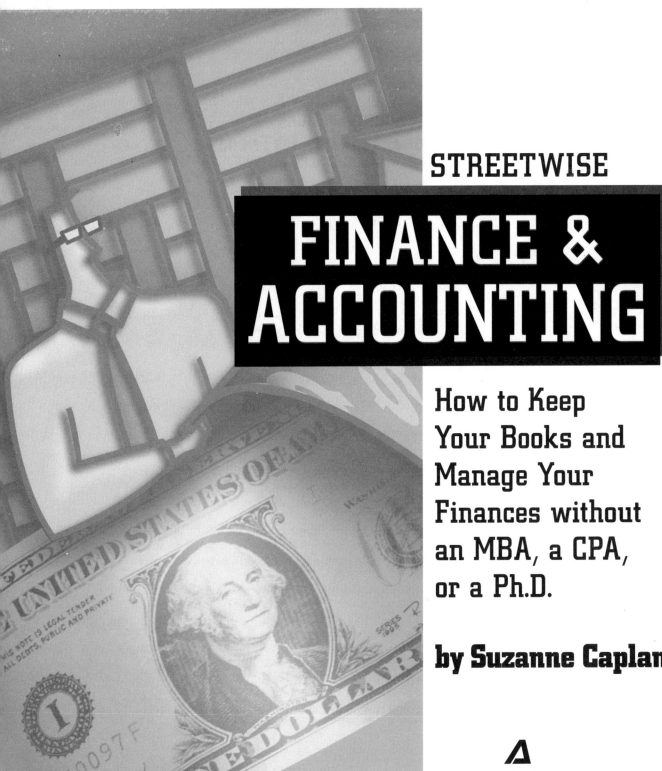

STREETWISE

FINANCE & ACCOUNTING

How to Keep
Your Books and
Manage Your
Finances without
an MBA, a CPA,
or a Ph.D.

by Suzanne Caplan

Adams Media Corporation
Holbrook, Massachusetts

To Tom Nunnally
Enterprise Bank
Mentor and Proudly, My Friend

Published by Adams Media Corporation
260 Center Street, Holbrook, MA 02343

ISBN: 1-58062-196-1

Printed in the United States of America.

J   I   H   G   F   E   D   C   B   A

Library of Congress Cataloging-in-Publication Data
is available from publisher.

This publication is designed to provide accurate and authoritative information with regard to the subject matter covered. It is sold with the understanding that the publisher is not engaged in rendering legal, accounting, or other professional advice. If legal advice or other expert assistance is required, the services of a competent professional person should be sought.
— From a *Declaration of Principles* jointly adopted by a Committee of the American Bar Association and a Committee of Publishers and Associations

Illustration by Eric Mueller.

This book is available at quantity discounts for bulk purchases.
For information, call 1-800-872-5627.

Visit our exciting small business Web site: www.businesstown.com

Contents

Part III: Setting Budgets and Controlling Costs

Part IV: The Source and Use of Capital

Part V: Strategic Planning by the Numbers

CONTENTS

PART VI: PROBLEM SOLVING BY THE NUMBERS

PART VII: KEEPING WHAT YOU EARNED

Acknowledgments

This would never have become a book without Sherry Truesdell, whose organizational talents have made a major contribution to my work. I am grateful. To my agent and friend, Laurie Harper, this road has been a challenge, and you have been steadfast at my side. You are valued.

To the dedicated folks at the Small Business Development Centers throughout the United States, you are my heroes, especially Catherine Kunzak in Pittsburgh and Mildred Holley in Little Rock. The courageous business owners I have met and worked with have taught me much about the drive and commitment we all need to be successful.

And to my editor, Jere Calmes, who helped keep the focus on providing all that the reader needed to become skilled at financial management, this work has benefited from your suggestions.

And to the people who tolerate me when I am in the middle of a book—you are the light at the end of my tunnel.

The success of any business depends on a number of critical factors, some of which may be more readily evident to you than others. What probably most easily comes to your mind is the sales and marketing of your company's products or services. After all, you must have customers in order to stay in business, so finding these potential buyers and meeting their needs is a very critical element. Meeting both the needs and the expectations of your customers is a function of the second factor, operations of your company. Do you produce and deliver the goods and services timely, in quality condition and with service that is efficient and pleasant? Let's assume that you have customers and they are, for the most part, satisfied. Is your role with the company complete? Not quite.

A banker friend of mine compares a business to a three-legged stool—one leg is sales, one is operations, and the third is finance. If any of these legs is shorter than the others, the stool will wobble and may very easily tip over. In many small and midsize companies, the financial management issues are completed by an outside accountant and reviewed minimally by the owner or manager or, worse yet, not at all. Decisions are based on the requirements of sales effort and the operating needs, and not driven at all by financial considerations. I see this every day in my consulting practice.

Why does this happen? Because the accounting and financial management is a detail function often handled by professionals who don't communicate well in a language other than "accountanteeze." And they are speaking to owners or managers who are often unknowledgeable about debits and credits and aren't sure what the questions should be, much less the answers. A common understanding is critical for any nonfinancial executive, and the mission of this book is to create the framework for this understanding.

> Accountants and business owners must find a common language.

Why You Must Understand Financial Reporting

Chances are that you are not doing any of the day-to-day accounting and this is a job you willingly have assigned to someone else. You do not even oversee the work as it is passed on to the company accountant in various forms such as a trial balance or monthend statement. These are reviewed for accuracy, and then you may be given copies. If they don't come accompanied with dire warnings, you pay little attention, so why change that now? The following are four major reasons to encourage you to learn and even master the financial management aspect of your business:

- The bottom line is the bottom line.
  Sales growth is important, as is new product development and efficient operations. But profits are always derived when the selling price exceeds the costs, and this information is found in detail on a profit and loss statement. The real insights are in the details, and the only way to find the information you require is to understand how a profit and loss statement is created. You can't improve the bottom line if you don't know what is impacting it.
- Financial management is critical to the planning process. You can operate your business for a limited time on good instincts, but in order to successfully plan for future growth and stability, your financial resources must be considered. Setting goals and determining budgets are signs of a healthy company since these are key elements of good financial management.
- To be knowledgeable is to be in control.
  Most business owners will be required to meet from time to time with bankers to review the progress and the needs of the company. Handing over a report that you do not understand does not build confidence in your banker, nor does being asked questions that you cannot answer. Although you might be able to defer to your accountant, the best impression will be left by you if you are in command of the information. For nonowners, understanding the financial details of the business is crucial to their success as well. Those in sales must understand the cost issues of their product or services in order to conduct effective negotiations with customers. Operations people are always looking for ways to make their jobs easier and more efficient, and many of these ideas

> Setting goals and determining budgets are signs of a healthy company since these are key elements of good financial management.

require capital. Understanding the budgetary realities as well as the cash flow issues can help them plan for well-timed requests.

- Unexpected surprises can destroy a business.
  Any owner or manager who pays attention to reports *only* when they are accompanied by dire warnings may well be acting too late. Once a financial crunch has begun, great effort must be expended in trying to change the circumstance. This is energy that needs to be used in other aspects of the business such as marketing and operations, and they will begin suffering by the neglect. Knowing how to monitor your business's financial position on an ongoing basis is the most effective way to manage the company successfully.

> Those in sales must understand the cost issues of their product or services in order to conduct effective negotiations with customers.

Financial Management Begins with Accounting

You need not acquire the expertise of an accountant or bookkeeper, but you will want to know how the system works. The origin of the numbers that go into income and expense accounts are an important feature of your system. How debits and credits work and how they track will aid in your overall understanding. This book is intended to give you the basic details of your accounting system.

We will start with the general ledgers that track all transactions that are made, and continue to learn about the chart of accounts that are established and how entries track through the whole system. How income becomes cash or accounts receivable and how expense is allocated will also be covered. Some specific issues such as accrual versus cash basis accounting will be explained clearly enough for any nonprofessional to comprehend fully.

Step Two Is Learning How to Read Reports

A number of different reports are generated on a monthly basis that must be understood and used. The most critical one is a profit and loss statement that will tell you how the company is performing. The balance sheet that accompanies this report will signal changes in financial condition. Also available are reports showing actual cash flow, meaning how much cash was available and how was it used. Cash flow projection can be used to create budgets. Payable and receivable agings are important managerial tools as well.

You will learn to use these tools as guidelines for setting budgets, and these budgets will be your primary aid in controlling your costs. You must have a projection of the available resources before you can plan to use those resources. In Section IV, we will cover the source and use of capital so that you can increase your knowledge of the various ways money flows into your business and what source you should plan on to meet the cash needs of your operation. There is a skill here that you will want to master.

Financial Knowledge Is Power

The last three sections of this book are meant to show you how to take what you have learned and put it to operational use beginning with strategic business planning. Learning how to make decisions that include *all* business considerations, marketing, operations, *and* finance, will surely enhance the profitability of your venture.

Let's take, for example, setting prices. The marketing aspect is driven by the need to be competitive, and the operational aspect is often driven by capacity needs or availability (such as attracting new business for slow times). The financial aspect must be driven by considerations about costs, that is, making sure they are covered but also having sufficient knowledge about the advantage (or, perhaps, disadvantage) of high volume. Many times there is an economy of scale in volume that allows flexibility in pricing. But you won't know this unless you master the financial side of your business.

Allowing the accounting functions to be done only by your bookkeeper, controller, or accountant without your understanding will deny you one of the strongest tools you need to build a successful venture, namely, how to make decisions that positively impact profitability and cash flow. Good planning may prevent future difficulties.

> Allowing the accounting functions to be done only by your bookkeeper, controller, or accountant without your understanding will deny you one of the strongest tools you need to build a successful venture.

However, should problems occur such as a general economic slowdown or pressures on your pricing created by aggressive competition, you will be able to problem-solve using your basic accounting and financial management skills. You will learn how to spot trouble signs before they become threatening and what steps to take. This book will cover increasing cash flow by aggressive collection techniques as well as well-planned asset sales. And should circumstances become more serious, we have also covered turnaround techniques.

And finally, it is not how much you make but how much you keep that really matters, and we will cover strategies ranging from the profitable use of excess cash to exit strategies. This book is meant to impact your personal financial health as well as your business.

Finance Can Be Fun

I have been speaking to and consulting with small business owners for more than 20 years, and during much of that time, I was also operating my own small manufacturing company. I know that the accounting side has often been viewed as both boring and confusing. I am including a glossary to clarify terms but also want you to understand that numbers tell a story, and when you learn how to read that story, it is far more interesting than you might have imagined. After all, you went into your own venture partly because of your personal competitiveness, and the numbers are how you keep score.

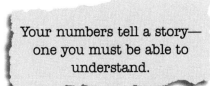

Your numbers tell a story— one you must be able to understand.

Keeping Track of Inflow and Outflow: Basic Accounting Practice

Summary of Part I

- **Understanding the language of accounting**
- **Creating your own record keeping system that gives you the most accurate data**
- **Tracing cash from income to expense**
- **Understanding the costs-of-doing business, those directly associated with a sale, and those that are overhead**

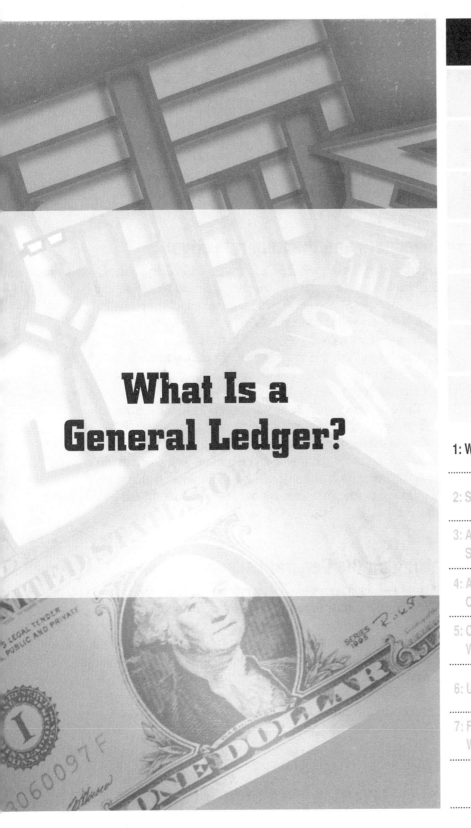

What Is a General Ledger?

The general ledger is the core of your company's financial records. These constitute the central "books" of your system, and every transaction flows through the general ledger. These records remain as a permanent track of the history of all financial transactions since day one of the life of your company.

Subledgers and the General Ledger

Your accounting system will have a number of subsidiary ledgers (called subledgers) for items such as cash, accounts receivable, and accounts payable. All the entries that are entered (called posted) to these subledgers will transact through the general ledger account. For example, when a credit sale posted in the account receivable subledger turns into cash due to a payment, the transaction will be posted to the general ledger and the two (cash and accounts receivable) subledgers as well.

There are times when items will go directly to the general ledger without any subledger posting. These are primarily capital financial transactions that have no operational subledgers. These may include items such as capital contributions, loan proceeds, loan repayments (principal), and proceeds from sale of assets. These items will be linked to your balance sheet but not to your profit and loss statement.

> The two primary financial documents of any company are the balance sheet and the profit and loss statement.

Setting up the General Ledger

There are two main issues to understand when setting up the general ledger. One is their linkage to your financial reports, and the other is the establishment of opening balances.

The two primary financial documents of any company are their balance sheet and the profit and loss statement, and both of these are drawn directly from the company's general ledger. The order of how the numerical balances appear is determined by the chart of accounts (which is covered in Chapter 2), but all entries that are entered will appear. The general ledger accrues the balances that make up the line items on these reports, and the changes are reflected in the profit and loss statement as well.

The opening balances that are established on your general ledgers may not always be zero as you might assume. On the asset side, you will have all tangible assets (the value of all machinery, equipment, and inventory) that is available as well as any cash that has been invested as working capital. On the liability side, you will have any bank (or stockholder) loans that were used, as well as trade credit or lease payments that you may have secured in order to start the company. You will also increase your stockholder equity in the amount you have invested, but not loaned to, the business.

The General Ledger Creates an Audit Trail

Don't let the word *audit* strike fear in your heart; I am not talking about a tax audit. Although, if you are called to respond to an outside audit for any reason, a well-maintained general ledger is essential.

But you will also want an internal trail of transaction so that you can trace any discrepancy (such as double billing or an unrecorded payment) through your own system. You must be able to find the origin of any transaction in order to verify its accuracy, and the general ledger is where you will do this.

Backup Documentation

The general ledger will tell you how and where the transaction came from, but you will need the original paperwork to establish the detail. Therefore, it is critical that you accurately file all the invoices and bills that were the source documents used in the journal entries. You will want to make your entry with an identifying number (such as invoice number, check number, or date) to make it easier to find the original. Equally important, you will want to create a special mark such as a distinctive red checkmark that will be put on each source document to establish that it has, in fact, been posted to the general ledger.

> But you will also want an internal trail of transaction so that you can trace any discrepancy (such as double billing or an unrecorded payment) through your own system.

Keeping the Ledgers in Balance

At the end of each month, a reconciliation known as a trial balance is created letting you (and your accountant) know that all the entries (debits and credits) are in balance. If one column is not equal to the other, it means that an item has been posted to one subledger but not the general ledger. You will review your general ledger to make a determination of which entry was not completed.

A computerized system will allow for an easily drawn trial balance, but it is a bit more time consuming on a manual system. Nevertheless, you should do this on a monthly basis since the fewer line items you must check for errors, the easier it will be.

> At the end of each month, a reconciliation known as a trial balance is created letting you (and your accountant) know that all the entries (debits and credits) are in balance.

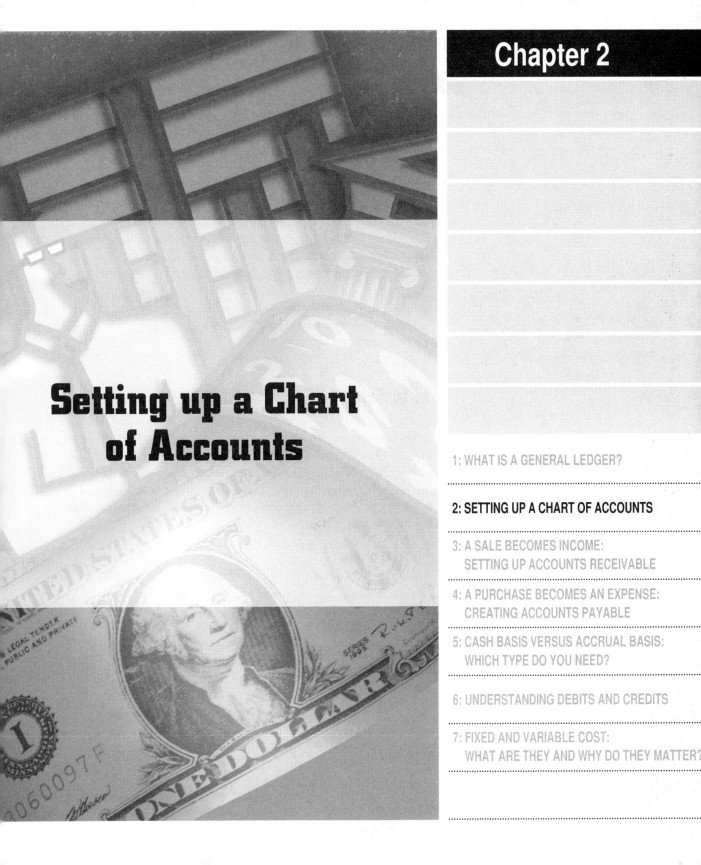

Chapter 2

Setting up a Chart of Accounts

Your financial records are meant to track all of your transactions for the purpose of keeping them in balance as well as providing useful data for management reports to taxing bodies and to use as decision-making tools. The chart of accounts is the key to this data.

What we are really looking at is a chart of account "numbers." If you were using a set of folders or even shoe boxes to hold receipts for the various transactions in your business, these account numbers would simply be the labels. There must be an account number that covers every type of transaction, including the source of your income and the type of expense you incur. At the end of any designated period (month, year), you will total the dollar amount in each category, and that will provide you with the numbers to create a tax return or a profit and loss statement.

> The accepted accounting method numbers them from 100 (or 1000) to 600 (or 6000).

How to Begin to Create a Chart of Accounts

First, you must learn the major categories that create the chart, and then you can work on the subheadings that will give you the detail you require. The accepted accounting method numbers them from 100 (or 1000) to 600 (or 6000). However, some packaged software uses 700 and 800 as well for the purposes of additional detail. It does not matter at all whether you use 100 or 1000. The meaning of each category is as follows:

100–Assets

This will include current assets such as cash and accounts receivable (which is considered to be liquid because it converts to cash as accounts are collected).

Current assets are numbered 110–149.

Fixed assets such as inventory, machinery and equipment, and real estate are numbered 150–199.

200–Liabilities

You will include current liabilities such as accounts payable, taxes due, and the current portion (one year's worth of payments) of any loan, and these will be numbered 210–249.

Your long-term liability such as the noncurrent portion of any loan and any other nonmaturing note will be numbered 250–299.

300—Equity Account

The amount of equity, meaning the difference between assets and liabilities, will be covered in this account number with one exception. Retained earnings have an account prefix of their own, 400.

400—Retained Earnings
500—Income

This is where you will categorize the various types of revenue that are received by your company that will be primarily income derived by sales. If you collect sales tax on certain types of sales but not all, here is where you can track that information so that you can easily report the numbers accurately.

The real use is as a management tool, which will be covered in greater detail a bit later in this chapter.

600–800—Expense

Each type of expense (material, labor, rent, utilities, and so on) will have its own account number. For the purpose of utilizing data for tax returns, separate accounts will be established for expenses that are not deductible such as payment of personal expense and the principal portion of any loan payments.

The use for management information will be covered later in this chapter.

> The real use is as a management tool.

Each Account Will Have a Name

Don't be concerned that you will have to memorize a series of numbers in order to record or understand the data that will be created by your chart of accounts. Along with each number, there is also a brief descriptive name that will be sufficient to tell the recorder and the reader what goes in that designated account.

For example, the income account is in the 500 category, but accounts may be broken out, as the following used for a shoe store:

501	Sales–leather sports shoes
502	Sales–walking shoes
503	Sales–sandals

Each category may have a subcategory as well, which gives greater detail such as sales by particular manufacturer. For example:

501-01	Sales–leather sports shoe–Analfi
501-02	Sales–leather sports shoe–Etienne Aigner
501-03	Sales–leather sports shoe–Kenneth Cole

> You can really create quite a large system that will give the most minute detail.

How Many Account Numbers Will Be Created?

That decision should be made by you in consultation with your company accountant as well as the internal controller or bookkeeper. You can really create quite a large system that will give the most minute detail. If you are doing it manually, the more account numbers, the longer it will take to do the day-to-day entry work. For those of you who are on an automated accounting system, the software you use may have limitations, but there should be more than enough numbers to provide the detail you will need.

If you are unsure in the beginning how many account numbers you will eventually want, don't be overly concerned because you will be able to add and change as the needs arise.

Who Should Create This Chart?

Most accountants, controllers, and some bookkeepers are perfectly comfortable setting up a chart of accounts–the broad categories are already established, and they will just follow a general formula. But it is really the input of management that will make this system generate information that has real value from an operational standpoint. You should know what detailed information would be useful in managing your business, and here is where you can arrange to have it compiled.

For example, on the income side, we are compiling data on the sales of your organization. You can plan inventory purchases, advertising focus, special sale periods, and even future directions for the business by knowing exactly what is selling and what is not. If you break down your sales income by specific product type, you can trace which items are not moving and plan a marketing effort or special sale to correct that.

On the other hand, if you see the growth in sales of a product line you weren't expecting to take off, you can focus more attention on encouraging this growth and plan increased inventory purchases as well. The amount of detail depends on the variety of product or services your business offers.

For some businesses, this detail is absolutely critical to their success. A restaurant, for instance, needs to know as much as it can about its sales broken out in categories such as food, beverages, lunches, and dinners. This information is important for staffing requirements as well as food purchases.

Expense Details Will Also Be Tracked by the Chart of Accounts

You will have expenses for material, labor, rent, utilities, office supplies, administrative help, and so on that will be deducted from your revenue to show if your company has produced a profit or a loss from conducting its business. The more detailed the information is, the greater control you can exercise over the operations to establish and maintain an acceptable level of profitability.

Let's assume you lump all of your labor into a single category and the number begins to grow as a percentage of sales. Your profits are going down and you want to investigate why. If you break down your payroll into subcategories and also use one for overtime expense, this will allow you to focus on a more exact cause of the rise in cost, and you will be able to take corrective action before it becomes a problem.

The following is the actual chart of accounts used by a plumbing contractor with a $2 million-plus business. The system is

> The more detailed the information is, the greater control you can exercise over the operations to establish and maintain an acceptable level of profitability.

computerized using Peachtree Accounting Software, and the chart was modified from their existing numbering systems. It does deviate from some other systems, as will other software packages.

Current Assets

10000	Petty Cash
10200	Citibank Checking Account
10600	Investments–Money Market
10700	Investments–Certificate of Deposit
10800	Citibank Checking–Interest Earned
11000	Accounts Receivable
11500	Allowance for Doubtful Accounts
12000	Inventory–Materials
14000	Prepaid Expenses
14100	Employee Advances
14200	Notes Receivable–Current
14300	Work in Progress
14550	Utility Deposit
14700	Other Current Assets

Long-Term Assets

15000	Furniture and Fixtures
15100	Equipment
15200	Automobiles
15400	Leasehold Improvements
15500	Buildings
15600	Building Improvements
16900	Land
17000	Accumulative Depreciation–Furniture
17100	Accumulative Depreciation–Equipment
17200	Accumulative Depreciation–Automobile
17300	Accumulative Depreciation–Other
17400	Accumulative Depreciation–Leasehold
17500	Accumulative Depreciation–Buildings
17600	Accumulative Deprec. –Building Improvements

> Current assets are those that will become cash within the year.

Current Liabilities

20000	Accounts Payable
23000	Accrued Expenses
23010	Accrued Rent
23100	Sales Tax Payable
23200	Wages Payable
23500	Federal Unemployment Tax
23510	Federal Income Tax
23600	State Payroll Taxes Payable
23610	State Unemployment Insurance
23800	Local Payroll Taxes Payable
23810	Social Security/Medicare
23900	Income Taxes Payable
24000	Other Taxes Payable
24100	Current Portion L/Term Debt
24200	N/P Bank
24210	N/P Stockholder
24700	Other Current Liabilities

> Current liabilities are obligations due within the year.

Noncurrent Liabilities

27000	Notes Payable–Noncurrent Portion
27300	Mortgage Payable
27400	Other Long-Term Liabilities

Equity

39003	Common Stock
39004	Paid-in Capital
39005	Retained Earnings
39007	Dividends Paid

Income

40000	Revenue
40200	Work in Progress
40600	Interest Income
40800	Other Income
45500	Shipping Charges Reimbursed
48000	Sales Returns and Allowances
49000	Sales Discounts

Expense/Direct

50000	Labor Costs/Direct
50100	Cost of Sales/Union Benefit
50500	Materials Costs
51000	Equipment Costs
51500	Subcontract Costs
57500	Cost of Sales–Freight
59000	Purchase Returns and Allowance

Expense—General and Administrative

60000	Advertising Expense
60010	Accounting Expenses
60500	Amortization Expense
61000	Auto and Truck Expenses
61500	Bad Debt Expense
62000	Bank Charges
62500	Cash Over and Short
63000	Charitable Contributions Expense
63100	Sponsorship Contribution
63500	Commissions and Fees Expense
64000	Depreciation Expense
64500	Dues and Subscriptions
65000	Employment Benefit Program Expense
66500	Income Tax Expense
67000	Insurance Expense–Liability
67100	Insurance Expense–Worker's Comp
67200	Insurance Expense–Health
67300	Insurance Expense–Disability
67400	Insurance Expense–Life
67500	Interest Expense
68000	Laundry and Cleaning Expense
68500	Legal and Professional Expense
69000	Licenses Expense

> Bad debts and bank charges can be very costly—watch them.

Office Expense

70000	Maintenance Expense
70500	Meals and Entertainment Expense
71000	Office Expense
71500	Other Taxes
71600	Real Estate Taxes
71700	Water and Sewer Tax
71800	Estimated Taxes
72000	Payroll Tax Expense
72500	Penalties and Fines Expense
73000	Pension/Profit Sharing Plan Expense
73500	Postage Expense
74000	Rent Expense
74100	Lease Expense–Equipment
74500	Repairs Expense
75000	Officer Salaries
75500	Supplies Expense
76000	Telephone Expense
76500	Travel Expense
77000	Utilities Expense
77500	Office Wage Expense
89000	Miscellaneous Expense
90000	Gain/Loss on Sale of Assets
90100	Corp Income Taxes

Use as much detail in office expense as you find helpful.

You will also notice how much detail is included in the general and administrative accounts. These expenses are critical to manage by using comparisons on a month-to-month basis to spot any changes early and make changes before they become an issue that affects the bottom line.

Structuring an accounting system that works as a tool for success takes the attention and input of managers and professionals alike. It is worth the work involved.

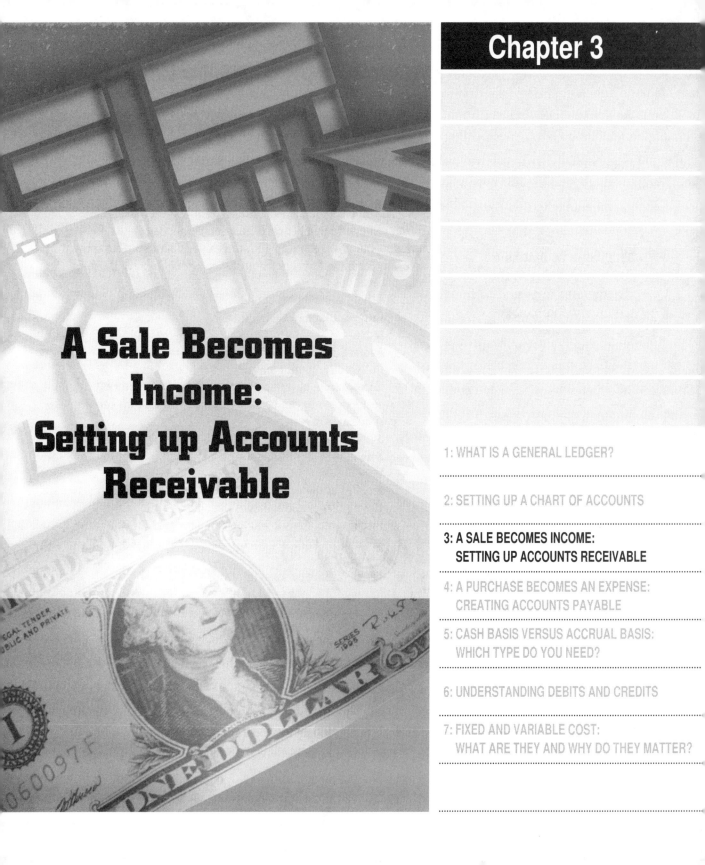

Chapter 3

A Sale Becomes Income: Setting up Accounts Receivable

The main reason you are in business is to provide goods or services to your customers. Success is a sale, and once that transaction takes place, your accounting system goes into action. The value of that sale becomes income to the company and is posted to the income subledger. If the sale is cash, it is posted to the cash account. If the sale is made on credit, it is posted to the accounts receivable.

You will need a number of different entries to complete this transaction, but it will all begin with the source document that is the invoice you generate for your customer. This should include the following information:

> The value of that sale becomes income to the company and is posted to the income subledger.

Customer data
Name
Address
Customer account number
Normal account terms (this should identify whether the sale must be cash or can be on credit based on a *credit check* or past business experience)

Sale data
Date of sale
Amount of sale
Description of goods or services sold
Income account #—if you are detailing your revenue to track the type of sales you are making, here is where you will classify this detail
Terms of the sale—cash or credit?

The first posting will be to the income (or revenue) account, which is number 500 or 5000 on most systems. It will be posted on the subledger as income and on the general ledger in detail. Now the second posting is to account for the result of that transaction—did you receive cash (check or the equivalent such as a credit card, which is paid by a third party such as the bank, counts as cash), or did you add the amount to your receivables? These will be posted to the asset accounts (100 or 1000) either in cash or accounts receivable. The subledger posting will then be posted to the general ledger.

Creating Accounts Receivable

In an automated system, you will have created a database with all the customer information needed to easily post any sale transaction.

Your receivable accounts are your customer accounts as well, so you will want to record as much information as possible so that your sales department can use the data as well. A cash sale does not need to be posted on to a customer's account receivable card because it has not resulted in money due, but posting by the sale and the payment will allow you to track a complete record of your customers' total purchases from your company.

Posting a Sale to Accounts Receivable

The first step here is to post the sale to income and then to the customer account card. In each case, you will want to identify the transaction by a date and invoice number that will allow you to refer to the source document.

Then you will need to add the current charge to any previous balances to get the current amount owed by that customer. This detailed record is critical for the effective collection activities of your business.

A computerized system will automatically update receivable balances; on a manual system, you will have to make sure that the step is done. Your accounts receivable total balance will show up as an important line item on the asset side on your balance sheet.

> The first step here is to post the sale to income and then to the customer account card.

Posting Payments and Other Credits to Receivable

When a payment has been received, it will be credited against the existing balance on your customer's account receivable card. The important step here is in making sure that the payment is credited against the exact invoice being paid. At the end of the month, you will want to determine the age of all of your outstanding customer accounts so that you can determine what monies are due from invoices that are over 30, 60, 90 days and longer. If you don't post the payment against the proper invoice, this task will be made very difficult and time consuming.

Sometimes payments are made out of order and must be identified and addressed. Was an invoice skipped because it was not received, or is there a problem with the merchandise or service provided under that invoice? You won't be able to address the problem if you don't have sufficient information. It is important to note as well when a short payment is made against an invoice. You must research why money has been withheld so that you can correct the problem and collect what is owed.

> There are several ways that customer balances may be reduced.

Transactions Other Than Payments

There are several ways that customer balances may be reduced, but you must learn how to handle these to keep your system in balance and your records accurate. The top three are as follows:

1. Credit memo. This is documentation allowing for an adjustment for defective merchandise or service, billing in excess of quoted price or incorrect charge for freight, and so on. You must create internal supporting documentation (a credit memo) and post from the number you assign that document. The amount of credit you allow will also result in a reduction of income since it will be deducted from gross sales (the revenue account).

2. Return of merchandise. This is a much easier transaction because it involves the canceling of the entire amount of the charge, but you must also remember to create an internal credit memo and a backup document. The amount credited will also be deducted from your sales (or income) account and will reduce your total volume.

3. Writing off a bad debt. This is an unfortunate reality for most companies from time to time. In 21 years in business, I wrote off only 5 accounts as bad debts, and you can keep yours down as well by following this advice. The first step is

making tough credit decisions going in. You want to make the sale but if you never get paid for it, what's the point. Be careful. However, the day may come when a customer is unwilling or unable to pay his or her bill. You should still make an active attempt to collect, even turning the account over to an attorney or collection agency. If that is unsuccessful, you can then assume that the debt is bad.

You will issue a credit memo to establish the internal procedure and post off the receivable. In most cases, you will also post the amount against sales. If your business is big and your system is large and very sophisticated, you may have a set-aside account already for bad debt, and in that case, this account will be charged instead of revenue. This is an unlikely scenario for most closely held companies.

Your accounts receivable are the lifeblood of your business; they represent the cash coming in to use for operations. Create and maintain this information accurately, and it will greatly enhance your performance.

> Your account receivables are the lifeblood of your business.

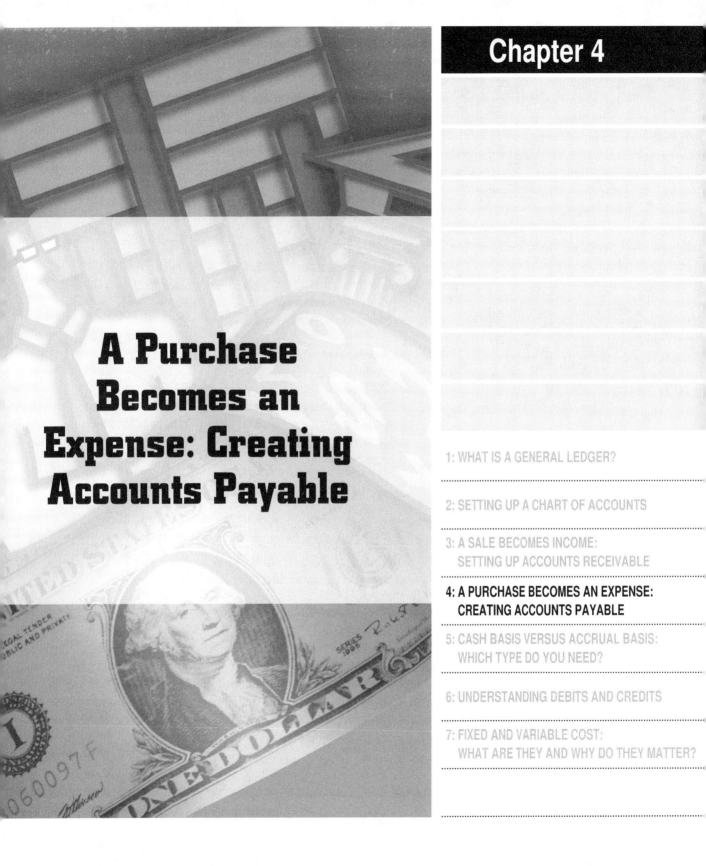

Chapter 4

A Purchase Becomes an Expense: Creating Accounts Payable

Each day you will spend money to buy material or inventory, pay employees, pay taxes, rent, utilities, and a variety of other expenses necessary to operate your business. The type and the amount of your expenditure becomes your detailed cost of operation. If you pay cash, it is simply expensed to the proper subledger. If the purchase is made on credit, then it is expensed to the proper accounts payable.

As with your receivable system, you will begin these multiple entries with a source document. This will be the bill issued by the company or individual you have made your purchase from. You will organize your vendor information much the same for payables as you did for receivables:

> **Vendor data**
> Name
> Address
> Normal account terms (this will tell you when the bill can be paid to receive a discount and when it must be paid to meet vendor requirements)
> Purchase data
> Date of purchase (critical because you will want to credit the expense to incur in proper monthly period)
> Amount of sale
> Description of goods or services purchased
> Expense account #—this is also very critical because you must disburse an expense to the proper account number where it converts to a number directly reflected in your profit and loss statement
> Terms of sale—was it paid or purchased on credit?

Your initial posting will be on the expense side, again taking care that the correct account number is chosen. The second posting is either from your cash account (reducing your available cash) or to the payables account (which increases your liability). The subledger postings will then be posted to the general ledger as well.

> As with your receivable system, you will begin these multiple entries with a source document.

Creating Accounts Payable

If you are currently on an automated system, most of your regular vendors will have been entered previously in your database so you may easily post any purchase or expense. Unlike the receivable side where you will want to enter any new customers for the purpose of sales and marketing information, an infrequently used vendor need not be entered under a separate vendor name if the purchase was made for cash. You may simply show the expense.

Your payable accounts connect to your expense accounts, so take care when you use one vendor for a variety of different expense types. For example, you may use your American Express card to buy a number of services and perhaps even material. The vendor is a single vendor, but the charges may be for travel, entertainment, office supplies, postage or air express charges, and even raw material (some suppliers will accept major credit cards). When the expense is posted, make sure it disburses into the proper expense accounts. This should be done when the purchase or charge is billed, and then, when payment is made, the transaction will automatically follow that trail.

> Your payable accounts connect to your expense accounts, so take care when you use one vendor for a variety of different expense types.

Posting Payments and Other Credits

The first test of any payable system is the ease of establishing sufficient information needed to schedule payments. This begins with the accurate posting of invoices that focuses on the payment due dates. You may decide to adjust that date to take advantage of a discount for early payment or to account if the creditor has given you more liberal terms such as extra dating for early orders of seasonal merchandise. Once the due date has arrived and you have sufficient available funds to make payment, you will begin the payable process.

The next step is to issue a check, which on an automated system, will also trigger a deduction from your cash account representing available funds at your bank. Chances are that you will issue checks in batches, and a good check and balance is that the total of the checks paid will equal the reduction in your accounts payable balance.

> You should cross-reference your check with the invoice number (and date), and you should also put the check number on the payable transaction as well as the original document.

You should cross-reference your check with the invoice number (and date), and you should also put the check number on the payable transaction as well as the original document. This transaction will be detailed on the subledger and carried to the general ledger.

Always verify incoming invoices to make sure that they are correct as to merchandise shipped or service provided, accuracy of quoted prices, quantity shipped, and condition received. Most invoices have statements to the effect that "all claims must be made in seven days." Finding out that there was a mistake a month later may deny you any recourse at all. A common error is to charge shipping incorrectly or charge it on the invoice and bill the freight to you as well. Protect your rights and your money.

Transactions Other Than Payments

If there are discrepancies or claims against a vendor invoice, make sure that you document the details and record them in the proper place. All reductions and, for that matter, increases will be posted against the original expense account charged. For example, if you return material that is substandard, you will reduce your payables when you post the credit and reduce your material costs as well.

Some of the reasons that credits may be taken against a vendor invoice are the return of merchandise, correction of pricing or quantity error, improperly billed freight, and deduction allowed due to quality or service disputes. Make sure that your vendor issues your company a credit memo to validate this adjustment. If they do not do so, you should issue an internal document to fax to them as notification; include this memo with your remittance and keep it attached to your original source document.

Managing Payables Are Key to Cash Management

How you record and track your accounts payable may really be a major contribution to your financial success. It can add to your positive cash flow by making sure that you take advantage of all trade discounts allowed, which will normally average 1 to 2 percent. On annual purchases of $100,000 per year, this will add $1,000 to $2,000 to your bottom line.

If your cash flow is tight, tracking payables will allow you to schedule payments that take into consideration the availability of cash versus the required disbursements. You won't pay one bill and deplete all available resources only to be surprised by a critical payment due only days later. Cash management is a key element of successful financial planning, and effective cash management begins with establishing and tracking good internal records.

> Tracking payables will allow you to schedule payments that take into consideration the availability of cash versus the required disbursements.

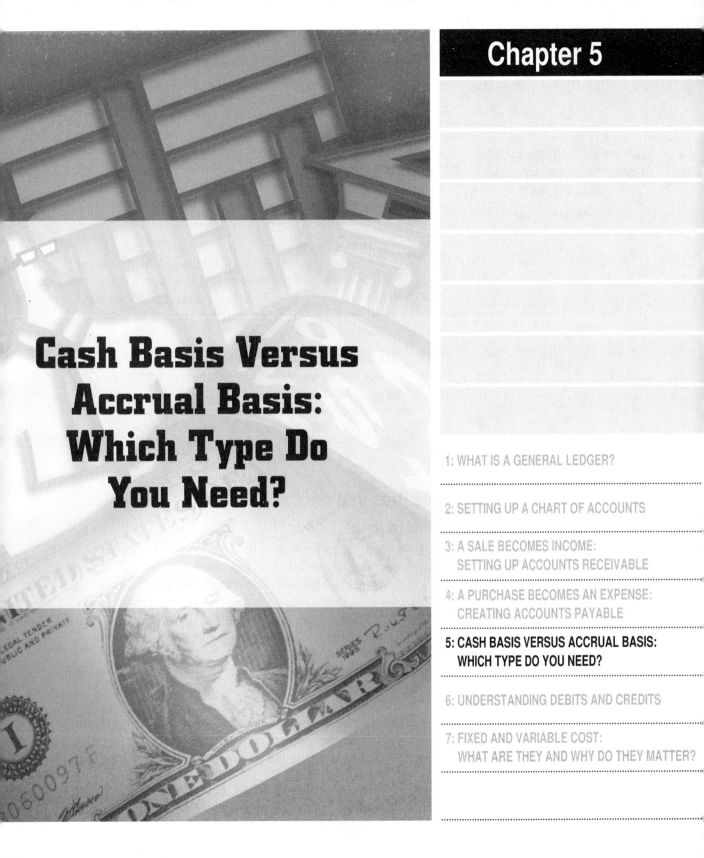

Chapter 5

Cash Basis Versus Accrual Basis: Which Type Do You Need?

> This method shows income (or revenue) at the time of payment.

Your accounting system may be established on a cash basis or an accrual basis, and it is critical for you to know which one you are using. The person (accountant, controller, bookkeeper, or the like) that sets up your books will often make the decision if you don't, and it may not be the wisest one. You should have an input in the choice.

Let's start off with the basic definition:

Cash basis accounting

This method shows income (or revenue) at the time of payment—a credit sale will not show up until it is paid. And expense is also recorded only when it is paid for so that purchases made on credit will not be disbursed until they are paid for rather than when they are billed.

Accrual basis accounting

This method recognizes income when it is earned even if it is not paid. *All* expenses also show when they are incurred whether they have been paid for or billed to be paid at a later date. Any obligation due, including taxes, will be shown as expense.

The Pros and the Cons

Cash Basis

Pros. It is any easy system to set up and run, and works well for a manual system. You can run it off your checkbook.

Only a very small business, particularly a service business that receives mostly cash and pays by cash or check as well, is a good candidate for cash basis.

A restaurant that pays cash to food purveyors and, of course, pays payroll (*including* taxes) on time is also a candidate for this accounting method. Other types of retail establishments may also be able to use a cash basis.

Cons. It is difficult to match income and expense in the same period because money may come in and go out at different times. For example, you purchase inventory for cash in May and sell it for cash in June. With the expense appearing in one month and the income in the next, comparing month-to-month progress is very difficult; the same applies in comparing one period from the current year to the same period of the previous year.

Perhaps more seriously, this system does not allow for good management control because unpaid invoices can pile up without being recorded, and the mounting debt will not be obvious and may jeopardize the future of the business. Unpaid taxes are often hidden in a cash basis system.

Accrual Basis

Pros. The revenue and expense match for any given period so an accurate profit and loss statement is more easily obtained. Period-to-period comparisons are also more relevant and can be used for planning and budgeting.

Accrual method will also allow management to keep on top of all financial changes and make any corrections as they are needed. Good cash flow management requires sufficient and timely information.

If there are a substantial amount of tangible assets involved, you will be able to account for depreciation only on an accrual system. This has a value since it is expense that can save the business taxes, and you should be made aware that the value of assets on your balance sheet will go down as they are used and depreciated. This will alert you of the need to eventually replace hard assets.

Cons. This is a far more difficult system to set up and operate. It is possible but very time consuming to create and maintain an accrual system manually so you will likely need a computer and some accounting software. In addition, the person hired to input and maintain this type of accounting system will be required to have a higher level of expertise and experience, and be a higher-priced employee.

> You will match the income and expense for the same period.

The Tax Implications of Cash Versus Accrual Accounting

Of course you will need to discuss all of your tax planning strategies with your accounting professional, but there are a number of advantages to accrual-based accounting beyond the use of depreciation deductions (which can be substantial). Toward the end of the year, you will begin to know how profitable the year has been, and you can make plans to minimize your tax liability.

This can be done on the income as well as the expense side because you are not just dealing with the exchange of money. If you receive a late year deposit on a sale but the actual transaction has not been completed and billed, you may not have to show it as income although you will process the payment into your system. On the expense side, you may want to make extra purchases of material such as printing and office supplies, repair equipment, or buy new tools so that the expense will be an offset against good profit. Remember that material that goes into inventory will have little effect because it will increase your assets, and larger equipment purchases will be capitalized and you will receive a deduction for depreciation only.

If the current year does not look like a profitable one, you can also plan to add income that will not increase tax liability by billing partially completed work in the current year period. You can also defer expense by asking to have bills dated for the new year to provide a deduction for what may be a more profitable period.

Changing from Cash Basis to Accrual

Even if you began your accounting system on a cash basis because your company was small and your accountant thought it would be easier, you can always make the change. For the internal record keeping, you will need a professional to make the adjustments and establish opening balances on all of your accounts. From a tax standpoint, you must notify the Internal Revenue Service within 180 days of the beginning of the year of your intent to change to accrual base reporting. It is a simple form that your tax advisor can file.

> Toward the end of the year, you will begin to know how profitable the year has been, and you can make plans to minimize your tax liability.

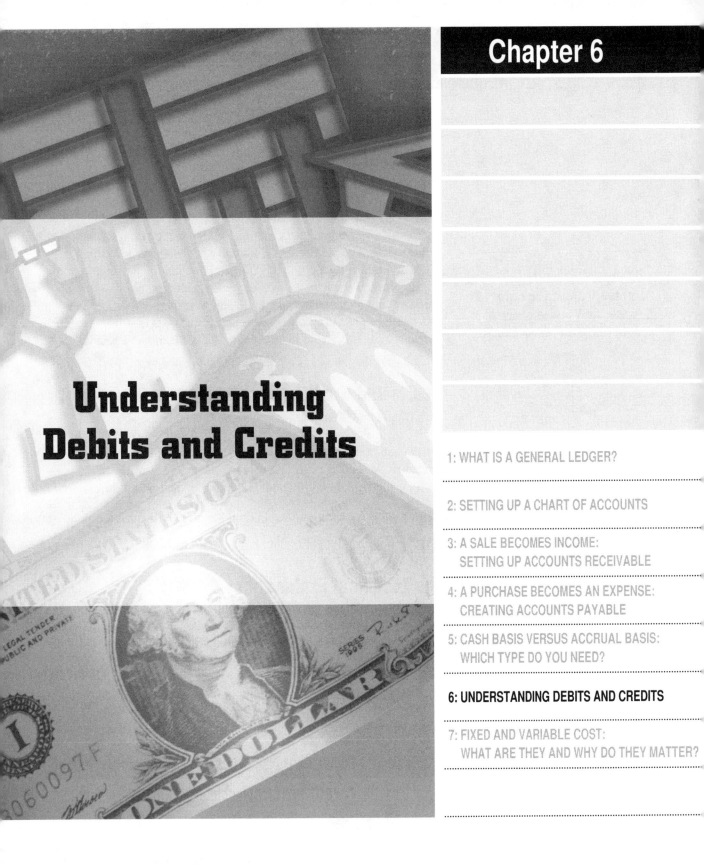

Chapter 6

Understanding Debits and Credits

There are two basic types of bookkeeping systems: a single entry type and a double entry type. Notice that I used the term *bookkeeping* and not *accounting* because a single entry system is a way of maintaining data but not an adequate way of accounting for transactions. Since this book is about accounting and financial management, I am going to limit myself to the double entry system. Understanding how this works will require knowledge of the basics of how debits and credits operate. It is far more complicated in theory than it is in practice.

In previous chapters, we have discussed debits and credits without using the specific title. A sale is credited to income and debited to either cash or accounts receivable. In some instances, a credit increases a balance, and in some instances a debit increases a balance.

> Each transaction is entered twice, and these entries *must* equal each other.

Debits and Credits Must Balance

Each transaction is entered twice, once on the debit side and once on the credit side, and these entries *must* equal each other. Although it may seem complicated, the logic is simple. If an invoice owed to you is paid, it must be removed from your accounts receivable balance. On the other hand, in return, you will add the payment to your bank balance. On the purchase side, when a bill is paid, you no longer owe it so it is no longer a liability, but your cash assets have been diminished by the amount of the check you have drawn.

The Technical Explanation

Accounts use a T form listing the debits on the left side and the credits on the right side. You will not use this type of system internally since you are likely on a computerized accounting system that will do it automatically. If you are still on a manual system and using double entries, chances are that your accountant will do adjusting balances on a monthly basis. For the sake of your increased understanding of the whole system, I offer the following explanation:

There are four basic account types: assets, liabilities, income, and expense.

This is what happens when these accounts are credited or debited.

Account Type	Debit	Credit
Assets	Increases	Decreases
Income	Decreases	Increases
Liability	Decreases	Increases
Expense	Increases	Decreases

For example, a sale for $1,000 made on credit:

Sales Income	$1,000 is credited
Accts Receivable	$1,000 is debited

These must equal each other.

Paying a bill for merchandise results in the following:

Cash	Credited
Expense	Debited

As you can see, each transaction has an equal and opposite transaction, and after all monthly (or yearly) business is completed, the balances should be equal.

Your debits and credits tie in directly to the two most important documents that a company generates—the balance sheet and a profit and loss statement—so accuracy is critical.

> Changes (reductions or additions) in the assets owned by your company and the liabilities owed by your business are the basis of your balance sheet.

Assets and Liabilities Are Reflected on the Balance Sheet

Changes (reductions or additions) in the assets owned by your company and the liabilities owed by your business are the basis of your balance sheet. The difference between the two is the net worth or deficit worth of the business, a number you must know and understand. The transactions you do on a daily basis will change these numbers, so you should understand how these changes are debited, which will *increase* assets and *decrease* liabilities, or how they are credited, which will do just the opposite.

Income and Expense Make up the Profit and Loss Statement

The income you credit on your transactions will show up on your monthend profit and loss statement, so it is important that this account is credited for all possible income items. The expense account must be debited correctly for all monies spent to generate that income so that at the end of the month, you will produce an accurate reflection of your profit and loss. A profit and loss statement is the report on the progress of your company; therefore, accurate and timely data that you understand and utilize is perhaps the most important tool you have for successfully managing your company.

> A profit and loss statement is the report on the progress of your company; therefore, accurate and timely data that you understand and utilize is perhaps the most important tool.

Basic Understanding Is Important

The actual posting of debits and credits on your ledgers and subledgers will likely be done by your controller, bookkeeper, or accountant. Someone along the way will use a computerized system to make the work easy. Therefore, the technical explanations are not necessary for you, but having the basic understanding is essential. These transactions are the basis for reports and information that are your roadmap to a successful operation.

Chapter 7

Fixed and Variable Cost: What Are They and Why Do They Matter?

By now you should have a working knowledge of how your accounting system has been set up and how transactions flow through. When establishing your chart of accounts, you must be involved in creating the accounts that best reflect the various types of expense you will incur operating your company. There are several general categories, the primary ones being fixed and variable, and these will be reflected on your statement as direct and indirect costs. Understanding these expenses and controlling them, as well as setting prices based on real costs, are the keys to profitability.

Direct and Variable Costs

These costs are directly related to the overall volume of your business. The more business you do, the more expense you will incur because each sale has the cost of material, product, or service directly attached to it. On the other side, the lower your sales, the less direct or variable expense you will have. It actually "varies" directly according to the volume of your sales.

For example, in a restaurant, the variable costs are the food and direct service personnel such as cooks and wait staff. The more meals consumed, the more food needed and the more employees required to cook and serve.

In a retail operation, each sale of merchandise has a direct cost, the price of the goods and the salaries of those who make the sale.

In a manufacturing operation, the variable costs will include raw material and the labor of all employees who are involved in the manufacturing process, including their direct benefits such as union contributions. Those employees, such as managers, are considered an indirect or fixed cost.

Once you have deducted your variable costs from your revenue, you will come up with your gross profit (profit *before* overhead and administrative costs are expensed), and you will also want to state your profit in a percentage figure, called your profit margin. Knowing this number will make setting prices more of a science and less of a guessing game.

> When establishing your chart of accounts, you must be involved in creating the accounts that best reflect the various types of expense you will incur operating your company.

Indirect and Fixed Costs

These costs are only indirectly associated with the sales volume of your business because they continue regardless of whether your revenue is high or low. Your landlord expects rent, and the office staff expects paychecks even if sales are bad. Additional overhead costs such as phone, utilities and equipment leases, and the use of office supplies will be there regardless of sales volume.

Perhaps most critical here is the interest payment on any loan the business might carry. This payment continues on a fairly steady path (it may fluctuate if the principal is being paid off as well) as a fixed expense regardless of the level of revenue. If the percentage of this cost gets too high, the expense can jeopardize the finances of the company because choices must be made to pay the bank or pay suppliers.

Once you have learned how to read these costs as a percentage of all costs, you will realize that as volume increases, the fixed percentage goes down and profits increase.

For example, your rent, utilities, administrative salaries, and interest, along with all other overhead, costs your business $150,000 per year. When your volume is at $300,000, that percentage of these costs is 50 percent, but when you increase the volume to $500,000, the cost percentage goes down to 30 percent (150,000 / 500,000), and the extra money drops to the bottom line, which is your profit. Understanding the volume–profit formula is important and will be discussed at greater length in Sections II and IV of this book.

> These costs are only indirectly associated with the sales volume of your business because they continue regardless of whether your revenue is high or low.

A Word About Semivariable Costs

Some costs that are listed under the indirect and fixed costs are, at least in part, semivariable. Your business will consistently spend money in these areas so that a portion of the line item expense is fixed. But as sales income increases, the costs of these items will go up as well. A good example is office expenses such as phone and postage. Your basic phone charge is fixed, but the more business you have, the more phone calls you will make and the higher the expense. Your mail volume will also increase, so the cost of postage goes up as well on high volume.

You should monitor a number of these semivariable expenses because they can easily get out of line. Travel and entertainment expense is one. Set up as a fixed expense, this is controllable and should be monitored. Perhaps the trickiest of these types of costs is sales and marketing expense. It may seem logical that sales and marketing expense stays steady or even decreases on soft sales volume, but in some cases it needs to go up as aggressive moves are made to increase revenue. This is a judgment call best made by an informed owner or manager.

Learning the basics of what is included in an accounting system is the first step to understanding the critical documents that will be produced by this work. Your balance sheet, profit and loss statement, and cash flow projections are important management tools. If you follow how they are created, you will be able to better analyze and utilize them.

> Your balance sheet, profit and loss statement, and cash flow projections are important management tools.

Understanding Financial Reports

Summary of Part II

- **Insights on your profit and loss statements**
- **What your balance sheet tells you about your financial stability**
- **How much revenue do you need to make a profit**
- **How to predict your future results**

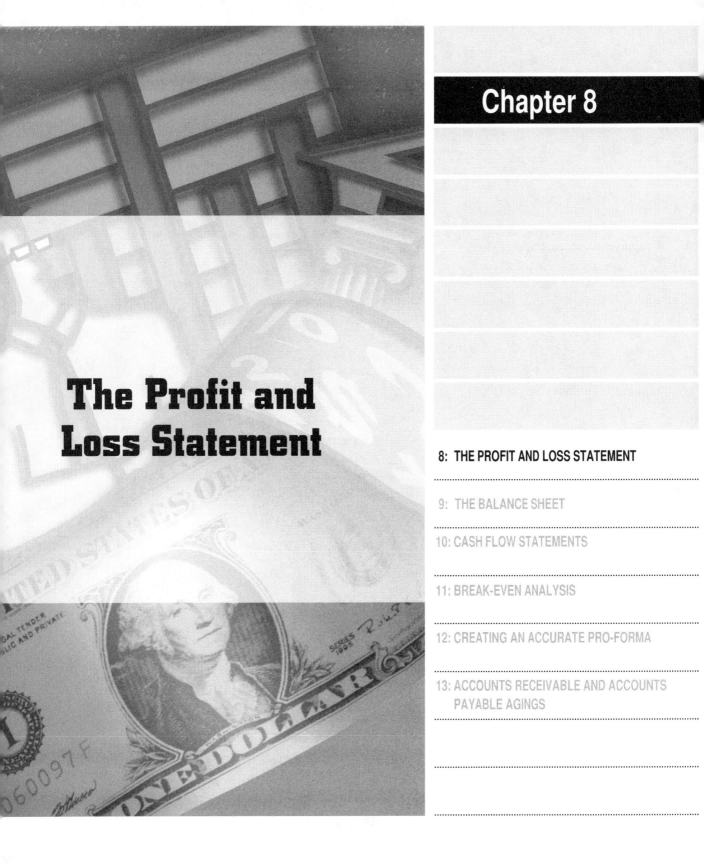

Chapter 8

The Profit and Loss Statement

At the end of each month, your company should generate a profit and loss statement done either inhouse on your computer or generated by your accountant. You should ask to see these as soon after the monthend closing as possible because if you are utilizing them properly, and you find problem areas, the sooner you institute corrective action the better.

The following is a very simple hypothetical profit and loss statement from a retail shoe store like the one used in the previous example:

> Cost of goods sold are direct expense. Administrative costs are indirect expense.

For the Month of January 199–

Gross Sales	$15,000	(1)
less returns	650	(2)
net sales	14,350	(3)
Cost of goods sold		(4)
products	7,200 ⎱ ∠83 ⊙⊙	(5)
direct labor	1,100 ⎰	(6)
←Gross profit	6,050	(7)
Less general & administrative expense		(8)
salaries	1,800	(9)
rent	600	(10)
interest	375	(11)
utilities	195	(12)
telephone	250	(13)
freight/postage	66	(14)
office supplies	70	(15)
sales and promotions	350	(16)
miscellaneous	240	(17)
Total expense	3,952	(18)
Net (before tax) profit	$2,098	(19)

Here are the basic details of each line item:
(1) This represents the total sales, cash, or credit recorded during the period.
(2) Returns may also be other allowances such as credit for quality problems. Any deduction from sales volume is recorded here.

(3) The net sales are the gross (total) sales less any allowable deductions.

(4) Cost of goods sold reflect the direct (variable) costs related to each sale. In general, this will be material and the labor directly associated with each sale.

(5) May be raw material or finished goods for resale.

(6) Sales labor, manufacturing labor, or any jobs directly related to the actual production or sale of each product.

(7) The gross profit is also called the operating profit. This represents your sales less the actual costs of those sales but *not*, however, the costs of operating the business.

(8) These are your indirect or fixed costs.

(9) These salaries are all the operating wages, including those of the owner or manager and all office, sales; and other administrative personnel.

(10) Rent for business premises.

(11) The interest on any business loan is deducted here, but the principal is not a deductible item. That payment comes from cash and is reflected on the balance sheet.

(12) Gas, water, and electric.

(13) Local and long-distance phone.

(14) All postage and incoming and outgoing freight that is not charged to customers.

(15) All supplies used for administrative purposes.

(16) This is a semivariable cost and includes in some cases advertising, direct mail, and so on.

(17) For some businesses, occasional expenses for repairs, small purchases, office cleaning, and so on will be covered here.

(18) The total of all general expense.

(19) The net profit before any income tax is paid.

Other items that will come under general and administrative expense are as follows:

- Payroll taxes—the employer's portion of FICA tax plus any state or federal unemployment tax.
- Auto and truck expense—if there are cars or trucks used for business purposes.

> Interest is a deductible expense; principal repayment is not.

- Leases—any equipment that is leased is expensed. On purchase agreements for vehicles or equipment, only the interest is expensed.
- Repairs or maintenance—if office equipment, delivery vehicles, or other machinery and equipment need repair or routine maintenance, this is expensed under indirect costs. These repairs will have to be made regardless of your level of sales volume.
- Depreciation—this is a noncash expense that will be deducted from your bottom line, monthly if you have a schedule available, or annually when your accountant makes year end adjustments. Though this is not a cash expense, it should be noted because as equipment gets older, it needs to be replaced, and this is how you express this in financial terms.

> You began determining how many and which categories you will use to identify types of income and expense when you set up your chart of accounts.

Your Chart of Accounts Creates Your Profit and Loss Statement

You began determining how many and which categories you will use to identify types of income and expense when you set up your chart of accounts. You may have as complex or as minimally detailed information as you want. You may set up a single account for all income, or you may segregate different types of income into individual accounts. For example, in our retail shoe store, they might list sales as follows:

Sale income
shoes
boots
sandals
leather care products
accessories

The point of this would be to determine if one type of product sale is going up and another product type is going down so that purchases of these items may be adjusted or promotions run to increase activity.

The same theory holds for all line items throughout the profit and loss statement. You may have several adjustments to sales besides returns, and you may want detail on these. A product return may reduce volume, but since you have the return inventory it won't reduce profit. A discount given for any reason *will* reduce profit.

On the direct expense side, you have the chance to find out exactly where your profit is by costing the merchandise directly against the sale.

For example:

Shoe store sells	$ 2,500	shoes
product cost	1,500	
difference is	1,000	profit
	or 66%	
Store sells	$ 2,000	boots
product costs	800	
difference is	1,200	profit
	or 150%	

> The cost of merchandise is a direct expense of the sale.

What the shoe store owner has learned from this is that the profit margin is higher on boots than shoes, so it is in his interest to inventory, advertise, and promote boots.

All of your expense detail has a story to tell particularly if you create enough categories for complete and detailed information. One critical example is salaries. The shoe store may pay only the owner and a part-time office person (sales staff are indirect costs). But many larger operations have officers (owners) salaries, managerial salaries, and office or administrative support salaries. Identifying these separately will give information regarding staffing costs as a percentage of total sales and will let the owner or manager know when overstaffing has become an issue or funds are available for additional hires.

The Key Is in the Percentage

Each item should also have a percentage (%) number attached as well as the dollar value. This is important because the key to profitability is to focus on budgets or goals as to what profit margins must be maintained and what expenses must be contained. For example, the rent or occupancy costs of many businesses cannot be over a certain percentage without causing serious damage to the bottom line. This is particularly true in the case of a restaurant—that cost must normally be kept to under 10 percent of gross.

Other expense items such as salaries and advertising and marketing may have target percentages as well. Their relationship to total volume affects your bottom line, so know your goals.

The use of percentages will also aid in period-to-period comparisons. If your volume varies from month to month or year to year, the only way to identify the outcome is to see how the percentages of profits and expenses change from period to period. Are your profits up or down? Are your expenses down, or are they creeping up? Once you know the target numbers, you will be able to create a budget.

A look at a more complicated profit and loss follows:

> The use of percentages will also aid in period-to-period comparisons.

ABC Contracting
Income Statement
For the Twelve Months Ending December 31, 1997

Revenues	$	%	
Fees–construction	2,480,878.27	97.88	(1)
Wrk in Prog–unbilled jobbing	41,434.81	1.63	(2)
Sales retrns & allowances	12,463.85	0.49	
Sales discounts	(50.10)	0.00	
Total revenues	2,534,726.83	100.00	
Costs of sales			
Cost of sales/union benefit	9,941.93	0.39	
Misc coded W	544.00	0.02	
Materials costs	436,056.29	17.20	
Equipment costs	4,064.95	0.16	
Subcontract costs	132,609.47	5.23	(3)
Cst of sales–sal & wages	728,992.71	28.76	
Cost of sales–chauffer	74,425.60	2.94	
Cost of sales/union benefits	245,139.32	9.67	(4)
Total cost of sales	1,631,774.27	64.38	
Gross profit	902,952.56	35.62	
Administrative expense			
Advertising expense	2,824.07	0.11	
Accounting expense	17,968.20	0.71	
Auto & truck expense	94,259.54	3.72	
Bank charges	605.02	0.02	
Charitable contributions exp	200.00	0.01	
Sponsorship contribution	100.00	0.00	
Commissions and fees exp	17,400.09	0.69	
Dues & subscriptions	129.00	0.01	
Gifts expense	48.72	0.00	
Insurance exp–liability	87,134.84	3.44	(5)
Insurance exp–work/comp	14,471.69	0.57	(6)
Insurance exp–health	24,778.45	0.98	(7)

Insurance exp–disability	223.00	0.01	(8)
Insurance exp–life	437.00	0.02	(9)
Interest expense	12,484.16	0.49	
Loan–principal	497.61	0.02	
Laundry and cleaning exp	2,339.21	0.09	
Legal and prof exp	3,450.00	0.14	
Licenses expense	3,789.51	0.15	
Maintenance expense	3,253.47	0.13	
Meals and entertainment exp	5,980.65	0.24	
Office expense	49,031.93	1.93	
Consulting fee	39,345.00	1.55	(10)
Real estate taxes	7,267.47	0.29	(11)
Water and sewer tax	602.90	0.02	
Estimated taxes	1,110.00	0.04	
Payroll tax expense	87,262.42	3.44	
ADP payroll prep exp	4,355.97	0.17	
Penalties and fines	2,936.21	0.12	
Pnsion/prfit-shring plan exp	8,154.20	0.32	
Postage expense	2,617.11	0.10	
Rent expense	60,500.00	2.39	
Lease expense–equipment	1,132.68	0.04	
Repairs expense	3,593.84	0.14	
Officer salaries	108,750.00	4.29	
Supplies expense	211.28	0.01	
Telephone expense	40,545.74	1.60	
Travel expense	42,491.39	1.68	
Utilities expense	4,601.67	0.18	
Office wage expense	142,858.44	5.64	
Adj.	(27.00)	0.00	
Miscellaneous	3,698.43	0.15	
City corp income taxes	659.87	0.03	
Total expenses	$904,073.78	35.67	
Net income	(1,121.22)	(0.04)	

Some of the more interesting aspects of this profit and loss statement are as follows:

(1) This is the total of all sales less those that have not been billed due to administrative problems such as waiting for a purchase order or release number.

(2) This work has been completed but remains unbilled. It is accounted for in the revenue because all labor and material costs have been expensed, so not to include this would impact profitability.

(3) In the case of this business, subcontracting lowers overall profit margins so a goal was established to keep this cost at 5 percent. Mark ups on subcontracted work is 20 percent, and on other work it is 36 percent.

(4) This is a totally unionized shop, and these are a portion of direct labor expense.

(5-9) The insurance expense was not lumped into one category so that the required insurance (liability and workers' compensation) could be separated from those that were voluntary (health, and disability, and life).

(10) This fee was for computer installation and management consultation. It is known as a nonrecurring expense since it need not be duplicated in future years.

(11) The building is owned separately but it is on a net/net/net so that real estate taxes are paid by the lessee.

The preceding statement contains a good bit of management information that may be used to monitor the progress of the operation. The next step would be to break down income into types of work that are more profitable so that these jobs may be aggressively pursued.

> Each category has detail that must be considered when interpreting a P&L statement.

Comparing Your Profit and Loss

Each industry has a certain level of expected performance, and you can check how your business is doing according to the norms. An organization called Robert Morris Associates does this business analysis and issues annual reports. These reports are specific to various types of businesses and consider the relative size of the business so that it is possible to make accurate comparisons.

A number of benchmark numbers are compared with a range of high and low performance so that you can see how your company is doing. You will find direct costs comparisons, including labor and material costs (percent of revenues). Gross profit margins are a real measure of how your business falls within its own industry.

On the administrative expense side, costs of employee benefits, occupancy costs, and interest paid are areas to review. The level of debt that you carry (and the interest paid) may seem high but be average for your industry because of equipment or ongoing technology costs.

> A number of benchmark numbers are compared with a range of high and low performance so that you can see how your company is doing.

Understanding Your Profit and Loss Statement Is the Key to Improving Profits

Most of the answers you need about how to improve your bottom line are found on your profit and loss statement. And if it isn't there, it surely is in the detail that makes up that statement; you can work with your accountant to have that information appear by changing your chart of accounts and creating new line items. Is there a hidden cost that has drained the profitability from your company? Look into line items on the increase and get detailed information.

You can project cost as well on your profit and loss by stating project income separately and project expense (direct) separately as well. A proportional allocation of overhead expense will show you exactly how much or how little profit you have made on a specific project. In Sections V and VI of this book, we will explain in greater detail how to manage and problem-solve using the numbers you generate. In the meantime, the first step is in understanding the document itself.

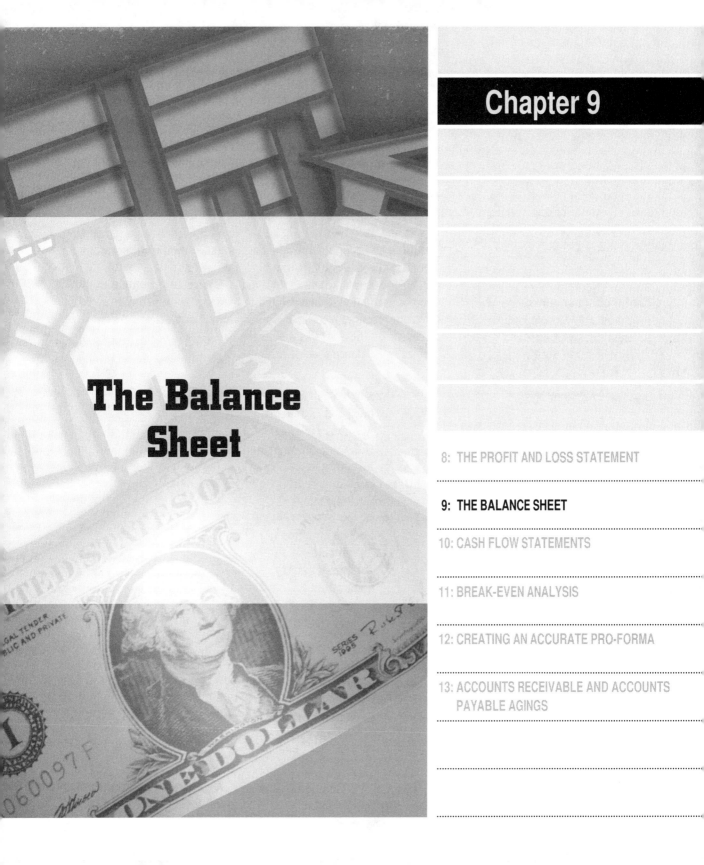

Chapter 9

The Balance Sheet

Second only to your profit and loss statement as barometer of the health of your business is your balance sheet, which is made up of a listing of your assets and liabilities. A look at this document will give you a good bit of information about the relative financial strength of your business.

Your chart of accounts will identify the various categories of assets and liabilities that will be shown on the balance sheet, and by crediting and debiting individual accounts, you will increase or decrease the values they carry.

For example, when a sale is made, it is posted (credited) to the income account and then debited to the asset account either as cash or as an accounts receivable. You will have a number of different accounts on the assets as well as the liability side of the ledger. Typically, a balance sheet is arranged as follows:

> Your chart of accounts will identify the various categories of assets and liabilities that will be shown on the balance sheet.

```
Assets
    Current assets
        Cash and cash items
        Accounts receivable
        Notes payable—short term
        Inventory
    Fixed assets
        Land and buildings
        Machinery and equipment
            Less depreciation (for both)
        Long-term notes—net value
            Total fixed assets
            Total assets

Liabilities
    Current liabilities
        Accounts payable
        Payroll taxes due
        Loans due (current portion)
    Total current liabilities
        Long-term portion of loans or notes
            Total liabilities
                Stockholder equity
```

The retail shoe store used as an example in the previous chapter would have a simple balance sheet like the one the follows:

Current assets
Cash in bank	$2,500.00	
Accounts receivable	650.00	
Notes payable	200.00	(1)
Inventory	35,000.00	
Total	38,350.00	

Fixed assets
Leasehold improvements	18,000.00	(2)
Total assets	56,350.00	

Liabilities
Current
Accounts payable -	15,000.00	
Payroll tax due	1,150.00	
Current portion loan due	2,165.00	(3)
Total current liabilities	18,315.00	

Long-term
Bank loan due	15,600.00	(4)
Noncurrent	34,915.00	

Net worth (Stockholder equity) $21,335.00

> Each asset less total liabilities give the net worth or equity in the business.

In the case of this business, there is no land, building, or equipment to list. If there were, they would be valued at their cost value first, then any depreciation already taken in previous years would be deducted and the *net* book value is carried on the balance sheet.

Other notes for the balance sheet listed are as follows:

(1) A company may have a loan outstanding to an employee or even a customer that is due in the short term, and it will be listed as current asset.
(2) Leasehold improvements are a nonliquid asset that has value as collateral to the company but not on a current basis.

There is little chance that cash can be realized quickly if at all for this asset.

(3) The portion of any loan that is due within the next 12 months is listed under a current liability.

(4) The portion (balance) of any loan that is due past the 12-month period is listed as a long-term liability. It is assumed that these payments will be made from future profits so that you need not have current assets to cover them.

> The solvency of a company is determined by its ability to retire current obligations from current assets.

How to Determine Solvency from Your Balance Sheet

The solvency of a company is determined by its ability to retire current obligations from current assets. Meaning, is it likely that your business can pay employees, creditors, and lenders in a timely fashion. You can look to your balance sheet to predict this liquidity by comparing the value of your current assets to your current liabilities. If you have more assets than liabilities, the solvency may be adequate. If they are even, a problem could occur such as inventory going out of style or out of date, and the money to retire debt would not be available. In that case, your payment possibilities may be very insecure. If you find that your liabilities exceed your assets, you are most likely facing an imminent cash flow problem.

You should pay attention to this warning and plan for immediate corrective action. Several alternatives will be discussed in Section VI on problem solving, but the primary goal must be to get more cash into the company without increasing current liabilities as well.

The shoe store that we have been using as an example has a good current ratio because their assets are $38,350 and liabilities are $18,315 giving them a 2 to 1 ratio.

What Your Balance Sheet Tells About Your Net Worth

The last line item on a balance sheet is often called net worth or stockholders' equity. That is the book value (your internal books that have included depreciation) on your tangible net worth. The values here are of all tangible property. The actual value of your company may be higher or lower due to a number of scenarios, and you may want to cast it in different light for different reasons.

For example, you may have equipment that still has tangible sale value although it has been fully depreciated on your books and therefore shows no value on your balance sheet. You may have substantial intangible asset value in items such as a well-established name or in proprietary information such as recipes for a restaurant or patents used in a manufacturing company. These may not show on your balance sheet, but they are value.

On the other hand, if your inventory has become obsolete and you still carry it on the books, the value of your business may be less than stated. On the machinery and equipment side, you may still carry a book value on equipment that is no longer in working order or that has become technologically obsolete such as computers. It is almost impossible to set an accurate value on used computer equipment because it has such a short shelf life.

The bottom line here is that the shareholders' equity listed on your balance sheet is only a starting point to determine the actual value of your business. As a going concern, you will want to set the value not on the net assets as expressed on the balance sheet, but rather the future earnings potential expressed by a multiple of the current earnings. We will discuss business valuation in the last section of this book.

Review Provider Changes in Your Balance Sheet

Perhaps the most important internal use of your balance sheet is to monitor any changes in your net value or solvency from one period to another. Are you building equity in the company or draining the value of your assets to keep the business going? Are you still as able this year as you were last year to retire current debts from current assets? A business is measured by its progress, which is increasing revenues with increasing profits and a stronger balance sheet. Pay attention to this document; it will give you very relevant information.

> Perhaps the most important internal use of your balance sheet is to monitor any changes in your net value or solvency from one period to another.

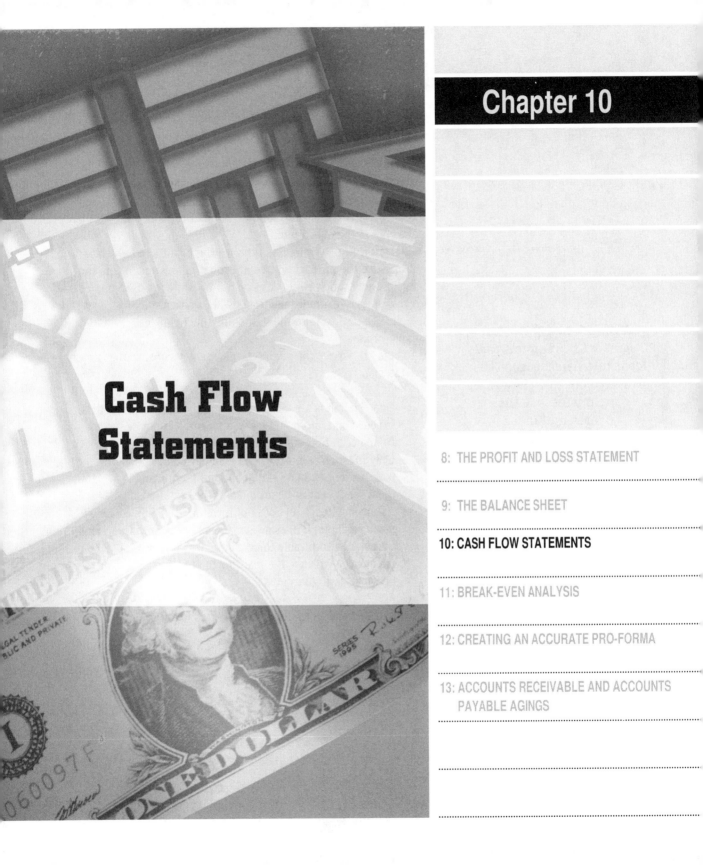

Cash Flow
Statements

It is possible to predict the flow of cash through your business on a monthly basis for up to a year in advance with some accuracy. A longer-term pro-forma (in advance) statement is a bit more speculative, but it can tell you how growth will affect your cash or how a loan will ease a cash crunch. And if you have loans that will be coming due at a later date, you will know whether the funds will be there to take care of the obligation.

A cash flow projection begins with the profit and loss statement because the primary source of capital in any business is the operating funds, and profits ease cash flow while losses strangle cash resources. Most new businesses will experience losses early on, so it is critical to know how this will affect your needed and available capital.

There are several things to remember when constructing a cash flow statement:

- Depreciation is a noncash item, and though it is deducted as expense on a profit and loss statement, it is not deducted from a cash flow statement.
- Only the interest portion of a loan payment is deductible from a profit and loss statement, but the principal payment (debt service) must be included in the cash flow.
- All income (revenue) does not turn into cash immediately in many businesses. If a sale is made on credit terms, you must wait for the receivable to be paid. There may be a 60–90 day lag in cash, which is the real source of cash struggle for a new or growing business.

You can format a cash flow statement as follows:

Income
    Less direct expense
            =   Gross profit
    Less operating expense (including depreciation)
            =   Net before tax profit

> A cash flow projection begins with the profit and loss statement because the primary source of capital in any business is the operating funds.

CASH FLOW STATEMENTS

Starting cash
   Plus revenue collection (or cash sales)
   Plus loan proceeds
      =   Total available cash
   Less direct expense
   Less operating expense (without depreciation)
   Less debt service (principal payment)
      =   Ending cash (this becomes the starting
             cash for the next period)

A simple cash flow statement may look something like this for a three-month period.

	May	June	July
Sale Income	$20,000	$22,000	$21,000
Direct Expense	11,000	12,100	11,550
Gross Profit	9,000	9,900	9,450
Overhead Exp (1)	7,200	7,200	7,200
Net Profit Before Taxes	1,800	2,700	2,250
Starting Cash	6,500	4,600	2,600
+ Collections	15,000	18,000	19,000
Total Available	23,500	22,600	21,200
Less Direct	11,000	12,100	11,550
Less Overhead (2)	7,000	7,000	7,000
Less Debt (3)	900	900	900
Ending Cash	$4,600	$2,600	$1,350

> On a cash flow, depreciation is not included as it is a non-cash expense.

(1) This overhead number includes depreciation.
(2) This overhead number has been reduced by $200 for depreciation.
(3) This is the principal payment on the company's bank loan.

You will note that in an average situation, the cash flow of a business is difficult to manage because even when you are making profits, the cash reserves can be going down. The reason for this in the simple model we used was that we began with a minimum of working capital.

How much you need will vary greatly from business to business and depend primarily on whether you sell for cash on credit. Another factor is whether you must purchase for cash or can use credit.

The toughest scenario is often found in new or early-stage companies that sell primarily on credit and have little established vendor credit for themselves. This means that their working capital requirements may be quite high. If you sell $50,000 of goods and get paid only 20 percent in cash, your cash will be far less than needed to pay bills and make inventory purchases for the next month. For example, you will receive $10,000 in receipts. For the current month, you may have $40,000 of expenses and without startup cash, the month will end on a deficit of $30,000. Beginning a new month with that deficit will create real problems in meeting day-to-day needs such as funding payroll and purchasing material.

Let's take, for an example, a profitable company that has no extra working capital beyond the revenues it generates and see what can happen in a period of three months:

> The toughest scenario is often found in new or early-stage companies that sell primarily on credit and have little established vendor credit for themselves.

	Month 1	Month 2	Month 3
Sale Income	$40,000	40,000	40,000
Direct Expense	24,000	24,000	24,000
Gross Profit	16,000	16,000	16,000
Overhead Exp	13,600	13,600	13,600
Net Before Tax Profit	2,400	2,400	2,400
Starting Cash	0	(27,600)	(40,000)
+ Collections	10,000	30,000	42,000
Total Available	10,000	(2,400)	2,000
Less Direct	24,000	24,000	24,000
Less Overhead	13,600	13,600	13,600
Less Debt	0	0	0
Ending Cash	$(27,600)	(40,000)	(35,600)

(handwritten notes in margin: 35,600 / 45,000 / 9,401)

This scenario has no debt service in it, only payment of operating expense. Even in month three when cash collections have started to rise, there is still a deficit in operating cash, and the business may be in jeopardy because of insufficient working capital. The only solution is to have a pool of cash reserves from initial investment or, less likely, a bank line of credit to draw on to fund the operations. It is difficult to get a bank to fund a startup, but to begin without adequate capital is to flirt with disaster.

Growth Puts a Strain on Cash Flow

Growth in sales revenues is a desired outcome for any business, but you must realize that without sufficient capital to fuel expansion, the goals may not be met. Working capital, which is important for any business, becomes more critical in a growth phase. It is possible to project cash flow requirements by doing a pro-forma projection. You can cast a number of different scenarios to determine the best strategy to employ for your own business. Several issues to consider:

- If you are primarily a cash business, growth will be much easier.
- Will your profits go up as revenue goes up because overhead is less of a cost?
- Can you increase collections of receivables to ease the need for capital?
- Can you secure additional vendor credit to ease the cash crunch?

A cash flow projection will aid you in predicting what capital requirements you will have during any periods of significant expansion. The following model will serve as an example of the growing cash needs during periods of growth. The hypothetical business has the following characteristics:

- Growth of 10 percent per quarter (over 40 percent annual).
- Most sales on credit terms—receivables turning in 60 days.
- Gross profit margins of 30 percent—net profit margin grows as sales increase.
- No current bank borrowing.
- Only adequate working cash going to current period.

> Working capital, which is important for any business, becomes more critical in a growth phase.

$$\begin{array}{r} 24\,000 \\ 13\,600 \\ \hline 37\,600 \\ 9\,400 \\ \hline 27{,}200 \end{array}$$

	1st Qrtr	2nd Qrtr	3rd Qrtr	4th Qrtr
Sales Income	$300,000	330,000	363,000	400,000
Direct Expense	210,000	231,000	254,000	280,000
Gross Profit	90,000	99,000	109,000	120,000
Overhead Expense	74,000	75,000	77,000	80,000
Net Before Tax	16,000	24,000	32,000	40,000
Starting Cash	120,000	36,000	5,000	(26,000)
+ Collections	200,000	275,000	300,000	320,000
Available Cash	320,000	211,000	305,000	294,000
Less Direct Exp	210,000	231,000	254,000	280,000
Less Overhead Exp	74,000	75,000	70,000	80,000
Ending Cash	$36,000	5,000	(26,000)	(66,000)

> Revenues and projects may be growing at the same time cash is becoming scarce.

You will note that when the revenue was growing, the profits were growing but the cash became nonexistent. The profits will be seen on your profit and loss statement, and the value of your assets will increase on your balance sheet even when cash is becoming critically short. Net (before taxes) profit during this year of growth exceeded $112,000, and this is the right time and reason to borrow funds to use as working capital. Once the growth has leveled off, operating cash flow will be sufficient to operate the company, and the loan may be repaid.

Your cash flow statement is an important document to help you determine when a cash crunch is coming and to assist you in determining how much money you will require as a working capital loan. Most borrowers will not be able to go back for a second round of financing in the early stages of a new loan, so asking for a sufficient amount in the beginning may be a key to the ease and success of your growth phase.

The Difference Between Profit and Cash Flow

Profit and cash flow are not the same thing, and every business owner should be aware of the difference. A company can have good cash flow but still be losing money. The airline industry is a perfect example of this. In the years that they were losing literally billions of dollars, their cash flow kept them aloft. Tickets were paid for in advance, but expenses were mostly deferred. Airplane lease fees went unpaid, as did vendors. For several airlines such as Continental, Pan Am, and Braniff, the leases finally caught up with them, and bankruptcy followed.

Both the profit and loss statement and the cash flow statement are important management tools. Use them together to understand how you are doing and to plan for the future progress of your business.

A profit and loss statement may be combined with the cash flow statement for a complete tool of financial management.

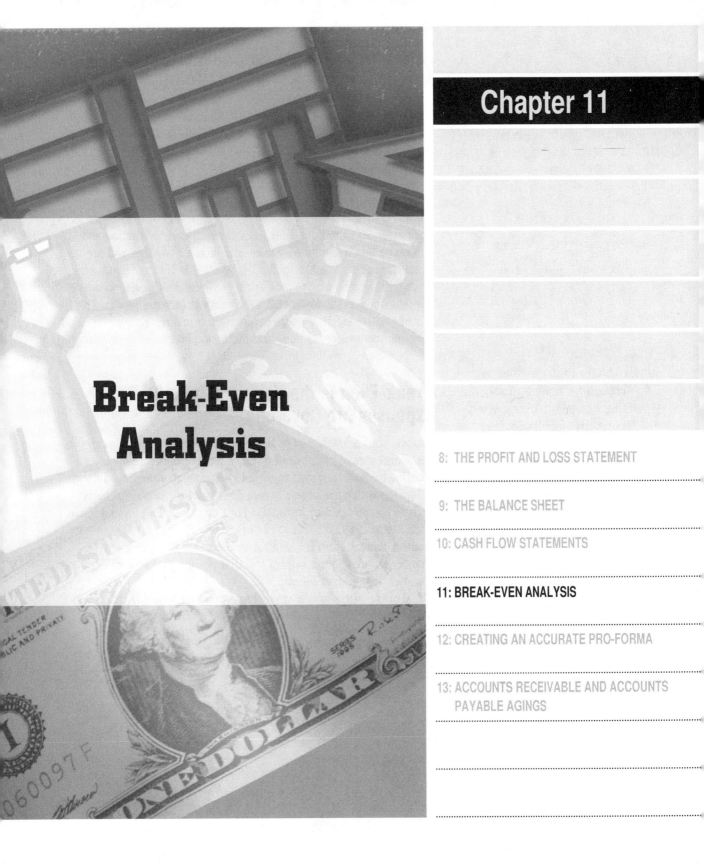

Chapter 11

Break-Even Analysis

This type of report is not one that is automatically generated by most accounting software, nor is it one that is normally produced by your accountant, but it is an important analysis for you to have and understand. For any new business, you should predict what gross sales volume level you will have to achieve before you reach the break-even point and then, of course, build to make a profit. For early-stage businesses, you should be able to assess your early prediction and determine how accurate they were, and monitor whether you are actually on track to make the profits you need. Even the mature business would be wise to look at their current break-even point and perhaps find ways to lower that benchmark to increase profits. The recent massive layoffs at large corporations are directed at this goal, lowering the break-even point and increasing profits.

> Even the mature business would be wise to look at their current break-even point and perhaps find ways to lower that benchmark to increase profits.

Break-Even Is the Volume Where All Fixed Expenses Are Covered

You will start a break-even analysis by establishing *all* the fixed (overhead) expenses of your business. Since most of these are done on a monthly basis, don't forget to include the estimated monthly amount of line items that are normally paid on a quarterly or annual basis such as payroll taxes or insurance. For example, if your annual insurance charge is $9,000, use 1/12 of that, or $750 as part of your monthly budget. With the semivariable expense (such as phone charges, travel, and marketing), use that portion that you expect to spend each and every month.

For the purpose of a model break-even, let's assume that the fixed expenses look as follows:

Administrative salaries	$1,500
Rent	800
Utilities	300
Insurance	150
Taxes	210
Telephone	240
Auto expense	400
Supplies	100

Sales and marketing	300
Interest	100
Miscellaneous	400
Total	$4,500

These are the expenses that must be covered by your gross profit. Assuming that the gross profit margin is 30 percent, what volume must you have to cover this expense? The answer in this case is 15,000—30 percent of that amount is $4,500, which is your target number.

The two critical numbers in these calculations are the total of the fixed expense and the percentage of gross profit margin. If your fixed expense is $10,000 and your gross profit margin is 25 percent, your break-even volume must be $40,000.

This Is Not a Static Number

You may do a break-even analysis before you even begin your business and determine that your gross margin will come in at a certain percentage and your fixed expense budget will be set at a certain level. You will then be able to establish that your business will break even (and then go on to a profit) at a certain level of sales volume. But your prestart projections and your operating realities may be very different. After three to six months in business, you should compare projections to the real-world results and reassess, if necessary, what volume is required to reach break-even levels.

Along the way, expenses tend to creep up in both the direct and indirect categories, and you may fall below the break-even volume because you think it is lower than it has become. Take your profit and loss statement every six months or so and refigure your break-even target number.

> The two critical numbers in these calculations are the total of the fixed expense and the percentage of gross profit margin.

Ways to Lower Break-Even

There are three ways to lower your break-even volume, only two of them involve cost controls (which should always be your goal on an ongoing basis).

1. Lower direct costs
2. Exercise cost controls
3. Raise prices

1. Lower direct costs, which will raise the gross margin. Be more diligent about purchasing material, controlling inventory, or increasing the productivity of your labor by more cost effective scheduling or adding more efficient technology.
2. Exercise cost controls on your fixed expense, and lower the necessary total dollars. Be careful when cutting expenses that you do so with an overall plan in mind. You can cut too deeply as well as too little and cause distress among workers, or you may pull back marketing efforts at the wrong time, which will give out the wrong signal.
3. Raise prices! Most entrepreneurs are reluctant to raise prices because they think that overall business will fall off. More often than not that doesn't happen unless you are in a very price-sensitive market, and if you are, you really have already become volume driven.

But if you are in the typical niche-type small business, you can raise your prices 4 to 5 percent without much notice of your customers. The effect is startling. For example, the first model we looked at was the following:

Volume	$15,000	
direct costs	10,500	70%
gross profit	4,500	

Raising the prices 5 percent would result in this change:

Volume	$15,750	
direct cost	10,500	67%
gross profit	5,250	

You will have increased your margin by 3 percent, so you can lower the total volume you will require to break even.

The Goal Is Profit

You are in business to make a profit not just break even, but by knowing where that number is, you can accomplish a good bit:

- You can allocate the sales and marketing effort to get you to the point you need to be.
- Most companies have slow months, so if you project volume below break-even, you can watch expenses to minimize losses. A few really bad months can wipe out a good bit of previous profit.
- Knowing the elements of break-even allows you to manage the costs to maximize the bottom line.

Once you have gotten this far in the knowledge of the elements of your business, you are well on your way to success.

When volume drops below break-even, controlling costs are critical.

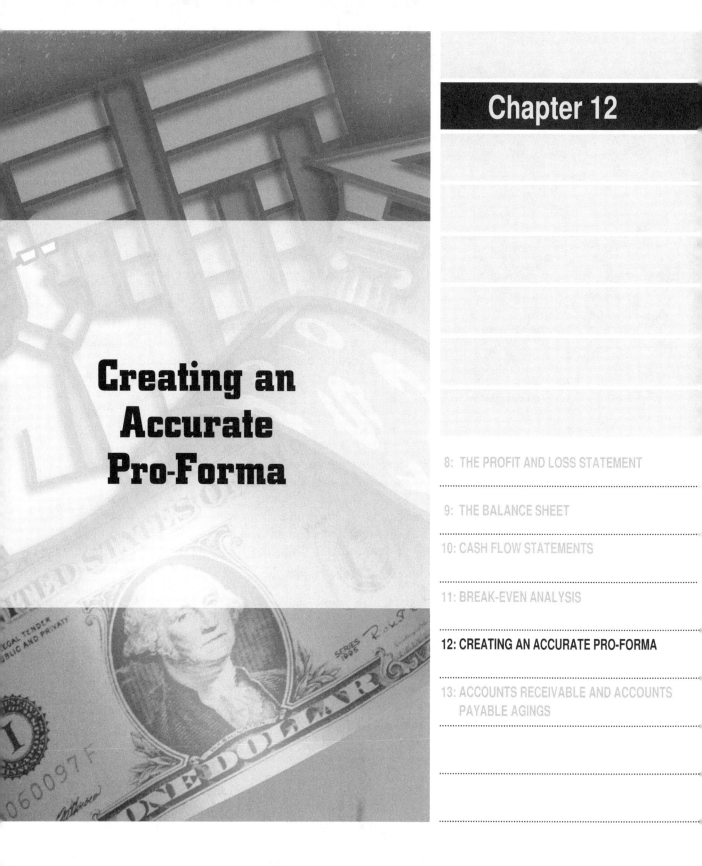

Chapter 12

Creating an Accurate Pro-Forma

There are a number of reasons you will require pro-forma statements, that is, profit and loss or cash flow statements that are projections of future performance. They will be a part of your initial business plan as well as part of any loan application that you will use for a number of reasons such as:

> A pro-forma statement predicts future performance.

1. Information to help you understand when your business will break even; when you will be able to draw a full salary and how much profit you may have to service debt or pay investors.
2. Documents required by any potential investors to help them make decisions about how attractive an opportunity your company presents.
3. To provide the bank or other lenders documentation of your projected ability to have sufficient cash flow to meet debt service.
4. To aid your growing business in planning for sufficient capitalization.

There are a number of ways to approach this task—ranging from the use of a spreadsheet software program that provides a formula you can use to project as far ahead as you wish, to the work of creating the numbers on a line-by-line basis using more in-depth analysis for each item of income and expense. The more effort you put into any pro-forma, the more accurate it is likely to be. Using a combination of analysis and formulas should meet the needs of most businesses.

A pro-forma profit and loss or cash flow statement may be done on a month-to-month or quarterly basis. The determination of what period you use may be made on the basis of how variable your income may be. If some months are far different than others in projected sales revenue (due perhaps to seasonal demand), it might be that a month-by-month report will give you a more accurate view of what to expect and what cash problems you may be able to anticipate. If sales are fairly steady, a quarterly projection will do.

Begin with a Pro-forma Profit and Loss Statement

The starting point of either report is the revenue from sales. This number is often the source of greatest miscalculation. Always keep in mind when you project your income that you are not setting goals, you are predicting what number you actually expect. This isn't a tool to be used as motivation for extra effort, it is to be used as a financial model—one that will allow you to manage the cash that the business will generate from operations as well as from secure outside resources such as loans or investment. An overly optimistic projection that is not met serves the interest of no one and may, if it is submitted to outsiders, undermine your credibility. Most of your cost number will flow from the revenue factor, so this becomes an important estimation.

The start up company must begin their research with a review of as much market and demographic information as possible. Learn as much as you can about the buying patterns that are typical of your product or service—things like the average check price in a comparable restaurant or the average purchase made of your product by each typical customer. This information is available through trade associations and industry groups. One of the benefits of going into a franchise business is the amount of this type of information that is readily available.

You can duplicate some of this research on your own, and there are resources available as well: your local business library, the Chamber of Commerce, and University-based organizations such as the Small Business Development Centers (SBDC). Many SBDCs (and there are over nine hundred centers in the United States) have marketing analysts available to assist you. They can show you how to find what you need.

After you determine how much your typical sale will be, then you must predict how many customers or clients you will serve. There are a number of variables here; mainly, knowing the total number of potential customers (the demographics) and factoring in your capacity (for example., number of seats in a restaurant, billable hours for a consultant, or production output). What percentage of the

> The starting point is revenue from sales—be realistic.

possible customer base (be conservative) will likely patronize your business and what will their average purchase be? Those two numbers will give you a prediction of your volume: The number of customers times the value of each sale.

New businesses seldom bring in the revenue they expect because the purchasing patterns of the public change very slowly. New customers are harder to find than you expect. Therefore, once you have made your projections, you may want to reduce them by up to 20 percent just to be on the safe side. You can always revisit the numbers and revise them, hopefully upward.

Any company that has been in business for a while has a track record to rely on. Remember, however, that in the normal course of business, you will lose some customers, and you may gain others, but only if you work at it.

Are you continually marketing? Again, pro-forma numbers are not goals—so be honest with yourself. What do you really expect to be the growth factor going forward? If you are doing little to be aggressive, they probably will be flat.

> Pro-forma numbers are not goals—so be honest with yourself.

Do Analysis on the Cost Side as Well

While it is likely you will have goals on the direct cost side that will allow you to generate the gross profit that you require, take the extra time to see if those predictions are accurate as the company grows. The cost of material may be affected by shrinkage (unsold goods) and that change must be reflected in your statement. A shoe store that marks up inventory 100 percent to generate a 50 percent gross margin may be seriously affected by the liquidation of unsold shoes to brokers who traditionally pay 30 percent of *cost!* Depending on the amount of shoes sold at this discount, that could cut gross profits in half. Do research and ask questions!

Your costs may be affected positively as well. As your volume increases, you may be able to make purchases in what is often called a "better column," that is a price break for higher quantity. And you may also be able to get prepayment on freight—a cost savings. Remember to account for that in any pro-forma that is planning for growth.

An Analysis of Labor Costs

You may have specific percentage goals for direct labor costs as well, but you must ask yourself whether those numbers will change as the business grows and matures. Some issues to consider:

1. New hires are not immediately productive–growth will cause you to increase your work force and there will be inefficiencies before there is the expected levels of increased production.
2. However, on the other side, the larger the production run, the more economical they may be. Set up times can be very costly and the larger the quantity, the lower the unit cost.
3. Once a job is ongoing, the work is normally completed more efficiently. Less man-hours per product or job/may be required.
4. The stronger you become financially, the more you will be able to invest in better technology thereby increasing productivity.

In short, when estimating what your labor costs will be, don't use a formula straight through the entire period. Consider what changes will happen to affect the cost as well as the productivity and reflect those realities in your expense.

> The larger the production run, the more economical they may be.

Indirect (Fixed) Costs May Vary

The reason these costs are referred to as fixed is that they generally do not change regardless of your volume. Most software programs will use the same numbers regardless of volume thereby increasing profitability. To some degree this is true, but there are circumstances when they will change and you will have a more accurate report if you consider these potential variances.

Take for example, rent. It would be easy to plug in a number that reflects your current lease terms including any cost escalations. But you may be underestimating what you will actually need in a year or two. Do you have sufficient space to house and serve the

> Salary increases are something to consider and factor into your pro-forma.

growth you are predicting? Will you have to expand and have you included the cost of that expansion in your pro-forma?

Other items down the line will have the same considerations. Office staff may be adequate to handle the current level of volume but you may have to add a clerk or a secretary to handle increased calls, letters, and billings. Or at least, you will be giving wage increases to current staff to reflect their experience and increasing work loads.

Salary increases are something to consider and factor into your pro-forma. If you are doing well, managers will expect raises commensurate with their contribution to that success. It is likely as well that you will increase your own salary.

The costs of benefits will go up, particularly health-care costs, which go up virtually every year ahead of the inflation rate. You may want to add benefits as your company becomes more established, and perks, such as cars, as well. These sorts of things aid in attracting and keeping desirable employees. Factor this escalation into your projections.

Postage, freight, telephone, and utilities will all have a certain level of increase. Here are cases where you may be able to use a percentage factor and just plug in the increases.

Remember Those Costs That Are Semi-Variable

The costs associated with sales such as marketing, advertising, travel, and entertainment are not fixed in the traditional sense. They will vary according to your level of sales. They will also reflect your business strategy—whether you are aggressive or more laid-back. If you have a marketing plan (and you should), put a number (budget) to your ideas and then use it in your pro-forma. Travel and entertainment may either be established based on a budget or on a specific basis such as knowledge of conferences and conventions that you will be attending. Will you be purchasing event tickets to use with customers? What real life expenses do you expect?

Now you should have a profit and loss pro-forma that is likely to be met by your actual operations and provide valuable information for planning. Next, you will use the same numbers in your cash flow projection.

The only difference with the cash flow is how much money you will collect in hand each month. If yours is a cash business, the answer is easy—the amount of sales. If yours is a credit business, you must predict what percentage of your outstanding receivables will be collected. Use your own terms as one factor and you can find industry norms from Dun & Bradstreet. An existing business has history to rely on—your receivable turnover ratio will give you what you need.

A Pro-forma Is Part of a Successful Strategic Plan

In business, being able to be proactive instead of reactive is a critical factor in success. In cash management, the main tool is your pro-forma. Take the time to make it accurately reflect your business and you will be prepared to take advantage of opportunities and deal with problems before they become serious.

A pro-forma is the best cash management tool you can have.

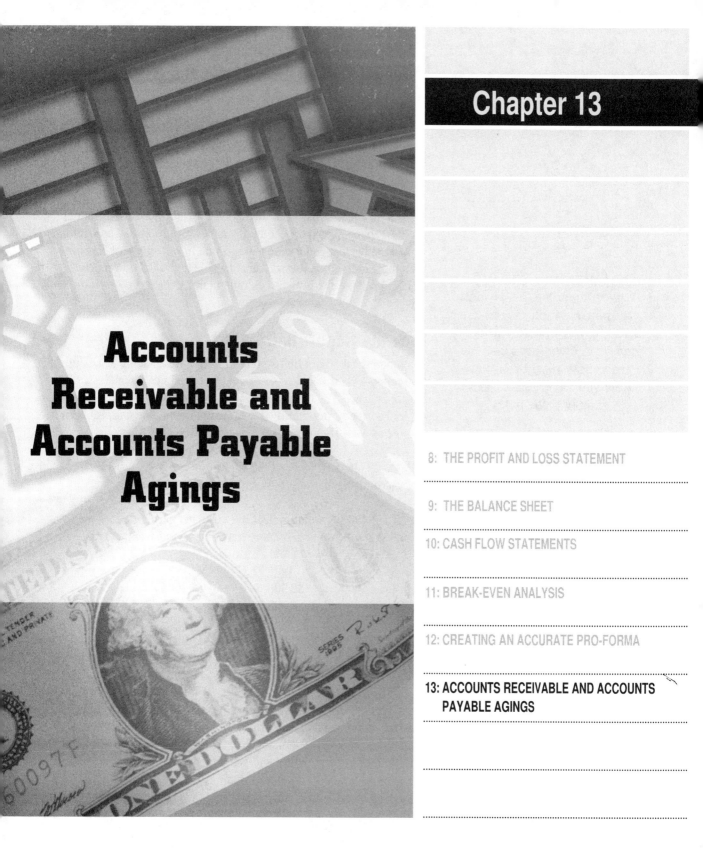

Chapter 13

Accounts Receivable and Accounts Payable Agings

These are more bookkeeping documents than strictly accounting ones, but they are important nevertheless. They are easy to understand and provide exactly what the name implies, a listing of your accounts payable and accounts receivable by the age of each invoice or bill. You will want to know not only how much money is owed to you but how long it has been owed because this information will tell you how soon you can expect money to be paid. You will also want to know exactly what you owe to vendors and how long your bills have been outstanding because you must be able to project how much cash you will require in the weeks and months ahead.

> You will want to know not only how much money is owed to you but how long it has been owed because this information will tell you how soon you can expect money to be paid.

How the Report Is Created

A computerized accounting system will generate an aging as an automatic report. Your bookkeeper or controller will need to make sure that the invoice date (for both payables and receivables) has been entered correctly and that the scheduled payment date has also been entered as well. The report will look as follows:

Days Outstanding	1–30	31–60	61–90	over 90
Account Name	Amt	Amt	Amt	Amt

The following would reflect five customer accounts, each owing several thousand dollars, some current and some beyond due dates:

	1–30	31–60	60–90	over 90	Total
ABC Corp	$2,500		$1,000		3,500
Blue Company	3,500				3,500
3X Corp		4,000			4,000
Joe's Store	1,000		1,500	1,000	3,500
XZY Dist.		5,200			5,200
	4,500	11,700	2,500	1,000	19,700

The total can be verified by making sure that the last column and the bottom column equal the same amount. You will have data of the total amount outstanding for each account, and you will know what amount is outstanding for each period.

Accounts that are over 90 days old should be verified to make sure that there isn't any dispute or they have not been paid but incorrectly posted.

From this report, you should be able to predict that your collections will be at least $14,200, which is 31–90 days old and perhaps some portion of the 1–30 day money as well. The over 90 portion is in question until verified.

Here is a sample of five vendors that you each owe several thousand dollars to:

	1–30	31–60	60–90	over 90	Total
CBA Supply	$1,500	1,800			3,300
Telephone Co	900	350			1,250
ZZ Leasing	800	800	800	800	3,200
XYZ Ind.	2,800	4,200			6,000
Bob's Supply		2,500			2,500
Total	6,000	9,650	800	800	16,250

The first step again is to verify that the totals balance on both the last and bottom columns, and then you can analyze your position. From this report, the good news is that the bulk of the payables are within 60 days. Perhaps the leasing company has let payments slide, or there may be some dispute over the terms or conditions of leased equipment.

This report gives the business owner information that a minimum of $9,650 must be paid against the payables over the next month plus any lease payment past due and current payments such as utilities that must be paid as agreed.

> An aging report will predict how much cash will be collected and how much will be needed.

Agings Are Management Tools

These simple, easy-to-read reports are key elements in good cash flow management. A good financial manager makes sure that they are issued, reviewed, and utilized.

Setting Budgets and Controlling Costs

Summary of Part III

- **How much money do you need to start a business**
- **What will your ongoing operations cost be**
- **Setting realistic budgetary goals**
- **Keeping overhead in line**
- **The hidden cost in labor and inventory**

Chapter 14

The Startup Budget

Every business plan includes a budget for the startup costs of the company, but the problem with many of these budgets is that they are often incomplete because of lack of complete information and unrealistic because of lack of experience. There are a number of key points to review when establishing a budget for startups that will prevent unexpected surprises from jeopardizing the success of your business. Several key issues are as follows:

1. Those expenses that are primarily for organizational costs (lawyers, and so on), space preparation, and equipment for long-term use will not see an immediate return. Borrowing money to cover these expenses may add debt service costs to your operation that you cannot afford in the early stages of business.
2. Don't neglect the costs of printed material (sales and marketing pieces), utility deposits, insurance coverage, lease deposits, and other less obvious charges you will incur.
3. A startup budget must include adequate reserve money to use as working capital. It is difficult to borrow this type of money from the bank for the first year or so of operation, but if it is not available, the business may not be able to grow to its full potential.

One-Time Startup Costs

> The first items on your budget should be those costs that you will pay only once.

The first items on your budget should be those costs that you will pay only once. In short, this is the cost to get you into business, and the return of this investment will come back over the years in the form of profits. If at all possible, monies for these expenses should come from equity investment and not borrowed funds. A combination of investment and loans is somewhat possible, but borrowing all the money to pay for startup costs may create an early cash flow problem as a result of the need to pay debt service before revenue has a chance to grow past the break-even point into real profitability.

The costs involved in a startup may include the following:
1. Legal and accounting charges for incorporation or partnership agreements, and so on. Fees to government entities for licenses or permits such as occupancy permits.
2. Site preparation, including leasehold improvements, fixtures, and any required rental or security deposits.
3. Utility deposits and phone installation.
4. Necessary machinery and equipment.
5. Printed material, including business cards, letterhead, and marketing material.
6. Initial inventory or supplies.

Your Need for Operating Capital

The most difficult component of your startup budget will be to compute how much cash you will need for working capital—money you will need to fund early losses (and there are likely to be some) and to smooth out your cash flow. You need to refer to any cash flow projections that you may have done as a part of your business plan and determine how much money may be lost in the early months. There are only two ways to fund those losses, with capital infusion or by acquiring debt, namely, not paying your vendors. This is not a good way to start a venture or to even run it if you have alternatives. So plan on having sufficient capital in reserve to fund early losses and to pay necessary expenses as cash flow begins to build.

Now is the time when you will put your cash flow projections and your break-even analysis to work. Take your first year's projected income and the year's projected expense, both variable and fixed, and that difference is approximately what you will require as capital. Remember the two variables from your statement; any depreciation is a noncash item and may be deducted, but you must include your principal payments on your loan, if any.

> The most difficult component of your startup budget will be to compute how much cash you will need for working capital.

Determine Your Market Entry Costs

The first part of your startup budget will likely be relatively straight-forward. You can do research on costs and get quotes on specific items. The second part, the working capital requirement, is far more subjective. You will not be starting your business in a vacuum; there will be competitive forces at work from the moment you open the doors. Doing an analysis of that competition is a part of the startup research you should be doing. How crowded is the market you are entering? Are you doing something that will differentiate yourself from your competitors? Are there sufficient customers to support a new player?

The honest answers to these questions will give you further guidelines on your working capital requirements. The longer it will take you to build an adequate customer base and the more pressure to keep prices (and therefore profits) down, the more capital you will need. For many new businesses, the key to ultimate success is to have the staying power in the beginning to remain in the game long enough to win.

> The longer it will take you to build an adequate customer base, the more capital you will need.

Be Conservative and Realistic

No doubt that a number of businesses have started on a shoestring, and you may be one that can pull it off. But a substantial number of failures are caused by too little working capital (the number-one reported reason), so the odds are not in your favor. Even if you must begin with less cash than you would like, at least begin with a realistic look at where you are and what your needs are likely to be. Then you won't be surprised when a cash crunch comes, and you can prepare temporary solutions to alleviate the situation. When you develop your startup numbers, be conservative with revenue projections and realistic with the cost of your venture.

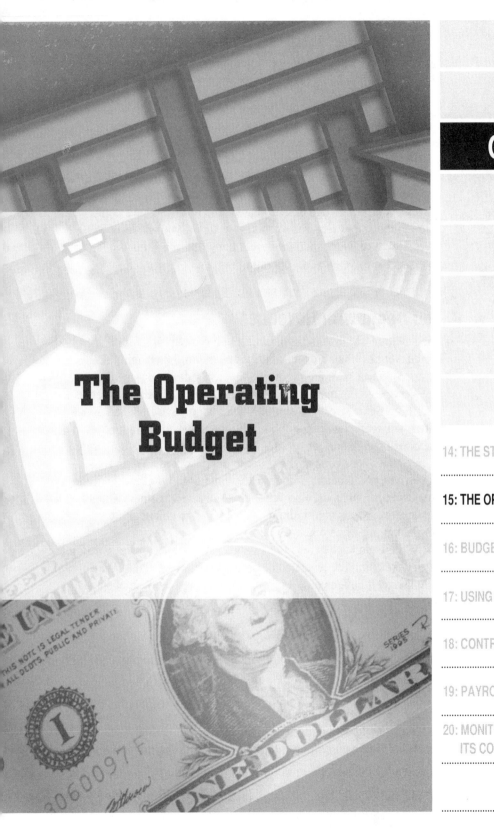

Chapter 15

The Operating Budget

Perhaps one of the most important documents you will create in the beginning is the operating budget that will set goals and targets for your first year in business and every additional year as well. The first of these budgets that you will do will likely be for your business plan, but you must not stop there. Remember that early on in the planning process, your knowledge base is limited, and once you have gone through the stages required to open your doors, you will learn a great deal from your experience. Over the years, your knowledge will be expanded by your actual operating history.

> The key to most budgets begins with the income from sales or operating revenue.

You Begin with Revenues

The key to most budgets begins with the income from sales or operating revenue. When most businesses are still in the planning stages, dreams of mega sales are prevalent, but reality dawns on opening day. Very often the most frequent surprise to new business owners is that the revenue stream (cash flow) never happens as they had anticipated. The reason is simple. While a business owner is wrapped up in the creation of his or her venture, few potential customers are aware or care that a new company is about to open its doors. When that day arrives, the expectations are seldom met as to how quickly these potential customers will discover and utilize a new business. One of the only exceptions is restaurants; people tend to go out and try a new restaurant when one opens.

So the message here is to be very analytical and conservative when developing the revenue line on your operating budget. When establishing it before you open your doors, do your projections and then reduce it by one-third. After the first 60 days in business, go back to that budget and test it against actual results. Make any adjustments, and then budget the whole year.

Set Goals for Your Direct Expense

The cost projections you make for your direct expense (labor and material) should be monitored closely during your early months in business to learn whether you have been on target or not. There may be some earlier variance if you have done any promotional pricing such as "grand opening specials." Ideally, you have provided for this in your startup budget (discounting causes losses and that costs money). In fact, if you want to determine the actual costs of your early promotional efforts, record your sales at their full price and create an expense account for the discounts given. The method is simple. For example, if your opening sale is a 20 percent off program, you might have recorded all sales at the selling price, so a $10.00 item would be shown as $8.00 of revenue. To track it better, you would record as follows:

Sales income $10.00
Admin. expense
    promotional discount $2.00

> There may be some earlier variance if you have done any promotional pricing such as "grand opening specials."

Now when you deduct your direct expense (material and labor) from your sales income, you will be able to track your *normal* costs and know your expected gross profit when the sale period is over.

Once the initial period is over, you must monitor your direct expenses to make sure that they stay close to your original estimates. Sometimes, you will see the margins shrink and you must find out the reason. Sometimes, it will be due to inefficiencies, and other times, the cause will be the pass through of price increases from suppliers or wage increases given to employees. The cost pressure will require you to raise your prices eventually—the timing and the amount will be much more successful if you are aware of the effect of these increases.

Waiting too long may cause you to lose money at a time when you can ill afford to (there is never a good time to lose money), and making your own pricing increase too conservative can damage your bottom line as well. Trying to readjust a second time will cause customers to take notice and perhaps resist. If the effect of material or labor costs are rising only marginally, you may be able to make internal changes to absorb these increases and avoid raising your own prices. Accurate and current financial information is critical to staying within your operating budget projections and keeping gross profit margins where you need them to be.

Budget Your Indirect Costs

Your fixed expenses come in three basic categories, and each is handled in a different way. The first could be considered the nonoptional and nonnegotiable. Items such as rent will fall into this category. Your landlord has set a price, and you have agreed to pay over a period. This cost is necessary and has been established by agreement. Other costs that fall into this category are:

> Spend time focusing on costs that are either optional or negotiable.

Utilities (other than phone)
Insurance (liability and workers' compensation)
Taxes (a fixed portion of payroll)
Debt service (interest is fixed)
Professional expense

Spending a great deal of effort on these items is a marginal use of your time. The only exception would be insurance if that is a *major* cost to your business. But few new businesses would get competitive quotes.

The second major cost of your fixed expenses are those that are more optional and at times negotiable. They may include:

Office salaries. (Keep an eye on this expense—staffing should be as tight as you can make it.)

Officer draw. (You should peg this number to a percentage of sales and keep it there. This is often the line item that creates the biggest problem when revenue is low.)

Benefits such as insurance, car and phone allowance, and vacation. (Curb the desire to be more generous than you can afford in the early stages of your business. Once a benefit is established, the costs become fixed and hard to reduce.)

Basic sales and marketing expense. (Early-stage businesses can utilize more effort and less cash and secure almost the same results. Don't throw money at marketing unless you have determined that it is absolutely necessary and you have budgeted for it. Use clever and free public relations efforts instead.)

And the final category of costs are those that we have described as semivariable: line items such as selling expense, travel, entertainment, phone (long distance), and postage and freight that will be tied to your level of revenue. Establish basic budget amounts that will represent the amount you expect to spend and allow this number to go up *only* if revenues increase and *only* by the increase in those revenues.

Your startup budget may look something like this:

	Jan	Feb	Mar	%
Sales income	$60,000	$70,000	$80,000	100
Material/labor	36,000	42,000	48,000	60
Gross profit	$24,000	$28,000	$32,000	40
Fixed Expense–Admin.				
Rent	4,000	4,000	4,000	
Utilities	2,500	2,500	2,500	
Insurance	1,500	1,500	1,500	
Interest	1,500	1,500	1,500	
Accounting	1,000	1,000	1,000	
	$10,500	$10,500	$10,500	
	17%	15%	12%	

As sales increase, fixed expenses go down as a percentage of costs.

Note that the necessary and nonnegotiable stays the same in dollars but goes down in percentage as sales go up.

Now those that are optional:

	Jan	Feb	%	Mar	%
Office salaries	$2,000	$2,000	3.5	$2,000	2.0
Officer's draw	3,000	3,000	5.0	4,000	5.0
Benefits	1,500	1,500	2.5	2,000	2.5
Marketing/promo	1,200	1,200	2.0	1,600	2.0
	$7,700	$7,700	13.0	$9,600	11.5

While sales are going up, more budget is being allocated to creating a benefit package and marketing and promotional material. The owner is taking a larger draw as well. Office staff has not increased. Given the increase in revenue, however, the total percentage of these fixed costs have gone down by 1.5 percent, increasing the bottom line.

Semivariable expense:

	Jan	Feb	Mar	%
Selling expense	$1,000	$1,160	$1,250	1.65
Travel	900	1,050	1,125	1.5
Entertainment	600	700	800	1.0
Phone	300	350	400	.5
				4.65%

> Create a formula for your operating budget and stick to it.

The cost goes up but the goal has been set to keep it at a constant percentage level. Working with this budget the percentage results will be:

	Jan	Mar
Sales	100.0%	100.0%
Direct expense	60.0%	60.0%
Gross profit	40.0%	40.0%
Fixed expense	17.0%	12.0%
Controllable fixed	13.0%	11.5%
Semivariable	4.65%	4.65%
Net before taxes	5.35%	11.85%

Creating a formula for your operating budget and sticking to it will keep your costs better controlled and sustain a healthy bottom line.

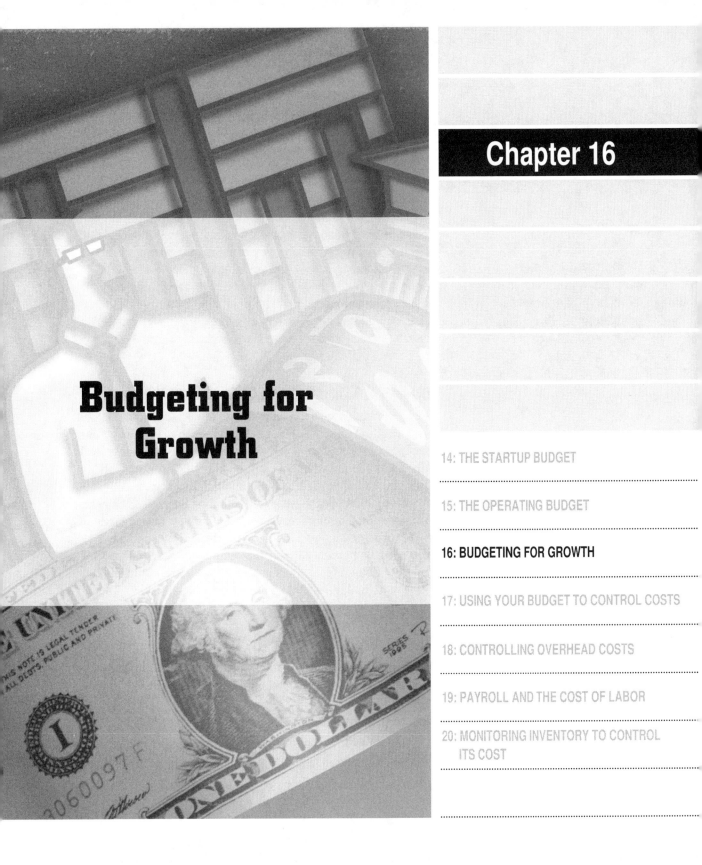

Chapter 16

Budgeting for Growth

The most common single goal expressed by new business owners is their desire to grow their business. Wanting to have a "million-dollar company" is fairly typical. Much thought must be given to what growth really means and how it will impact, positively and negatively, the stability and possibly future of your venture.

The first admonition here would be to remember that it is not the top line (total revenue) that matters, it is the bottom line or profit that really counts. If you are willing to sacrifice most of your profit, it isn't that difficult to grow a company to a fairly large size. Selling your products or services cheaper than your competition is likely to get you a substantial share of the market, but the lack of positive cash flow is just as likely to threaten your very existence. So although growth is an admirable goal, profitable growth is what you should strive for.

> Thought must be given to what growth really means and how it will impact, positively and negatively, the stability of your venture.

You Must Control the Rate of Growth

Rapid growth may seem like an exciting prospect—consider the adage "build a better mousetrap and they'll beat a path to your door." But if too much happens too soon, you may be caught without the funds or the human or material resources to meet the demands. A customer base that is unsatisfied is one that seldom returns. The other potential problem is not having sufficient capital and stretching your cash and credit too thin. Unpaid vendors or, worse, unpaid taxes could seriously undermine the future, particularly if it results in credit being withdrawn, supplies not being shipped, or collection action being instituted. So it is important to understand the dynamics of growth and the strategies to manage it comfortably.

The Stages of a Growth Cycle

There are three basic stages of growth, and each requires different expenditures and different efforts.

Stage One: Entering the Market

This is a high-cost stage because most of your cash resources are going into development and marketing efforts, which are long-term investments. New revenue may be slight at the start of this stage because demand is just being created in your targeted customer base. The accuracy of your market analysis is critical here because your spending must be kept in line with the expected revenue and profits of the product or service that is being launched.

For example, you would not spend $100,000 to launch into a market where the total potential sales would be less than $500,000. That would burden your revenue with a 20 percent cost of just creating the sale. But you might well spend the same $100,000 to be a player where there are millions of revenue to be had over a number of years. This stage should take three to six months to develop for a smaller company; only a very large and stable organization can afford a longer market entry cycle.

Stage Two: Fulfillment

This is the high-effort stage that also has a need for substantial capital but will have a revenue stream attached as well. Once the orders are in hand, it may be possible to borrow a substantial portion of the needed money from a lending source. This is the profitable stage of a growth cycle, and the money earned must be utilized carefully.

High demands will be made of staff at this point, and it will be tempting to just add folks until the workload is relieved.

There is a caution here. Remember that new employees are seldom very productive until they are properly trained and experienced. This will increase your direct costs, and while your volume is growing, your operating profits may be sufficient enough to offset these inefficiencies, but a period of slow or no growth will be made more difficult if your gross profit margins are smaller. Now is the time to use the percentages you established as goals on your operating budget. If labor is meant to be 25 percent of your costs, don't let it get higher than that. Perhaps everyone will have to work a bit harder but overtime may be preferable to new hires.

There are other problems with a slew of new hires. Benefits add to the cost of labor, and it is often cheaper to pay time and a half in wages to an existing employee who has already covered his or her benefits. And there is the human side as well. Keeping a core group

> The accuracy of your market analysis is critical here because your spending must be kept in line with the expected revenue.

of employees fully employed over the long haul is preferable to a revolving door of new hires when things seem very tight. It is difficult to lay off a worker, and you are somewhat likely to keep too much staff when things level off or slow down.

Material or inventory also must be watched during times of rapid growth. When sales begin to take off, it is difficult to set inventory levels because you are often running out of items. Depending on deliveries from your suppliers, this can become a critical problem. It is natural to want to stock as much as you can. Keep careful watch on line items and when the stock begins to grow, take action. Unsold inventory while carried on your balance sheet as an asset will not turn into cash until sold. Ultimately, it may have to be liquidated at a deep discount or written off, which will impact your bottom line.

Stage Three: Renewal

Once demand has leveled off or competition has come into play, you will have the task of reenergizing your sales. This is also a high-effort stage and often needs little cash as labor and material are being cut back to meet demand. Sales may be coming from old contracts or discounted goods, and when this part of the cycle has ended, if a revitalization of products, services, or strategy has not been implemented, sales may begin to disappear altogether.

> You must budget cash resources during the growth and profitability stage that can be used for development and marketing.

You must budget cash resources during the growth and profitability stage that can be used for development and marketing of the next phase of your business life. Although your bank may step forward as a lender during the actual growth phase, few lenders are willing to make loans to a company losing steam. Capital must be on hand or internally generated.

The Three Major Elements to Manage Growth

1. Sufficient capital must be available. Drawing on your profit and loss statement and cash flow projections, determine how much capital will be required before the cycle begins. Set up a line of credit at the bank that you can draw on as needed.

Increasing vendor credit may also be a form of capital during this period.

2. A full-blown strategic plan must be in place. Your marketing plan is step one, and the production or operational plan is step two. Know how you will create demand for your products or services and how you will fill that demand. Be specific about key elements such as employment levels, space needs, and equipment requirement.

3. Put in place sufficient leadership to manage a high-growth period. This is where the rubber meets the road with regard to delegation, and the successful entrepreneur will bring in good managers and allow them to operate at full capacity. They must have decision-making authority and should be given budget responsibilities as well. This rapid growth cycle is a challenge opportunity and needs good people working on all cylinders to take advantage of it.

The Budget Is the Goal

From day one of your operation, you should monitor your progress against the budget you've created. For controlled growth and profitable growth, this budget review process is the key. Know your goals in costs and profit margins, and establish limits on money spent. You'll be able to be proactive in securing the capital you require and in maintaining the profit level you need and deserve.

> From day one of your operation, you should monitor your progress against the budget you've created.

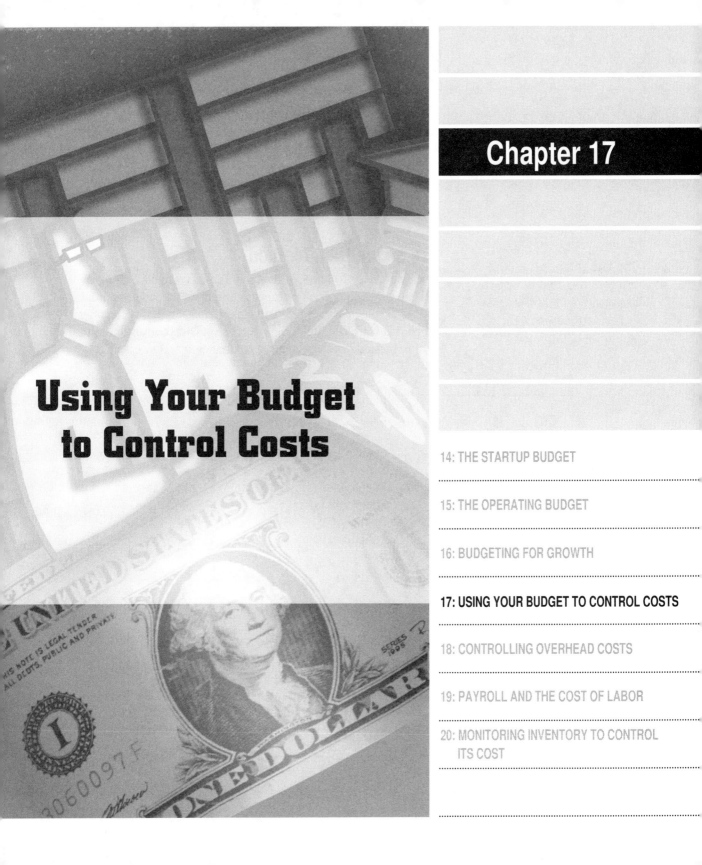

Chapter 17

Using Your Budget to Control Costs

Your budget must be a vibrant document, one that is well considered and that is used on an ongoing basis. Use it as a historical reporting system. Don't look at how you've measured up to your goals months or even weeks after a period has closed. Check the important elements (direct costs as one example) far more frequently.

Use a Line Item Method

When you created your chart of accounts, you created a list of general categories such as office expense or repairs and maintenance. For the purposes of your profit and loss statement, those categories are all that is needed. But for the purpose of cost control, you may want to break down these items into subcategories. For example:

> For the purpose of cost control, you may want to break down these items into subcategories.

- Utilities
    - Gas
    - Electric
    - Water
    - Sewage
- Office expense
    - Supplies
    - Equipment leases
    - Postage
    - Temporary help
- Insurance
    - Liability
    - Auto
    - Health
    - Life
    - Workers' compensation

This will give you detailed information on exactly where the money is being spent so you can monitor and correct any serious excesses. Comparing your fixed expense to the budget and the amount spent a year earlier on the same items is a good way to see if you are still in line.

Monitor on a Regular Basis

Even when the trend is exactly where you want it to be, don't give up the regular habit of monitoring costs against budget. You can create a statement that looks like the one that follows:

	Budget 1999	Actual Jan	YTD	+/-
Sales				
Cost of goods				
Gross profit				
etc.				

If you had anticipated sales of $600,000 for 1999 and your sales for January were $42,000, then the top line would read:

	Budget 1999	Actual Jan	YTD	+/-
Sales	$50,000	42,000	42,000	(8,000)

You will know at a glance whether you are over or under in any budget category, and then you can research the line items if necessary to identify and correct any problems.

Give Budget Authority to Managers

A critical element in delegation of work and authority is assigning responsibility for expenditures and bottom line outcomes. At the beginning of each period, identify the amount of money budgeted for each department manager and ask them to create a list of priorities. Then on each reporting period, check the results of their expenditures against the amounts budgeted. Perhaps you can include an incentive program for those who come in under budget. Whether in the corporate world or the world of small business, it is human nature to spend all the money in the budget because there is always some piece of equipment to upgrade or replace, or there is some inventory

> At the beginning of each period, identify the amount of money budgeted for each department manager and ask them to create a list of priorities.

that is difficult to source and creates the desire to stockpile. Put a prize on resisting that urge, and don't forget to explain all the reasonings behind budget decisions.

Be Prepared to Sacrifice

A healthy business can bring a good return, long term, to a prudent operator. Don't make the mistake of choosing short-term satisfaction at the risk of long-term stability. Keep all the expenditures within reason until the company is well on its feet and able to easily afford them.

Don't make the mistake of choosing short-term satisfaction at the risk of long-term stability.

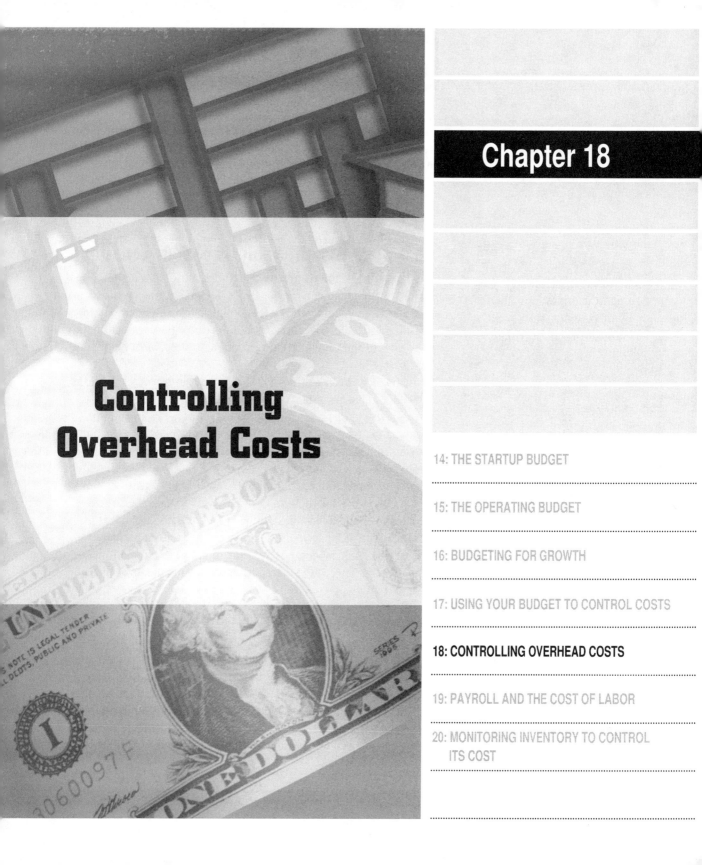

Controlling
Overhead Costs

The time to begin a control system on the cost of your overhead is before you open your doors. You will be making a number of choices at that time that you will live with for many years to come. The primary source of this overhead expense is your business location and all the costs associated with that space such as utilities and taxes.

Do a Cost–Benefit Analysis of Your Location

It is certainly glamorous to have a luxurious office in a high-rise building with a fabulous view or to operate in a quaint storefront in a trendy shopping district. But it is not glamorous to be unable to pay all of your bills and worry about future profits. Many considerations go into choosing a business location, but cost *must* be high on the list.

Much has been written and talked about in recent years on the growth of home-based businesses. From a pure cost perspective, this can be a way to operate with a minimum of overhead. In addition, there are tax advantages as well because you can deduct a portion of your housing expense for the space used strictly to operate your business.

But a home office is not for everyone. For your venture, it may be difficult to meet with clients, you may find too many distractions, or you may even be violating zoning laws. For the independent professional such as an accountant, consultant, or sales representative, this may be the most cost-effective way to get a start in a business, particularly if you tend to meet with most of your clients at their place of business.

Locating a retail business is a far more difficult choice because your success may depend on whether customers find you accessible, and you will want to draw on existing commercial traffic as well. If your products are unique enough to make your business a destination and your customer base is expected from a wide geographic area, you can be more flexible in your space, with personal security and perhaps good parking being key criteria. Study the demographics of any area you are considering and talk to other store owners. For the most part, they should be cooperative about giving you

> There are tax advantages as well because you can deduct a portion of your housing expense for the space used strictly to operate your business.

information because if you move in, that could mean more customer traffic for them.

Manufacturing and distribution businesses have the most options because they can operate out of a variety of locations; the main criterion likely would be the space being adequate for the need of the operation. If a labor force will eventually be hired, good public transportation may be an issue, as will having additional space for future expansion.

There are business image issues involved with the location of any company as well as the look of the offices or store. Most potential customers for big-ticket items expect to conduct their business in somewhat luxurious accommodations, but often the need for high-cost space is overrated. Well appointed, moderately priced offices can work nicely.

Using your original profit and loss projections as a guideline, determine the maximum percentage of revenue you can afford for occupancy (including rental, utilities, and any other space-related costs) and keep to that budget. If you have done a three-year pro-forma budget you can total those dollars for each year knowing that what you can afford on opening day may be only a small fraction of what will fit into a reasonable budget for the future. Don't, however, prespend the money you hope to be earning down the road. Keep your cost to the total budgeted amount. It also may be possible to structure a lease that will meet your cash flow expectations by making the rent in year one less than the rent in year three. If you find a good, well-priced business space, try to get an option on additional years as well. Moving can be costly and disruptive to any business venture. You want to keep the choice open to stay on if the space works.

> Good public transportation may be an issue.

Controlling the Cost of Administration

In the early days of a new company, the founder and perhaps a family member will fulfill many of the roles required to run the business, including that of secretary and bookkeeper. As the company grows and the transactions increase, staff will be hired to handle this work.

This often is the type of work that entrepreneurs find confusing and less challenging than the other tasks such as sales or operations. Paying little attention to what tasks are required and how they can be best accomplished often results in administrative overhead that is in excess of the need. This function may almost become a business within a business, and insufficient questions are asked about this aspect of the overhead on the assumption that it is required.

The benchmark here as well is the amount established in the startup or ongoing budget. If this amount is exceeded, look around for savings. One way is to contract out for some services. Unless you have a very small payroll, an outside service is bound to be more economical and often more accurate. Outside services have the systems to do this easily and efficiently. You also might consider using a lockbox service provided by your bank to process your receivable checks. Money will be deposited quickly, and you will receive the information to post to your accounts.

If you have short-term projects or temporary high-volume times, perhaps the answer is to hire a temporary worker from an agency. The cost may be a bit higher, but you won't be increasing your payroll on a permanent basis. Once hired, it is too easy to keep an employee on even when he or she is not a necessary expense. Learn to resist the urge.

> Unless you have a very small payroll, an outside service is bound to be more economical and often more accurate.

Controlling the Costs of Professionals

Your accountant, attorney, and perhaps a consultant may well be necessary advisors to your business, but they are expensive ones as well. You must be careful about how often you use them and for what purpose since most charge by the hour or any fraction thereof.

For your accountant, you will want to schedule at least quarterly meetings to go over your progress and verify the accuracy of your internal books. The more process work you can do at your own office, the more money you can save on these professional fees. Most businesses can utilize prepackaged software such as Quicken or Peachtree, and with these or more sophisticated custom systems, you can generate internal profit and loss statements.

Have them reviewed periodically so that if you have made mistakes, they can be corrected early. You will also want to schedule a tax planning meeting with your accountant at least 60 days before the end of your year, and he or she will assist in closing the year and prepare your tax returns as well.

For your attorney, you must be well organized and your questions well thought out before calling him or her. What may be annoying or upsetting at the moment may not be urgent and may not require an immediate answer. With the passage of time, the issue may resolve itself, and you won't have acquired a legal bill to discuss it. Certainly, if you have real legal problems either threatened or in process, you should turn them over to your lawyer, and you should *not* sign leases or contracts that have not been reviewed by counsel. But be prudent about how often you call and how long you talk.

Any consultant who you hire to handle a project or give advice should give you a written proposal of the scope of his or her work and a firm quote of the price. Make sure you get progress billings on a timely basis and halt any work that goes over budget until it can be reviewed.

Small Stuff Adds Up

A number of line items, such as office supplies, postage, phone charges (particularly cell phones), and the dump category called miscellaneous, may be small individually but can easily get out of control and effect the bottom line. The best monitoring device here is a strict adherence to dollar amounts budgeted as well as percentages. As volume increases and these costs appear almost inconsequential, it is easy to cease any review at all, but it's a mistake as well. Allowing any expense categories to go unmonitored is inviting an escalation of costs, which during slow times, can cause a problem.

For example, your phone bill was budgeted at $400 a month, a small percentage (2 percent) of your expected $20,000 sales. As volume grew, more and more folks wanted (or needed) cell phones, and the bill jumped to $1,100 a month, which was approximately 3.5 percent of revenues, now at $30,000. This may seem like a relatively

> If you have real legal problems either threatened or in process, you should turn them over to your lawyer.

small increase and surely one that can be managed. But sales go soft from time to time, and should yours fall back to $20,000, this cost would increase to 5 percent of revenue, which could be a problem. Cell phones are one area where costs can mount quickly, and you become dependent on the convenience. Be careful to monitor closely.

Be diligent about your targets.

Begin with a Plan and Stick to It

From the time you create your initial pro-forma statement and operating budget, you must think of the numbers you establish as serious goals. Diligence in meeting these targets will result in a healthy bottom line and the flexibility to weather tough times and take advantage of good ones.

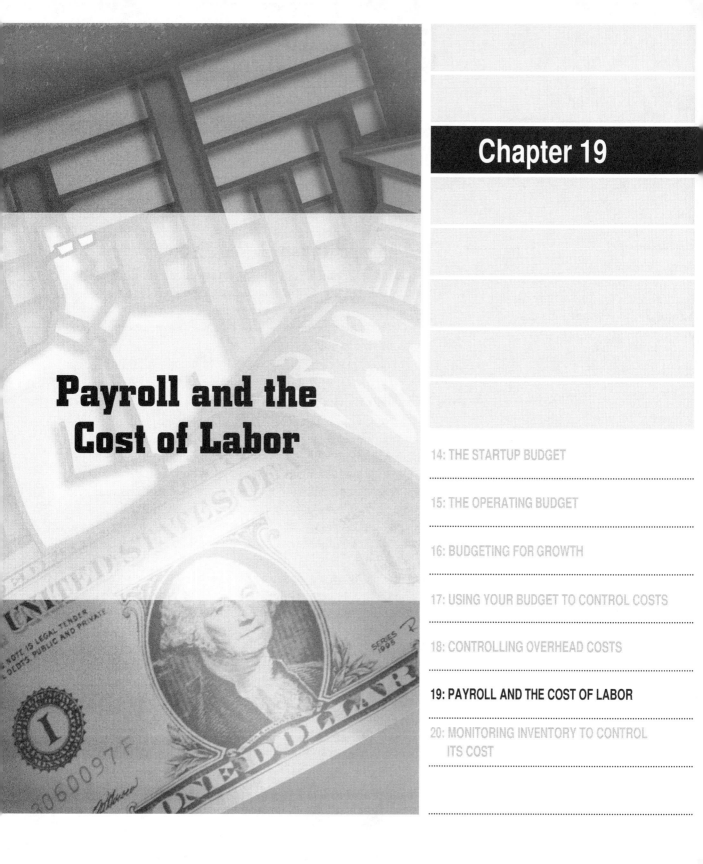

Chapter 19

Payroll and the Cost of Labor

For many businesses, particularly those in the service industry, such as restaurants or manufacturing companies that are labor intensive, the cost of payroll is the single largest line item on the profit and loss statement. Therefore, these are costs that *must* be budgeted and must be monitored for progress.

The Administration of Your Payroll

The two key elements in establishing an effective payroll administration system are, first, setting company policy regarding pay and, second, determining how often payroll will be done and who will do it. These are the decisions made by the business owner, and they should be well thought out not just made on the run.

> Set policy with regard to pay and determine who will do it.

Establishing Payroll Policy

Unless you are utilizing union labor and subject to a negotiated contract, the parameters (within the law) of payroll are yours to set. You will likely negotiate vacation time with new employees and ultimately set a companywide standard such as one week after the first year, two weeks after year three, and three weeks after year five. It is best to be conservative going in; you can always loosen the policy, but it is almost impossible to take time back once it has been given. The same goes for paid holidays such as Thanksgiving, Christmas, and so on. Decide how many you can afford and be conservative. The day after Thanksgiving is appreciated because it makes a four-day weekend, but it is not necessary. The last portion of these "time off days" are sick time and personal leave. Find out what is typical in your type of business; you want to be competitive to attract the right people, but again be cautious in the beginning.

Consider this: If you give two weeks vacation, five holidays, and five sick or personal days, that is a total of 20 days. The work year is 260 days long, and that means that almost 8 percent of your labor costs is being paid for nonproductive time. As we go along and look at other benefits, you will see how expensive employees are—far beyond the wages you think you are paying. Remember this when setting budgets. The average "extra" cost of each employee is 35 percent, so a $40,000-a-year person is actually a $54,000-a-year person.

Getting the Payroll Processed

If you have a small number of employees and a good computer system, you can do your payroll processing in-house. But as your numbers grow and the type of information you want gets more complicated, sending this task out to an outside service makes far more sense.

Make sure that the person who tracks and transmits your payroll keeps accurate records; the use of a time clock is one good way to be sure all hours worked are correctly maintained. Vacation days as well as paid time off should be scrutinized to be fair to both employer and employee.

Benefits Can Be Costly: Keep to a Budget

Without adding anything additional, your payroll is increased by approximately 24 percent by the cost of vacations, FICA (Social Security) contribution, unemployment insurance, and statutory workers' compensation insurance. But that does not end many benefit packages that may also include health (including dental) insurance as well as life insurance plus perks such as car expense, which may be required in certain circumstances. This can add up in a hurry and, if not controlled, may make the company unprofitable or uncompetitive.

Again, be cautious at the outset because adding benefits is far easier than trying to reduce them. Full health coverage for a family can easily cost $600 per month, or $7,200 per year. For an employee earning $40,000 per year, this is an 18 percent add-on and would increase the benefits to a total of 42 percent (24 percent established by vacation, tax, and other insurance), making the cost closer to $60,000. This is a fairly high place to start unless you are working in a competitive situation for specific skills or talents.

The issue of company cars as a benefit is a difficult one as well. The total cost can be substantial and remains fixed regardless of the

> Make sure that the person who tracks and transmits your payroll keeps accurate records.

productivity of your employees, normally sales personnel, because the cost isn't tied to any set level of sales. Why not start with a reimbursement plan (mileage and perhaps a gas card), and if the cost seems to be justified, you can consider the car as well; just remember that insurance will also be a cost, as will maintenance, parking, and all other incidentals.

For many companies, payroll for both direct and indirect labor is *the* largest line item. Remember that there are costs beyond the pay itself, and keep them in line by creating and sticking to a budget.

> Why not start with a reimbursement plan (mileage and perhaps a gas card).

Payroll Taxes

Keep in mind that you must budget for those taxes that are add-ons to your payroll. First is the federal FICA tax, which is for Social Security and Medicare. You will also pay a tax to the Internal Revenue Service as well as your state for a contribution to the unemployment fund. The percentage on the FICA tax is fixed at 7.8 percent but the unemployment tax is variable depending on the status of your account. The more people who collect, the higher the fee. Know how much and when these payments are due and take great care that you have set aside the money to pay them.

It is a serious mistake not to pay your taxes on a timely basis. The late fees for not filing and not paying can be enormous and add up to a 50 percent penalty to the taxes you owe. Once this unbudgeted and unaccounted cost is added to a company's expenses, profits go out the window and cash flow is strangled. And trying to avoid payments won't work because the taxing bodies have strong powers of enforcement behind them. This is a situation to avoid at all costs.

Keep Employment Levels in Check

The administrative side of labor costs is producing the payroll, keeping benefits in line, and paying taxes on a timely basis. The managerial side of this is keeping the proper number of employees to do the job and at the same time not overstaffing. This cannot be done with just a casual attitude; it takes diligence and the commitment to not only monitor the costs but take actions to keep them on budget.

You will start with your direct costs, those that will rise or fall in direct relation to the amount of revenue being generated. You will base a great deal of your financial future on establishing a gross profit margin, so keeping the labor part of this equation in check is a key element. It may also be a balancing act since you don't want to lose skilled, trained, and talented employees because you can't provide enough work for them to make sufficient wages.

If you find the trend over a two- to three-month period is that the percentage of labor is going up in relation to sales, you must investigate the cause. A single month is too soon to tell because the variation may be caused by work done but not billed in that month, or temporary equipment or production problems.

If sales begin to trend downward and you make no change in your labor force, the percentage is bound to go up. The answer is not easy but it is clear: Hours must be cut back or layoffs must occur. No business owner likes this reality but not to do so may jeopardize more jobs than the few being readjusted. Putting everyone on a 36-hour work week may help spread the discomfort evenly, and sometimes employees will be willing to try this for a limited time.

When sales remain the same or even go up a bit and the cost of labor goes up as well, you have a productivity problem. Before looking at individuals with a thought that they are not pulling their weight, review the other elements of the work as well. Are the tools, machinery, and equipment all in good working order? Has material inventory been arriving on time? Are there other bottlenecks that might be costing extra labor time? Once this review has been completed, meet with managers and other employees. Let them know that there are exact goals in terms of labor costs and ask them to help in meeting these goals. If you have made them in the past, you should be able to reach them now.

> If sales begin to trend downward and you make no change in your labor force, the percentage is bound to go up.

Sales and Administrative Labor

There has been previous discussion in this chapter about the goal for administrative labor—keep an eye on it and know what people are doing and what is unnecessary work tasks. There is other overhead labor to consider as well.

Owners or officers should fix their salaries or draw as a percentage of gross revenue and keep it there. If sales go up, the draw can as well, but by the same token, if sales go down, so must the draw. To do otherwise would be foolish, risking the future for short-term reward.

Finally, there are sales salaries. They may be commissioned and therefore fixed to a percentage of sales. The problem can come in when there is a draw against the commission and one or more salesperson are not covering their draw. Few small companies actually charge back to draw but it can be costly not to. Normal expectations are that it takes time for anyone in sales to get up to speed, but to carry them for any length of time is a luxury few small businesses can afford.

> Owners or officers should fix their salaries or draw as a percentage of gross revenue.

Payroll Is a High Ticket Item: Keep It in Line

Whether it is the administration or the management of labor costs, the need is always there to be attentive about all aspects of this part of your business. Create a realistic budget and monitor progress against goals, and take action where indicated. In many companies, this is the major force in bottom line management.

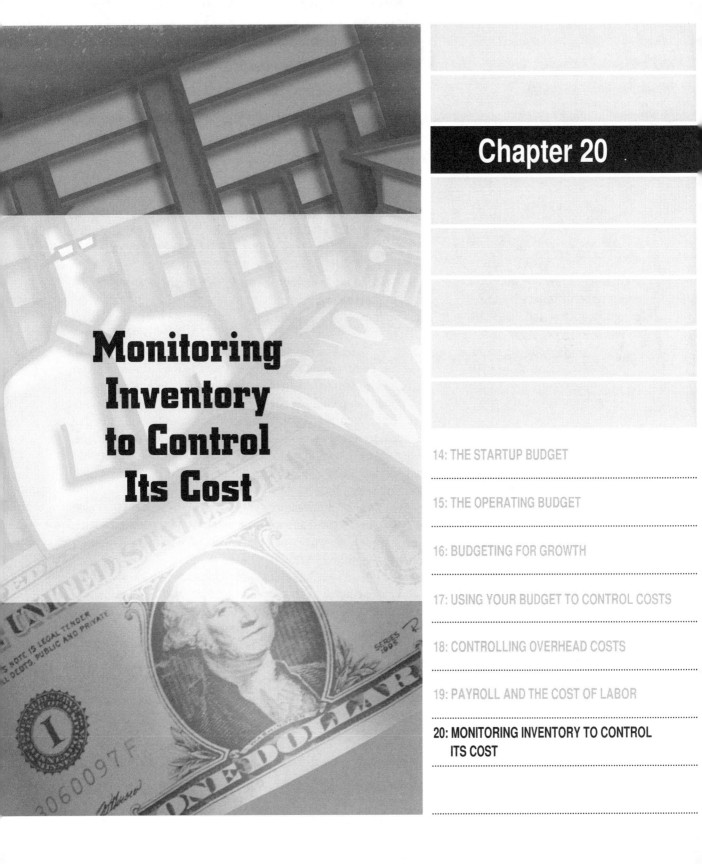

Monitoring Inventory to Control Its Cost

> You must create and maintain separate records to properly monitor the purchase, the use, and the remainder of existing inventory.

The second major expense of any business is the cost of inventory, so setting a reasonable budget and adhering to it is worth the extra effort. And it will require effort because you must create and maintain separate and detailed records to properly monitor the purchase, the use, and the remainder of existing inventory.

There are different types of inventory for different types of businesses. For a retail establishment, it is the finished goods ready to be sold. For a restaurant, it is the food waiting to be cooked and served. For a manufacturing operation, it may be raw material, partially completed work in progressed or finished goods ready to be sold and shipped.

When inventory is purchased, it goes on the books as an asset of the business. When inventory is sold, it becomes a direct expense against that sale. The problem most often exists in the time between these two events—when something happens to diminish the value of the inventory, you must be able to account for it. In a retail store, your goods can go out of style before they are sold, and lose their value. In a restaurant, the food can spoil and have to be disposed of. In a manufacturing operation, you may have mistakes that ruin the value of what is being produced. And in all cases, inventory can be lost or stolen. The way to prevent this is to create and maintain a good inventory control system.

The basis of an inventory control system is to enter (*after* having physically checked) all incoming material and track it through to sale. Depending on what type of business and what type of inventory, your systems will vary greatly.

The system used for a retail operation may be fairly simple. Each item is entered in an inventory log or if at all possible, on a database that will keep it "on hand" until it is sold. A sale will withdraw the item from your database and also compute the exact direct cost of the sale. If your system is manual, a physical inventory will have to be taken to determine what remains in stock.

Most wholesale- or distributor-type businesses must have a computerized inventory system in order to be of value to their customers. Whereas the retail store physically shows most of their goods directly to the customer, the wholesaler does most of its business via telecommunications, and instant information on availability is critical.

For a restaurant, a weekly physical inventory is necessary to provide ordering information and establish food costs. If the target percentage is maintained (usually around 30 percent) very little else is required. When food costs go up, investigation must begin.

The most complicated inventory control system is one set up for any type of manufacturing operation. The material must be managed before, through, and after the manufacturing process for a number of reasons. One is to track it, the second to value it because the value increases as the labor component has been added, and the third is to monitor the cost of production. You will require a combination of a database and a physical count for the following three types of inventory to be maintained:

1. Raw material—must be verified and entered into the system when it is received.
2. Work in progress—must be physically counted and entered identifying the stage of completion.
3. Finished goods—unless you hold finished product in inventory, this is usually accounted for as it is invoiced to customers.

> Whether the inventory is maintained on a database or a manual system, there must be backup documentation maintained at all stages.

Setting up the System

You must begin by designing your transaction report for completion at the times inventory is received or it is counted. Whether the inventory is maintained on a database or a manual system, there must be backup documentation maintained at all stages. All transactions (receipt of inbound goods or record of physical counts) must be dated and signed by the person responsible for the count. If you find any irregularities, you'll know where to go to begin to look for the problem. You will also want to keep records of the location of the inventory and any other relevant comments.

How to Cost Your Inventory

You will want to keep a running total of the value of your inventory because it represents a major item on the balance sheet as well as the cost side of your profit and loss statement. There are a number of accepted ways of inventory valuation; you may choose the one that best reflects the most favorable profit scenario for your business while minimizing your tax liability. The following are the major inventory valuation methods:

> Inventory is a major asset; keep an accurate record of its value.

1. At Cost (or cost average)—This assumes that your costs change from time to time, both increasing and decreasing. You will value each incoming inventory shipment at its actual cost, and at the end of the period, the total inventory will be valued at the average cost of the item. For example:

   Jan   1,000 items purchased @ $1.00
   Feb   1,000 items purchased @ $1.20
   Mar 1,000 items purchased @ $1.10

   You have purchased the items at an average cost of $1.10 per unit, so at the end of March when you do a physical inventory, the remaining balance on hand will be valued at $1.10 each.

2. First In/First Out (FIFO)—This is based on the assumption that goods purchased first are sold first. You will base your price only on the first price paid, for instance, in February, you will cost inventory at the oldest or $1.10 price. This method will increase your net income and therefore increase your tax liability.

3. Last In/Last Out (LIFO)—The opposite of FIFO, you assume that the cost of an item sold is based on the lowest price you paid for inventory. If prices are on the rise, this reduces your net income and the tax liability as well. For a newer company, this tax advantage may be of help from a cash flow standpoint. But remember, when prices are on the decline or you make a particularly good purchase, your income may be increased and taxes may be artificially high.

4. Lower of Price or Market—If your material or inventory costs go up and down on a regular basis, you may want to choose this more conservative method of costing. You may choose the lower of the two; the actual price paid or the current market price. This method tends to reflect current market conditions.

You will not be making the choice on your own; much of the advice will come from your accountant. But since you know the special conditions of your own business better than your outside professional, you should actively participate in this decision so that the information you get reflects the best choice that is available to give you the management information you need and tax benefits you want as well.

Writing off Inventory

Virtually no business sells or utilizes all the inventory it purchases. Products go out of style, food spoils, and customer demands change. At some point, the unsold and, perhaps, obsolete inventory will have to be disposed of either by discount sales, liquidations, or writing off and donating to a nonprofit group. This decision has implications to both your balance sheet and your profit and loss statement, so it must be made only after serious consideration.

If you write down an inventory item that had a cost of $5,000 and make it 50 percent off at $2,500 due to any factor, you will show a loss of $2,500, and your assets will be lowered by that amount. If you are concerned about your current profits, perhaps because you are still trying to find permanent financing at your bank, you may be reluctant to do this. You can avoid it over the short term, but it isn't always a good idea.

The real issue for you is knowing exactly how your business is doing so that you can make corrections and adjustments that will improve your performance. If you avoid the fact that a certain percentage of your inventory will likely not sell at full markup price but have to be sold at or below cost, you will not be accounting for that

> At some point, the unsold and, perhaps, obsolete inventory will have to be disposed of either by discount sales, liquidations, or writing off.

fact of your business, and this is one that must be taken into account when you price your goods.

The direct cost of your material must include the cost of that product that will not be sold at full price or, perhaps, not sold at all. For example, you buy 100 pairs of shoes at $30.00 and sell them at $60.00. On first reading, it appears as if the direct cost of your product is 50 percent. But assume that 15 percent of your inventory has to be sold at 20 percent below costs just to move them. The equation now looks different.

> The direct cost of your material must include the cost of that product that will not be sold at full price or, perhaps, not sold at all.

Bought 100 pairs of shoes @ $30.00	=	$3,000.00
Sold 85 pairs @ $60.00	=	$5,100.00
Sold 15 pairs @ $24.00	=	$360.00
		$5,460.00–net
		per unit of $54.60
Cost of direct merchandise		$30.00

With an average sale price of $54.60 and a cost of $30.00, the direct cost is 55 percent, not the 50 percent that you might have assumed. This store must now base its pro-forma statements on a direct cost of 55 percent in order to be accurate about its operations.

Writing off inventory can be done either when the sale is below cost or liquidation actually happens, or at the end of a period when you are pricing a physical inventory. You may also find a way to benefit from this as well because if you know that it is eventually necessary and you have just had a very profitable quarter or year, the write-downs could lower your taxable profit and actually save you money. So plan for this as you create your business projections.

Managing Inventory for Profit

Having your money tied up in inventory can cause a number of problems, the most difficult one being a cash flow shortage. The result will be a need for outside capital that will normally be borrowed funds, adding interest to the cost of doing business. Therefore, it is far preferable to keep less inventory on hand than to have to finance it.

A number of benchmarks can be used to determine the dollar amount you should have in inventory and many variations within various types of industries. A retail store that sells seasonal merchandise will want to keep far less in stock than a store that sells staple items. Over the years, manufacturers have tried to employ a just-in-time system, meaning that material is shipped regularly as it is needed with little kept on hand. Restaurants order food on a weekly or even daily basis because of spoilage. You must learn the norm in your own industry and tailor it to meet the specific circumstance of your company.

Delivery or lead time from your suppliers will be a key consideration. When you are new and somewhat unproved, you may not be getting the same type of service that you will get when you become a larger customer. So if you find out that you can't control your inventory as well as industry norms in the beginning, set a goal and strive to meet it.

The two key benchmark numbers you will see are how many times you "turn" your inventory and how many days (weeks or months) of inventory you have on hand. They are fairly simple calculations. You turn your inventory when you sell it, so if you sell $10,000 worth of goods and have a material cost of 50 percent, you have sold $5,000 of your inventory. If you carry $15,000 worth of product, you turn (or sell out) inventory theoretically every three months (3 x 5,000 = 15,000), so you have four turns per year. Using those same numbers, you note that you have three months (90 days) worth of inventory on hand.

Where it gets complicated is in the area of obsolete, unusable, or slow-moving inventory that is carried from month to month without any change. This is another reason to clean out stock on a regular basis so that you can accurately monitor the performance of your inventory. One additional reason and perhaps a timing mechanism is that a number of states have a floor tax based on the value of inventory. Why pay tax on something that may have little value?

A good system of control that is monitored regularly will provide excellent information for you to use when ordering merchandise and pricing your goods. These skills will add real dollars to your bottom line.

> The two key benchmark numbers you will see are how many times you "turn" your inventory and how many days (weeks or months) of inventory you have on hand.

The Source and Use of Capital

Summary of Part IV

- **Where and when is additional capital required**
- **What are the best sources of capital, i.e., investment, debt, or asset liquidation**
- **How capital comes in and is spent in a normal business cycle**

Chapter 21

The Needs
for Cash

Every business owner needs to have an understanding of the cash requirements of his or her business so that he or she can plan for the availability of capital when needed and from the appropriate source. The positive cash that flows in and out of a business is a critical measure of how it is performing currently and a predictor of how it is likely to perform in the future.

There are three stages in the business cycle when level of cash resources are most critical. The first is in the startup phase, then as a healthy operating unit, and ultimately for the desired growth.

Startup needs have already been covered earlier in this book and they include the one-time investment in establishing the business and furnishing its physical requirements such as machinery, equipment, and leasehold improvements. The final but very critical need is to meet operating cash needs until break-even revenue is achieved and profits are realized.

The operating unit has need for capital on an ongoing basis— this is cash above and beyond that which flows through the company in the normal course of doing business. The internal cash flow generated by sales revenue is the working capital and is not considered in this equation. However, the excess cash (profits and retained earnings) is very critical to this mix.

> Every business owner needs to have an understanding of the cash requirements of his or her business.

The Use of Cash for an Operating Company

There are four basic categories that describe the need for cash in an ongoing business operation. They are as follows:

1. The Purchase of assets. The need to buy machinery, equipment, vehicles and other tangible assets is the most primary need for cash. The purchase of land and buildings would also be covered by this capital need. The payback from these purchases will be midterm or long term, and that aspect of the return must be taken into consideration when looking for a source of cash.

   The other asset purchase that likely will be made is to purchase additional inventory that when sold, will turn into accounts receivable or cash. This is a shorter-term payback.

2. The repayment of debt. Again, outside the working capital (internal cash flow) expenditures is the need for cash to pay back the principal amount on all loans whether from stock-holders or from outside lending institutions. You cannot pay either one of these parties from existing cash flow without jeopardizing the liquidity of the company.

3. The repurchase or redemption of equity (including buyouts of other stockholders). There are times when those having made investments in your business (perhaps even yourself) will need to withdraw some of those funds. As in the payback of any borrowings, this can be done only with cash that comes from sources other than the net operating cash that flows through the business.

4. Funding losses. This is the most difficult need for cash because it is not as optional as the first three. Few businesses plan to lose money, yet most do early on. Unfortunately, there are times when the trend begins and, if left uncorrected, can go on for a long period. This cash drain can be the most life-threatening to any company because few sources of capital are truly appropriate for replenishing the losses of cash from operations.

The Need for Cash for Growth

The major need for cash when a company goes into a growth mode is to purchase additional assets. Most of them will be of the fixed and tangible variety such as land, buildings, machinery, and equipment. These are long-term (or midterm) payback items, so the source of the cash must match the return of the investment.

Other growth cash requirements may include increasing levels of inventory to support higher sales. If inventory turns remain at effi-cient levels, this cash need will be short term since the goods will turn back into cash or receivables when sold.

At times, the growth strategy will include a period of losses as new products are created or markets are being opened. As in the operating unit, this cash need is a difficult one to meet, and it must be minimized so far as possible. Growth creates a shortage in cash

> Growth cash requirements may include increasing levels of inventory to support higher sales.

flow even when operations are profitable. Having losses during this period can risk the cash position and ultimately the solvency of any venture. This is the main reason that overexpansion can be a dangerous strategy if not planned for and fully understood.

Growth creates a shortage in cash flow even when operations are profitable.

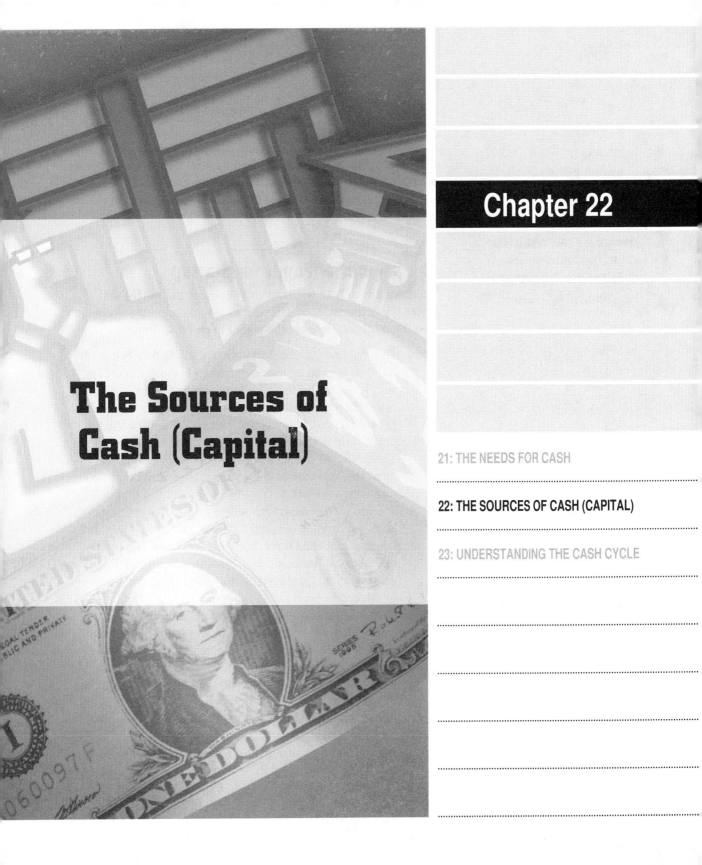

Chapter 22

The Sources of Cash (Capital)

There are three periods in the life of a business when there is a need for cash from sources other than operating revenue. The needs were described in the previous chapter, and now the sources that might be available and appropriate for each circumstance will be covered as well. The match of source to need is a key strategy in successful business management.

The Sources of Funds for Startup

There are a variety of ways to secure cash for the startup and early-stage business, some more difficult to secure and some more risky than others. Here are the eight top choices:

1. Personal savings. The most optimum way to go into a small business is to invest your own savings because you can let your investment ride for the long term and build up equity rather than having to pay yourself a cash return. The buildup of stockholders' equity is also a very good sign for any lending institution when it comes to ultimately making loan decisions. After all, if you're willing to invest your money, they know that you have both the confidence and the commitment in the venture.

   Too few entrepreneurs are willing to save to start a new business; they are too anxious, once they get the idea, to take the time. And if you use all of your savings, you may face personal financial problems during lean times when your salary may be low or nonexistent. Keep everything in balance.

2. Family and friends. Family members and close friends may lend or they may invest, and it is a very individual decision whether you should ask or even accept these funds. When you have a great idea and limited access to capital, it may be too easy to look around to anyone and everyone who is close to you to put in some money. Think carefully.

   Be very honest and very realistic about how long you will need the cash and what the rate of return or payback will be. Use your pro-formas to plug in any numbers for return and

> Personal savings is the most frequent source of funds for start-ups.

decide how soon a payoff or payback can occur without compromising the financial strength of the company. The only business funds that should be used for this purpose are excess profits, and they may be a long time in coming.

3. Outside investors. If you have formed a sub S corporation, you can look to outsiders to invest in your business venture. Your business plan and pro-forma should give them sufficient information to make their investment decision, and you are required to approach only sophisticated investors who understand the risks. Be sure to add a caveat to your plan acknowledging the speculative nature of any investment in a new business venture.

4. Personal lines of credit. This is a very frequently used method of raising cash, and it may be a very risky one. If you draw against the equity in your home, you put the very roof over your head on the line, which you may someday regret. However, it is usually preferable to drawing on credit card advances, which are likely to have a high rate of interest and can easily bury you without even reducing principal.
Any personal loans you use to start your business will require immediate repayment schedules (unlike some longer-term business loans). These payments may be hard to meet and will reflect on your personal credit should payments be late or missed. Be cautious.

5. Sweat equity. If you have done your pro-forma correctly, you have accounted for the eventual salary you will receive as the CEO. However, if you can work for reduced or, in some instances, no wages for a while, this sacrifice will add value and, in the end, equity to your company.
Customers will be paying prices that have margin built in for the owner's draw, and you will be leaving it in the company as excess cash.

6. Vendor credit. The money you will need for tangible assets (machinery and equipment) as well as inventory may be loaned by your vendors in the term of credit or an open account. You may find deals where you can lease what you need and pay it off as you make the money from utilizing it.

> A personal line of credit may be risky and credit card advances carry a higher interest rate.

It never hurts to ask for credit, but don't be surprised if you have to earn it by developing a track record. Perhaps you can begin with a 50 percent payment in advance and the balance on terms. The risk will be less to your vendor, and you will be able to develop higher credit limits.

7. Bank loans. Over the past several years, a number of large (and some small as well) banks have been marketing home equity loans under the pretension that they are business loans. These loans are really more personal than business, and you should think of them in that way. It is very difficult to find any bank financing for a business startup because you will have no track record to establish the likelihood of repayments. One exception might be if there is some equity or collateral (such as buildings, equipment, or even patents) available from the beginning.

8. Customer deposits. A little considered place to find capital is directly from the customers you will serve. If you have gone into business to fill a specific need of one or a group of customers, they may be willing to advance money to help you pay for all or part of the materials and labor you will require to help get you up and running. Just remember that deposit money is for specific use and to divert it for other expenses could be a problem when the time comes to deliver what's on order. If you are producing for special order, it is always good policy to secure some money up front.

> Two seldom considered sources of capital are vendor credit and customer deposits.

Cash for the Ongoing Business

There are four major sources of cash for the existing business, and they are as follows:

1. Retained earnings. This is your *net* income after tax plus any depreciation that is not a cash cost item. This profit represents positive cash flow from operating activities and represents the *best* source of cash for any business.

2. Borrowed funds. This could be additional loans from owners, family members, or friends. It may also be the trade credit you receive that is actually a short-term loan from your vendor.

3. New investment. This may be additional invested funds from any source, including the owner, but often is a sale of equity (a percentage of the business to a new outside partner). This may be a good source of *new* money during the early stage of a venture when both the cash and the extra input of a new investor may spur growth into profitability.

4. Sales of assets. This should be done as an orderly liquidation of unnecessary equipment or inventory. This action may have a cash benefit, but it will have a negative effect on the profit and loss as assets are written off, particularly if they are sold below book value. Many cash-strapped companies consider this and determine only after it is too late that the financial reports have reflected this as a serious loss of asset value and net equity.

   If assets are completely nonperforming, such as equipment no longer in use at all, this still should be considered. It may be possible to footnote the financial reports to account for this as a one-time occurrence.

The Source of Cash for Growth

Funding growth internally through the use of retained earnings is the most optimum way to do it, but in reality, virtually all companies fund growth with the use of borrowed funds. A key to the successful use of these funds is to make sure you have borrowed a sufficient amount of money and that the loan payback is appropriate to the increased profit stream created by the growth.

New investment is also possible to fund a substantial growth that would allow for dividend return on the investment.

> Funding growth internally through the use of retained earnings is the most optimum way to do it.

The Source Must Be Sufficient and Matched

You do not have to utilize only a single source of cash, you may, and likely will, use a number of different options. Use your profit and loss statement and your pro-formas to predict how much you will need and how the cash will flow through your business.

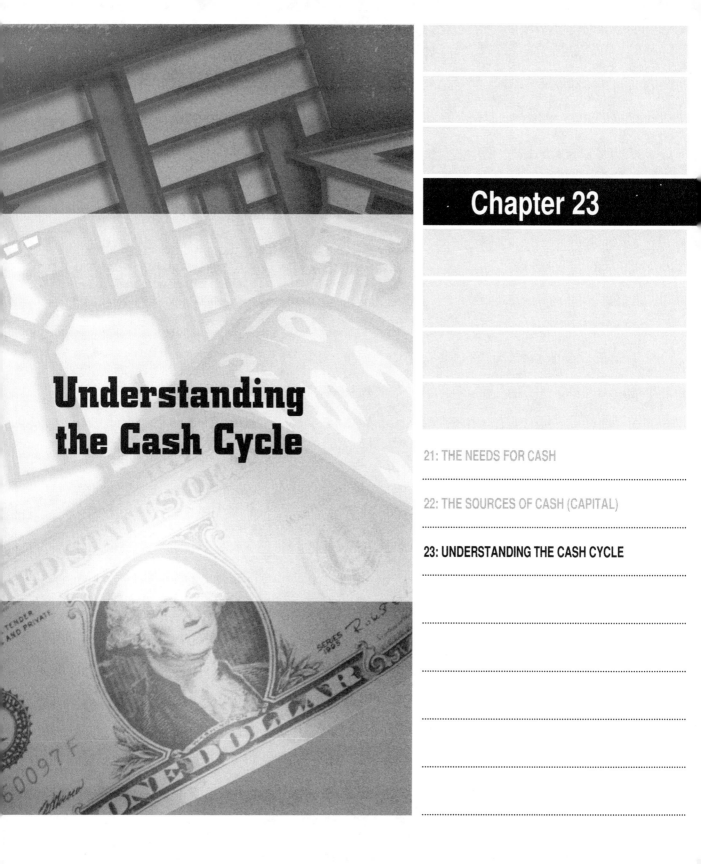

Understanding
the Cash Cycle

Chapter 23

Throughout this book, the focus has been on how to keep records and how to understand the meaning of those records. The reason that any owner or manager needs to understand this aspect of business management is simple. Cash (or capital) is the fuel that powers the entire operation, and running out of it or running low risks the success of the venture. The final step of this basic understanding is understanding the flow of cash through its cycle.

Money comes into a business through the sources described earlier in this section either in the form of startup capital, operating capital, or outside capital (investments, loans, assets sales). Once the capital is in the business, its internal use is to pay for material, labor, and all overhead expense.

The asset side of your balance sheet will show you how much capital (accounts receivable and inventory) you have been able to acquire in reserve. On the other hand, your profit and loss statement will show you *only* how you have been able to utilize your sales revenue to make profits or lose money. The profits you make will build equity on the asset side of the balance sheet, and any losses you suffer will show up on the liability side and be a net offset to your equity.

Cash flow, when viewed alone, can be a very misleading gauge of how your business is doing. It is possible to have a positive cash flow for a period while the business is losing money. On the other hand, a negative cash flow may be a problem even at times when a business is making a profit. Growth is the chief source of this problem.

The cash cycle is about smoothing out the timing of cash in and cash out by the use of capital other than just operating revenues. Learning when it is appropriate to borrow money or when it is necessary to seek additional investors or to sell off assets is a key financial skill. If you learn to integrate the information found on both your balance sheet and your profit and loss statement, you will find several keys to this decision making.

> It is possible to have a positive cash flow for a period while the business is losing money.

You Cannot Borrow to Finance Losses

There is a difference between the startup losses most businesses experience and any operating losses sustained by an ongoing business. But it is difficult to finance either of these through the use of borrowed money. The reason is simple: There will be no reserve of cash building up in order to pay back any loans.

The two losses are different, however. The ones suffered by most new companies are expected and are actually more the cost of establishing a new venture than anything else. Until revenue grows to a break-even point, these losses will be a reality, but they are building the name, reputation, and position of the company in the marketplace. Any going concern has an intangible value, and though it may not show up on a balance sheet, you are establishing this intangible value during this startup phase.

But there is good reason to use investment money to fund these losses rather than borrowed funds, even those that come in the form of vendor credit. The payback from this early stage may be long term, but lenders and vendors will want their money sooner than you are likely to see profits come on stream.

It is very difficult to fund losses of an ongoing operation through the use of borrowed funds either by voluntary lenders (a bank) or involuntary lenders (suppliers who are not being paid). As the losses drain liquidity from your reserves, it becomes increasingly less likely that you will be able to repay obligations. Few banks will be willing to lend money to a business operating in the red.

Selling assets may raise cash to meet obligations, but you may be in reality conducting an internal liquidation and run out of assets before you run out of debts.

As soon as a business drops to a low profit or break-even situation, action is required to turn it around so that positive cash will flow in to prime the pumps. Don't wait until actual cash becomes short.

> The payback from this early stage may be long term, but lenders want their money sooner than you are likely to see profits.

Growth May Be Funded with Loans

On the other hand, the use of borrowed money to fund growth is very acceptable. You will be purchasing assets such as inventory, and when the products turn into cash, these funds will be used to pay down the borrowings from lenders or vendors. Both are usually receptive to being funders of a growing business as long as it is profitable.

> The best source of capital is profits.

Profit Is the Best Answer

The best answer for a small business is to generate profits. This can lead to successful borrowing to solve the timing problem. And the business should build up a liquidity cushion (cash reserve) to cover the unexpected losses that could happen to any business and to build the base for future expansion. Then, your company will genuinely be in a position to consider the *best* source of cash before the need for a cash outlay.

Strategic Planning by the Numbers

Summary of Part V

- The elements, cost, and competition of a pricing strategy
- Creating a cost-effective market plan and budget
- Knowing which loans are best for your business
- Using ratios to analyze your financial performance
- Whether it is preferable to lease or purchase equipment

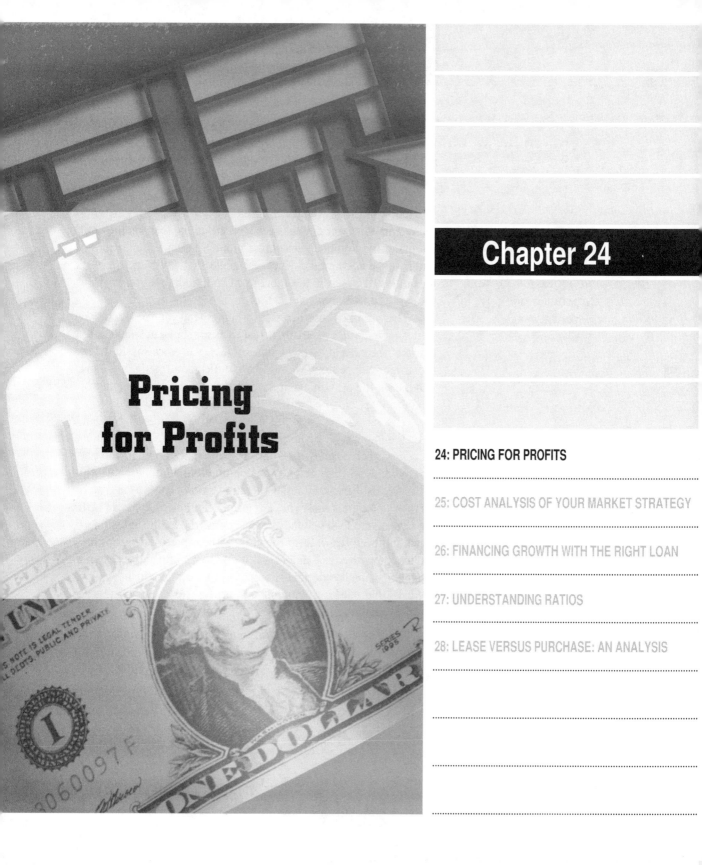

Pricing
for Profits

Chapter 24

A number of different elements are involved in creating a profitable business. One of the most important is setting prices that will generate adequate volume and still provide healthy profit. When you create your pro-forma, don't just estimate the total sales volume you expect to achieve; you must predict it on an item-by-item basis—in short, how much of what will you sell and what will you charge for each item. What you can charge above the actual cost will provide the first critical number, your gross profit. These are calculations that must be made carefully because neglecting any costs will result in margins that may be too short to let you produce a break-even at your startup level of revenue.

There are two considerations when pricing your product or service. The first *must* be what the real costs are, but you should also be aware of the current market competition. If you price substantially above your competitors, you will have difficulty attracting new customers. On the other hand, it never makes sense to leave money on the table by pricing below what the market is willing to pay.

The only exception to this is when you are positioning yourself to be the low-cost alternative hoping to generate substantial volume. Since few small business startups have this expectation, it won't be covered in depth with only the admonition that a business with this strategy must have substantial operating cash to cover what may be very serious early losses. The best example of how risky it can be trying to generate high volume at low prices is the airline industry, which has been strewn over the years with corpses of new, upstart carriers that have tried and failed. The problem often arises when a stronger competitor decides to fight for the business the new kid on the block has tried to siphon off with pricing. Few new business ventures can sustain the fight.

> The most important is setting prices that will generate adequate volume and still provide healthy profit.

Step One Is to Know Your Direct Costs

You must be able to account for all the direct costs of labor or material that you have in the product or service that you are pricing. If you are looking at the retail or wholesale business, the product cost is *not* just the unit cost that you pay the manufacturer. You must take into account several other elements. One is the incoming freight, assuming that it is charged to you. When your volume is low in the beginning, that will often be the case. Eventually, you must determine what it will take to get freight prepaid because these dollars can make a difference. If freight is $10.00 per 100 units, add the 10 cents to the direct cost number you are using for a cost figure. This charge may be paid as an administrative expense, but for the purpose of establishing a selling price, it's best to consider it as a cost of the product itself.

The second, and often the most important, "hidden" material cost is that of shrinkage, the amount of product that will go unused or unsold. New businesses often don't expect this phenomenon and don't take it into account at all. If you have no track record, the prediction of how much this will be is purely speculative, but you must consider at least some percentage. For the sake of this example, we will assume 10 percent of your inventory will go into a sale or liquidation. Therefore, every $1.00 of cost will be raised to $1.10 to adjust for this. Then you will include the price of freight, which we will assume to also be 10 cents if 100 units ship for $10.00. The correct material cost will be $1.20 and not $1.00. This is a substantial difference, and if you neglect to use the correct total, you may substantially underprice your goods.

If you have a direct labor component to add (for manufacturing primarily), you will also need to consider the hidden costs of labor as well, which include the benefits, including vacation, taxes, and insurance. The typical number is 30 percent, so if your labor cost is $10.00 per hour, your actual cost is $13.00 per hour. If you have five hours in a product, the direct cost is $65.00, not $50.00 as you may have assumed. These extra costs also will most often appear in the administrative overhead column of your profit and loss statement, but again, for the purpose of pricing, you must take them into consideration.

Many startup companies are surprised at how marginal their profit is after a few months in operation because they assume that the prices they established have built in sufficient markup. Not accounting for these "extra" costs is the primary miscalculation that explains that outcome.

> You will also need to consider the hidden costs of labor.

Step Two Is to Establish Gross Profit Markup

Once you know exactly what it costs to purchase, produce, or provide the product or service of your company, you can calculate the markup that will give you the gross margin you need for a profitable operation. If you are a startup, you will rely on the pro-forma you did as a part of your business plan. If you have been operating, you will have some history to rely on, but early history isn't always accurate. You may be carrying some overhead expenses that are startup related and therefore will be nonrecurring, and these will increase your overhead number. Or you may not have paid the full cost of some expenses such as taxes or insurance, which will understate your overhead. Try to use all the information available to establish a very reasonable cost of operations and determine what gross margin you will need at break even to exceed these expenses and make a profit.

For example, your overhead costs are $300,000 per year and you have established your break-even to be $600,000 gross with a 50 percent gross profit margin. Each product or service that you deliver must be priced at over twice the direct cost to give you the margins you need.

Therefore, if a product costs $100 to get out the door, you want to sell it at $200 or more if possible. There is value in putting some room in your quoted prices to provide a cushion for discounts or the possibility of bad debts.

> If you are selling a branded retail product, you probably have little room to set prices that are higher than others.

Factor the Competition in Your Pricing Structure

If you are selling a branded retail product that has an established selling price, you probably have little room to set prices that are higher than others. Your goal will be to keep your overhead in line so that the margin you can get will give you the profits you need. For many commodity products, the markups are limited as well since customers have a resistance to items above a certain price ceiling. But many new businesses are based on niche markets, hard to get or very specialized products or services, and the pricing here has far more latitude than a more generic business.

Determine the range for similar products or services in your community (or wherever you may sell if it is statewide or national) and set a benchmark for the highest and the lowest prices you can find. Determine the characteristics of the other providers of these products—items such as:

- Convenient location
- Free delivery
- Evening and weekend hours
- Liberal return policy
- Extra customer service
- Customized production, logos, printing, etc.
- Credit terms

Determine where your business fits in terms of these criteria because they will likely have perceived value to your customer. Are you high on the value-added score, midlevel, or low? Your price range should be in line with the level of service provided by your business.

If your cost and your desired profit is covered or exceeded by the competitive price level, your goals should be met. If not, you have decisions to make. The question becomes can you lower your cost or raise your level of service?

Added Value Means Added Profit

The most effective way to justify pricing that may be above the midline is to differentiate your company from the competition by providing products or services that are unique or exceed the expectation of your customer. A clothing store that offers free alterations, a food store offering online ordering or delivery, a furniture store offering design services, or an auto repair service with evening and weekend hours are all examples of special value-added extras that make premium prices seem reasonable.

> The most effective way to justify pricing that may be above the midline is to differentiate your company from the competition.

Before setting your prices on the low end of the range, look around for ways to enhance your products or services that will justify the higher price. A little creativity and a little effort could result in a healthier bottom line.

Cutting Prices to Create Demand

This is a very risky strategy for a smaller business because you must be aware of how much of an increase in volume you need and can expect in order to determine the validity of such a move. Most business owners would be surprised to learn exactly how great of an increase in volume is needed to offset a lower price. Consider the following example.

Selling price of widgets is $10.00 each, and the direct cost is $6.00 each. The company is currently selling 1,000 widgets per month. Their profit and loss statement shows the following:

1,000 units @ $10

sales income	$10,000
direct cost	6,000
gross profit	4,000

If a price discount of 10 percent were instituted, the profit and loss statement would look like this:

1,000 units @ $9

sales income	$9,000
direct cost	6,000 (now 66%)
gross profit	3,000

With a 20 percent increase in sales, you would see:

1,200 units @ $9

sales income	$10,800
direct cost	7,200
gross profit	3,600

> To analyze the value of a price cut, you must know how much of an increase you can expect.

At a 20 percent increase in volume, a substantial increase for any business, you will still have lower gross profits.

Widget sales would have to go up a whopping 35 percent in order to achieve the same gross dollar profit. The profit and loss statement would look as follows:

1,350 units @ $9

sales income	$12,150
direct cost	8,000
gross profit	4,150

A 35 percent (or one-third) increase in volume is a substantial jump and won't happen without aggressive selling effort (at a cost) and at least some increase in the overhead expense for handling, billing, record keeping, and so forth. It is very possible that a 10 percent price cut even with a 35 percent sales increase may *lower* your bottom line after a great deal of work and effort to make it happen. Know the implications *before* you make the decision to lower selling prices. It may be impossible to get them back to your needed margins without customer resistance.

Raising Prices May Damper Demand

A certain percentage of your customer base may be very price sensitive even if you are providing a valuable service along with the products. Any price increase could lower your sales volume, and that knowledge dissuades many businesses from raising prices even when costs go up. You may be as surprised at the results of lowering prices in terms of its impact on gross profits.

Assuming the same unit price of $10.00, direct cost of $6.00, and unit sales of 1,000 per month:

Current profit on items sold—1,000 units @ $10

sales income	$10,000
direct costs	6,000
gross profit	4,000

> It is very possible that a 10 percent price cut even with a 35 percent sales increase may lower your bottom line.

Price increase of 10 percent and volume decrease of 20 percent results in the following 800 units @ $11.00:

sales income	$8,800
direct costs	4,800
gross profit	4,000

This profit is *equal* to the original one, and a volume drop of 20 percent is highly unlikely because many customers have established buying patterns that won't be changed that easily. What's more, overhead will probably be less because of lower levels of handling, billing, and other administrative costs. Higher prices and lower volume often result in a healthier bottom line.

> Higher prices and lower volume often result in a healthier bottom line.

Setting Prices Is Setting Expectations

When a new business opens, the early months will establish its identity to a new customer base. They learn about your products or services and the quality of what you deliver, and they make a determination of the value they received from doing business with your company. A portion of this value equation is predicated on the price range of the products or services. A high-priced restaurant or shop attracts customers who expect a good deal for their money. Midrange establishments may draw a crosssection of potential customers with open expectations, but a low-priced outlet invites price comparisons since that is the driving force. You have one chance to impress; make sure you're ready.

The midrange strategy is likely the safest. Deliver more than customers expect, and you will begin to gain loyal followers. Provide less, and you will have a difficult time bringing in sufficient numbers to make the venture go.

Changing Prices After Opening Day

A business that has been open for a few weeks or a few months and has not met the sales projections set in the pro-forma may decide that a change is needed, but not necessarily a change in pricing strategy. Before cutting any prices, remember how much more volume you will need to make your profit goals. Try upgrading products or services to justify your current levels of markup.

If you find that you have underestimated your costs, raising prices *may* be an answer, but consider other solutions as well such as lowering direct costs (finding alternative, lower-priced supply sources, for example) or the current overhead. When an increase is inevitable, add new items or services or an accompaniment. You want existing clientele to absorb these raises without much notice.

Perhaps the best way to let the market (customer base) give you feedback about how they perceive the value of your goods or services is to set pricing a bit high and offer various discount incentives. Opening specials, lower prices for volume or at specific times of the day, or promotional items will give you a chance to see what price point creates the greatest customer traffic. Critical to this information is very detailed and accurate record keeping.

How Much Profit Is Enough?

An honest, fair markup is whatever the customers accept as a value to them. If you can purchase at a good advantage, you should benefit from this work. If a business is to grow and thrive, it needs a healthy profit. Even though there are times that all companies take losses due to circumstances outside their control, it all averages out in the end.

Your ability to understand and control your costs and to understand and meet your customers' expectations are the key elements in successful pricing strategies.

> If you can purchase at a good advantage, you should benefit from this work.

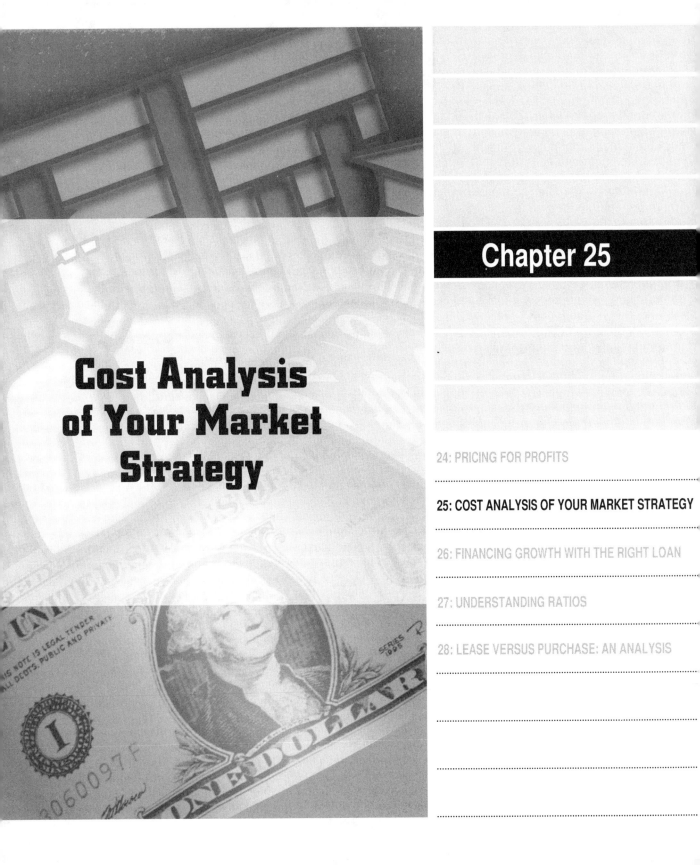

Chapter 25

Cost Analysis of Your Market Strategy

Most small business owners are not quite clear on exactly what marketing really means, much less how much money to allocate for expenditure on any effort in this area. The answer that most choose is to do minimal marketing at best or identify some money to that line item and throw it in the hands of any outside vendor they can find. When sales don't go up in six months, they grumble to themselves that they knew it wasn't worth it in the beginning and cut the budget. Wrong answer. Marketing is important to growth and profitability, and it must be maintained as an ongoing business necessity.

First, you must understand the difference between sales and marketing. Marketing creates business opportunities; sales is the transaction. Marketing is a long-term investment; sales may bring immediate return. Marketing is part art and part science, and you can use your financial skills to quantify how much money to commit to your marketing effort and to monitor how it is doing as well.

For a startup business, marketing is more theoretical and driven by availability of capital although there is the need for this effort. But the analysis is still the same.

> Marketing is important to growth and profitability.

Begin by Determining the Value of a Customer

Each customer who walks into your doors, calls you on the phone, or makes a written inquiry is important to you. Although some customers will be frequent and major, and others will be occasional and less important, they will have an average economic benefit to your company. You can determine how much this is by finding out the average revenue per customer as well as the average profit per customer.

For existing businesses, this information is found in the financial history of the company. The revenue per customer is determined by dividing the gross dollar volume by the number of active clients. If you've had sales of $500,000 with 50 active customers, each one has averaged $10,000 of activity. A new company must estimate the total amount they expect the *average* individual customer to purchase.

Don't get caught up in the dream customer; you won't have many of those. You will, instead, have a variety of small and midsize customers along with those of major importance.

Now you want to know how much the average customer contributes to your gross profit dollars. Relating to your net profit may be misleading because that number is very volume sensitive. The gross profit number will tell you what you need to know in terms of "real dollar" impact.

If your gross profit margin is 40 percent and each customer makes annual purchases of $10,000, then each contributes $4,000 to the company's gross profits. That is a way to put a dollar value on each customer. Now you can more knowledgeably decide how much you wish to spend to generate a *new* customer.

Look at your pro-forma to see how much in the way of overall dollars you have allocated to marketing expense—what percentage is that of total overhead expense? Let's assume that your overhead is $180,000 and you have allocated $18,000 to the marketing category. That equals 10 percent of your expenditure. You may want to say then that 10 percent of the $4,000 of gross profits is what you wish to spend to bring in a viable new customer.

Then, when analyzing the value of any new marketing plan, you can use as an overlay the fact that a new customer should have a $400 maximum target cost to develop. It should not be a hard and fast rule but merely a baseline for decision making. Don't be tempted to spend $10,000 on an advertising campaign that is designed to meet the attention of a small number of people. If you find only six to eight new customers as a result, you will lose money on the effort!

The most important work in any new marketing effort is to make sure that you have identified the target. That means that you know exactly who your likeliest customer will be. Look at your existing customer base for the answer to that question. What characteristics do they have in common? Age? Location? Income level? Education? These factors and a whole lot more will tell you as much as you need to know about the potential you have with any new customer. You are meeting the needs of specific people, and additional people from the same demographic and interest group are your best candidates.

> The most important work in any new marketing effort is to make sure that you have identified the target.

If you sell to businesses, the questions are similar. What are they by total sales volume? Location? Industry? Are they locally owned or publicly traded?

This is a job that you or someone in your office can complete, or you may hire an outside firm to do the work. Don't try to reinvent yourself by throwing dollars at changing your marketing strategies; listen to the voices of those who have stated their opinions of your company with their purchasing dollars.

> Don't try to reinvent yourself by throwing dollars at changing your marketing strategies.

Use a Rifle Not a Machine Gun

Once you know where your target is, you want to reach them in the most cost-effective way you can. If your current customer chooses you because your place of business is conveniently located, don't diffuse your dollars by advertising all over your city or doing a broad-based direct mail piece. Spend your allocated dollars doing as much as you can to saturate your local area.

If your customer base (business clients) come from a specific industry, spend your dollars in publications going to decision makers in that special industrial group. Have a booth at their trade fairs and create solid marketing material as handouts. With current desktop publishing capabilities, this can be done in-house at a reasonable cost. Or a small graphics firm can provide camera-ready material that can be taken to a printer to produce high-quality brochures and promotional material.

Be very cautious before being talked into any high-volume or high-saturation marketing ideas. They may seem glossy and sophisticated and feed your ego, but it isn't likely that they will contribute to your bottom line. Always remember that the cost per new customer is a benchmark for determining a cost-effective program.

Plan a Budget and Stick to It

Whether you use a professional marketing consultant or do the work yourself, as in all other aspects of financial management, creating a realistic budget is step one to success. Know what you can afford to spend, establish what would be desirable to spend, and set your target at a balance between the two. Remember also that you may want to try a variety of programs—media advertising, direct mail, co-op promotions—so don't spend the bulk of your dollars on one project.

Underspending may also not be desirable when it comes to your marketing budget because it usually indicates that you have ceased putting any effort in this area. Since the effects of these programs are long term, you may not see a downturn in business, and you will begin to think it doesn't matter. But it will eventually and, at the least, slow your progress and, at the worst, erode your current business. Your customer base will always have a certain proportion in change, and you will need to find new customers to replace the ones that leave. Keeping your name and image in front of the public is a good part of the solution to that problem.

> You will need to find new customers to replace the ones that leave.

Financing Growth with the Right Loan

Chapter 26

Adequate and timely business financing may be the most critical factor in the success of a venture, yet it is an area most confusing to many owners and one of the issues that they are not educated enough to ask the right questions. And the strongest resource for those answers, the experienced lender, is no longer a part of the banking scene for virtually all large banks. The role that has replaced the lender, that of relationship manager, is more of a salesperson than a lender.

Over the past decade, there has been much consolidation in the banking industry as well as centralization and automation of many banking procedures. In cities where there were once four or five major banks, there are now only one or two. Many of the midsize banks have been purchased as well, so it is almost impossible to develop a relationship with a banker who is an experienced lender and can serve as a long-term resource for your business. Many of the branch personnel simply serve as administrators, accepting loan applications and passing them on to another department. Few have actual lending authority (the ability to approve loans up to a certain amount).

Business loans under $250,000 are almost all credit scored, meaning that a combination of information about the business (length of time in operation and gross volume) and the owner (personal credit history) are fed into a computer and matched against standardized answers. Answers come quickly, but appeals are difficult. Loan proposals are not reviewed as lending criteria.

Smaller banks such as S&Ls are now doing some commercial loans, and new boutique banks are springing up to meet the neglected small business market. These are often single-branch institutions that specialized in small business lending. Other business lenders such as the Money Store and GE Capital are also possibilities since they are SBA guarantee lenders. You may find a good resource list at your local SBA office.

In many communities, there are government development organizations that also lend money, often at below market interest rates. The borrowing process may be fairly long and arduous, and the decision process even longer. Where timing is an issue, this may not be a good choice.

> Business loans under $250,000 are almost all credit scored.

Your first job will be to find the best source of capital for your business and that should be done before you are going to need it. Ask other members of the business community and stop in and talk to the most likely candidates. It may make good sense to have more than one lender in your sights before you even begin to apply so that you have a fallback position.

Step One: Determine How Much You Need

Whenever you apply for any kind of a loan, the amount of the request is up to you. Asking for too much may precipitate the loan being refused, but asking for too little may be just as critical a problem. Far too many companies determine soon after borrowing that they do not have sufficient funds to complete the growth needed to complete early stage goals and take advantage of market opportunities. You must look beyond the next few months and determine how much you will require over the next several years and frame your request for that amount.

There are loans and lines of credit that make these funds available, but you do not have to draw them until you need the capital. Therefore, you won't be acquiring any interest expense until the funds are put to use.

Using your existing profit and loss statement to determine your actual costs and profit margins, you should be able to create a proforma cash flow that will give you the guidelines for how much cash you will need to complete the planned growth cycle. Once your operation has become cash positive, you can also project how much you can afford to commit to a repayment schedule. Remember, loan principal payments come from profit, so you must be in the black to comfortably pay debt service.

Since you will not be able to go back for more capital, at least not in the early stages of your loan, build in sufficient cushion to meet all of your needs. A banker may come back and offer less, but if you've been overly cautious, less may simply not be enough.

> It may make good sense to have more than one lender in your sights before you even begin to apply.

Step Two: How Long Will You Need It?

After you know how much capital you will need, the next question is how long will you need to keep outside financing before you will be in a position to pay it back. Financing may be either short term (less than one year), midterm (one to five years), or long term (more than five 5 years). Various types of loans may be structured to meet the specific needs of your company.

Short-Term Loans

Normally established as a line of credit, you may draw on available funds as you need them until the maturation of the note within a year. This type of loan is meant primarily to meet short-term cash flow needs rather than long-term growth strategies.

Typically, if you had a large order and needed to buy material and pay labor to finish the job and then wait until the receivable is paid, a short-term note is what you need. But don't think that you can use this as a funding source over several years as you begin to build your business to the next level. A line of credit, if well collateralized and handled in a manner acceptable to the bank, may be renewed year after year, but there is no guarantee. In fact, it may even be increased, but you won't know that until you go for an annual review. Then, it may be too late to find a new lender, and you will find yourself critically short of capital.

If this is the only commitment you can get from the bank, it surely may be best to take it, but discuss other possibilities as well when applying for a loan.

> A line of credit may be renewed year after year, but there is no guarantee.

Intermediate-Term Loans

The normal term on these loans is from three to five years, and they are typically the more traditional installment type, but there is one hybrid that is a cross between a term and a line of credit that may be just what you need. Called a nonrevolving line of credit, the loan is drawn down over a period, usually up to a year. During that time, only interest payments are made, but once the full amount is drawn, the loan terms out over a period of years with regular principal and interest payments. Perhaps your growth involves some expansion that you are doing over a period of months, not all at once. You may need new equipment, and you may need to improve the space. Once the work is complete, the additional revenue and profitability makes it possible to retire the loan. Then it will be easier to make the installment payments.

When purchasing a single piece of equipment or doing an expansion project that will be completed all at one time, the typical installment loan is what is needed. You will get the loan proceeds in one lump sum, and you make monthly payments on a regular basis over a period of years until the loan is repaid.

Long-Term Loans

If you know that it will take some time to generate a return on the investment of your borrowed funds, you need a long-term loan with a payback period of more than five years. The most common need for this type of financing is the major expansion of your business, perhaps including the acquisition of real estate and the purchase of major equipment accompanied by a substantially higher level of inventory. After an expansion, few businesses can expect their sales revenues to increase overnight; you will have to grow into your new capacity. This type of loan is partially speculative since it is difficult to insure that greater volume and profits will follow their planned goals. Many long-term loans need additional collateral or guarantees like those offered by the SBA or other government entities such as state and county development agencies.

> When purchasing a single piece of equipment the typical installment loan is what is needed.

What Collateral Must You Pledge?

Few banks give completely unsecured loans these days, so be prepared to pledge some collateral as security for your loan. The shorter the term of the loan, the more flexible the banker can be with regard to the type of security that he or she requires. Most likely, you can use your inventory and your accounts receivable as assurance that if the loan is not paid as agreed, assets have been pledged to meet the obligation. In case of default, the bank may look to your customer to make his payment directly to the bank as settlement of your loan.

For midterm and long-term loans, more scrutiny is given to type and quality of the collateral. A long-term loan must have security that will be of value for as long as there is an outstanding balance. Machinery and equipment will age and lose its value, and some inventory will inevitably become worthless. This should help explain the reason that banks require collateral far in excess of the loan–to cover the shrinkage of value of your assets over the years.

Many business owners become offended and object to the fact that UCC (Uniform Commercial Code) forms are filed on all business assets while the loan is being repaid. However, once the balance has been reduced over time, it may be reasonable to ask for a release on certain collateral to allow you more flexibility in planning.

Remember that all assets that are secured by the bank are legally under their control, and you can't take action like selling a piece of equipment (or even trading it in) without the permission of your banker. This may be the basis of the problem for many business owners: They become a captive to one bank because all of their collateral is tied up there. Don't be afraid to ask for a release, it may take some compromise such as sharing proceeds (to pay down the loan) if you sell off equipment. But you won't know unless you ask.

> A long-term loan must have security that will be of value for as long as there is an outstanding balance.

Personal Guarantees and Personal Collateral

Most banks require personal signatures on all small business loans particularly if the venture is new. The rationalization is that if you're not willing to take the risk, why should they? There was a time when a spouse (husband or wife) had to sign as well, but since many couples have jobs and assets of their own and are not willing to do so, this has become more negotiable. You can take a stand on this requirement, and you may very well be successful.

The most likely personal collateral used these days is the equity in your home, which takes the form of a second mortgage. Real estate has tangible value, and the banks feel most borrowers will work hard to save their homes, so these loans are fairly safe. If you have other financial resources such as cash instruments in the form of certificates of deposit, you may be asked or want to offer them as collateral on an otherwise borderline loan. You should be able to leverage a cash instrument a bit because it is very liquid as opposed to inventory and machinery, which would require great effort and expense for a bank to sell. Be prepared to answer any reasonable requests and to negotiate the deal that best secures the bank but protects your personal finances as well.

The Small Business Administration

The SBA of the modern era is no longer a direct lender of funds to small business. Instead, their main focus has changed to be a guarantor or underwriter of loans made to eligible small business. This allows the banks to be more flexible with terms and their own level of risks because it limits their exposure.

The SBA has also succeeded in substantially streamlining its required paperwork, a move that greatly enhanced its attractiveness to smaller banks. The work involved in placing an SBA loan in the past was so great that a number of banks would not take on these types of customers. Any bank profit was eaten up by the cost of labor of working with the SBA, but that has changed and so has the turnaround time. Approvals that took months now take days or at the most weeks. Funding is not always available, but this aspect has improved as well. The SBA has become decidedly more customer friendly.

The downside for the bank is a fee of 2 to 3 percent, which is usually passed through to the borrower. There are regular status reports to file. The downside for the borrower is that virtually all of your collateral will be tied up and it's harder to get releases from a joint bank and SBA participation loan than a direct bank loan. Call your local SBA office for more information and a list of their most active lenders. An SBA guarantee may be the extra push you need to secure the financing you require. Learn all you can before you apply. For women needing small loans, a preapproved process is available.

> The SBA is no longer a direct lender of funds to small business.

Special Types of Loans

Beyond the standard demand note or line of credit and business installment loan are a number of customized loans designed to meet specific needs. The following are some but not all of the loans that may meet the needs of your business.

Contract Financing

If you literally have a single large contract that will take time and cost money to complete, you may be able to take this one piece of business to the bank and finance it alone. If the customer is a known, stable company, this will be a lot easier because the bank will be more secure that you will be paid.

You will want to present the contract document along with your own cost analysis to your banker and a schedule of when you will need funds and how you expect to be paid by your customer. The contract will be the security for the loan, and all money paid will be used to pay down the balance of the loan. You will keep the profit at the end. Your bank may also require that the customer send jointly drawn checks (made out to the bank *and* your company) to insure that they will be paid when you are. This all depends on how high the risk and how established you or your business is.

> The contract will be the security for the loan.

Accounts Receivable Financing

This is a line of credit based solely on the value of your receivables. As they grow (usually meaning that you are having higher sales and not slower collections) so does your loan balance, and it is paid down again as you get paid. You receive cash for your work sooner than if you had to wait for a customer to pay.

The first step here is to determine how much of your receivables would be eligible for such a loan. Accounts that are more than 60 days old will not usually be considered since they are showing signs that they will be difficult to collect. Also "work in progress" billings would not be eligible because final payment might be in question.

Step two is the determination of what percentage of the "eligible" receivables will be used as a basis for your line. The likely percentage will be 80 percent, meaning that if you have $100,000 of receivables, you can borrow $80,000 against them. As your sales go up, the value goes up and you can borrow more. For some companies, this becomes almost a permanent type of financing with the loan almost never going down to zero. As long as your receivables are good, the loan is fairly secured to the bank.

Care must be taken to continue to collect on these accounts because a receivable aging will have to be submitted to the bank on a regular basis. Accounts that go beyond the agreed period will be discounted, and the collateral value will go down accordingly. In fact, an account with a few old invoices could be declared ineligible, so pay heed.

The only real drawback to this type of financing may be the interest rate charged. It is an expensive loan for the bank to manage so they will charge a higher rate, possibly 2 to 5 percent over other rates. Make sure that this does not compromise your profitability or you will defeat your purpose.

Factoring

Factoring is also based on the value of your receivables, but it is not a traditional loan. Instead of borrowing against your receivables, you sell them to a lender who then collects the money directly from your customers. As bills are paid, the amount outstanding to the factor goes down. As you do more business and bill your customers, you get the money almost instantaneously since it is usually wired directly into your account. Your factor will do all the collecting necessary.

The credit decisions are based on the creditworthiness of your customers, not your business. For those companies that are new with little track record but having AAA-rated clientele, this may be one way to get working capital solidly built up to profitability. Costs here can be quite high, even higher than receivable financing, so make sure that your own profit margins can afford it.

> Care must be taken to continue to collect on these accounts because a receivable aging will have to be submitted to the bank on a regular basis.

In addition, the collection activity may be very vigorous and could offend your customer. You will have no control over what is done, so before you make a decision to go with a factor, check his or her history with reference to collections; that is, does the factor demand interest on *any* invoice over 30 days and does he or she allow time to settle any disputes. And if your industry has little or no history of factors (the garment industry uses them regularly), consider the effect on customers.

Inventory Financing

Available only through larger banks and commercial financing businesses is a loan most often described as floor planning. Most often seen in the auto industry to finance a car dealer, other big-ticket items such as furniture and appliances may use it as well. The benefit to the borrower is allowing for larger than normal inventory during times when demand is high and having in stock merchandise necessary to make the sale. When the inventory is purchased by a customer, the loan amount (the cost) of that item is paid to the bank.

> When the inventory is purchased by a customer, the loan amount (the cost) of that item is paid to the bank.

It takes a larger and somewhat more sophisticated bank to do this type of financing because it takes a higher level of monitoring. Close supervision of inventory levels, including surprise audits, are desirable. This has a cost and interest rate that may be fairly high although an aggressive bank that is looking to do loans with the buyers may absorb some of these costs if you agree to a referral to that lender.

Consignment

Consignment loans are not offered by traditional lenders but sometimes offered by suppliers instead. You receive inventory physically, but the title remains with the vendor so no transaction of purchase, payable, or asset goes in to your books. Once you have used or sold the inventory, it is billed to you and becomes your payable. These loans are offered by very aggressive vendors but seldom offered to new customers without a track record.

Asset-Based Lending

Some finance companies offer their own version of a small business loan, which isn't really a loan for the business but a loan against specific assets that secure the loan. These assets may belong to you personally or they may belong to the business, but they will be fairly saleable like real estate or easily moved inventory.

You may be able to borrow more from this type of a lender because you must put up 100 percent security. But remember, they are well prepared to foreclose and sell off assets if you run into any problem. If the money is needed and you can put it to good use, it makes sense; just be cautious.

No One Size Fits All

You don't go to a bank and get money. You must find the right amount of money and the right term and conditions in your loan. If you can't find a lender and feel you need help, go to a professional loan packager. He or she will be able to help you fashion the loan you require. They are usually paid a portion of the proceeds.

For excellent free help, you can call on any one of the more than nine hundred Small Business Development Centers located at colleges and universities throughout the United States.

> You must find the right amount of money and the right term and conditions in your loan.

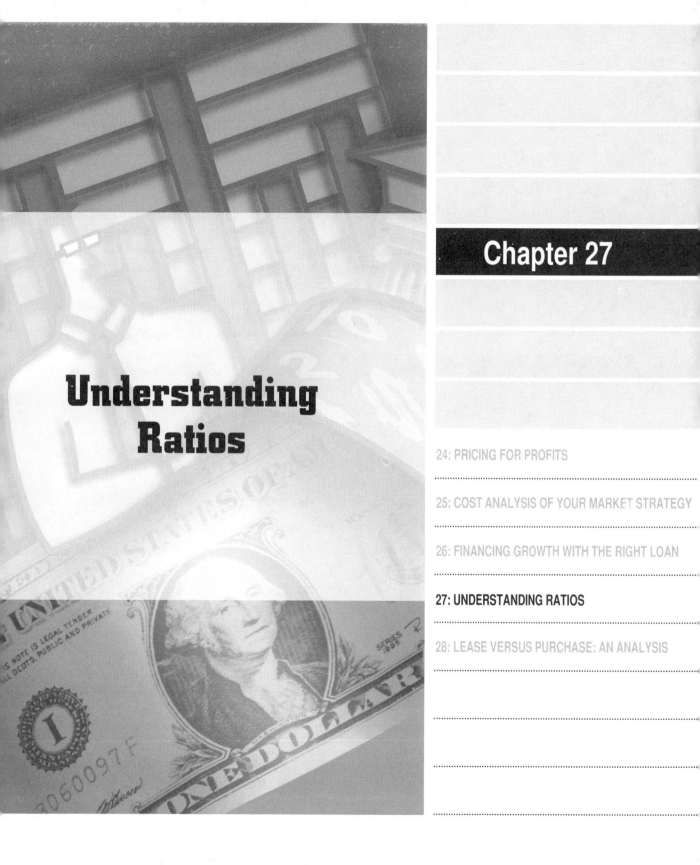

Understanding Ratios

Chapter 27

A number of different ratios can be very effective as an indicator to any small business owner about the financial progress of his or her company at a given point in time. Financial ratios are impartial measuring devices of the financial trends of all types of businesses.

These ratios do not have to be difficult, and though a financial analyst may use dozens, you need to look at only six or eight and not all on a regular basis. You are mostly looking for trends (assuming that you begin within reasonable norms), and if you spot a downward trend, you must analyze the numbers further and watch for the signs of improvement or further deterioration.

You will also want to compare same periods (third quarter to third quarter or yearend to yearend) to track your progress. Many businesses have seasonal highs and lows in sales activities or times when discounting is necessary and profitability down. Customer payments may also go down during certain periods of the year, frequently during tax time. Learn to understand this form of financial data, but also learn to use it wisely.

The most common ratios are as follows.

Current Ratios

This is a measure of your company's liquidity, that is, your ability to pay current liabilities when due. You will find the numbers on your balance sheet.

Take your current assets
    Cash
    Accounts receivable
    Inventory
and divide the total by your current liabilities
    Accounts payable
    Current portions of loans (due within 12 months)

As an example, if you have $100,000 in assets and $50,000 in liabilities, then your ratio is 2 to 1, which is what is often considered the norm. However, in some businesses, such as a restaurant that

> If you spot a downward trend, you must analyze the numbers further and watch for the signs of improvement or further deterioration.

carries few receivables and little inventory so that assets are all in cash, a lower ratio would be considered acceptable.

The trend over a period is important here because lower ratios represent less working capital, and if you begin to spot a declining trend that does not stabilize, it is an indication that a cash crunch is on its way with your obligations exceeding your capital and perhaps action from unpaid vendors or lenders.

Quick Ratios

Another version of the current ratios is determined by dropping the inventory from current assets and dividing the remaining assets (cash and receivables) by liabilities. The primary reason to do this is to account for inventory that may be slow or difficult to turn and therefore may not be as liquid as anticipated in the current ratio scenario. Instead of the 2 to 1 ratio expected in the current category, you may now expect a ratio of 1.3 to 1, meaning $130 in assets for each $100 of liabilities.

Each business is different, and you should know what is relevant to your company. Assuming that your inventory is typical but a certain portion of your receivables are written off, you should make your adjustments accordingly.

You can create a blended ratio by deducting a portion of either your inventory or your receivables and using that adjusted number. As long as you compare like to like numbers, you will get a good picture of the current financial picture as well as the future trend for your business.

> Quick ratios drop the inventory from current assets.

Profitability Ratios

You want to track both the gross profit margin and the net profit margin on a trend basis using same period-to-period comparisons. You will use the percentages and not the actual numbers.

If your gross profit margins begin to slide, it is a sign that direct costs have gone up and pricing hasn't kept pace. The most logical solution is to raise current prices so that the gross profit margin percentage you need is restored, but if your current competition is stiff, you may not be able to do so. Then the change has to come through greater scrutiny and control of the material and labor costs that make up your direct costs. New, lower-cost vendors or increased productivity must be sought.

If net profits begin to drift downward, you need to look first at whether gross margins are trending down as well. If they are, the culprit could be primarily a pricing issue. If your gross profit is steady and your net is trending down, the causes are either soft overall sales or escalating overhead costs. These must be kept in control at all times but particularly when sales are soft.

> If net profits begin to drift downward, you need to look first at whether gross margins are trending down.

Debt-to-Worth Ratio

This number is calculated by dividing total debt (current and long term) by total equity (sometimes called shareholders' equity on your balance sheet). In other words, if your debt is $300,000 and your equity is $100,000, your debt-to-equity ratio is 3 to 1. This is the upward limit of what most lenders think is safe.

This ratio is a sign of leverage: how you are able to use equity to generate additional capital to invest in ongoing operations. In the early years of any business, growth is financed primarily through debt, but once that period is complete, this ratio should stabilize and begin to go down. Any long-term trend of rising debt to equity could be dangerous because at any time lenders may decide to refuse further credit, and a cash crunch could follow.

The more stable the assets (such as cash instruments or saleable real estate), the higher the debt-to-worth ratio can be.

Return on Equity Ratio

This is found by dividing the net equity by the net profit earned by your company. For instance, if you have $200,000 of equity in your business and you earn $20,000 in profits, your return is 10 percent. The reason to review this number is to determine how your investment in your business is working for you. Would you be better off if your money was invested in other vehicles such as money market funds, common stocks, or bonds?

A small business is a greater risk than other standard investment instruments, so your return surely should exceed what you
would earn elsewhere.

Receivable Turnover Ratio

You calculate this ratio by dividing annual sales by the total dollars of outstanding receivables. For example, $300,000 of annual
sales divided by $50,000 of outstanding receivables gives you a
turnover of 6 (times per year). To get the number of days, you divide
6 into 365, and you come up with 61 days. This means that it takes
you an average of 61 days to collect on an outstanding bill.

Determining this number gives you a guideline with reference
to cash flow projections since you will know that your receivables
take (on average) 60 days to collect. Therefore, if sales are up by
$20,000 one month, that cash will not likely be available for 60 days,
and you will have a cash flow shortage. This is a critical formula
when doing a cost flow analysis.

All businesses should have an aggressive collection plan, and
this is one way of tracking the success of your collection activity.
Watching the trend come down to 48 days means what you are doing
is working, and if the trend goes the other way, you will know that it
is not.

> This number gives you a
> guideline with reference to
> cash flow projection.

Inventory Turnover Ratio

You begin with the annual material costs of goods sold and
divide it by the inventory. For example, if under direct costs, you
show a cost of $300,000 and you currently have $50,000 worth of
inventory, you turn your inventory 6 times a year. Divide that number into 365, and you come up with 61, your turns in days.

This is a key indicator of how well you are managing your
inventory. If the number of days go up over a period, it can mean
that you are not selling a portion of your merchandise at all and
product is just being carried from one month to another. Or you may
be over ordering in anticipation of higher sales that haven't material-
ized. You may have a good bit of your working capital tied up in
inventory, so you must manage it carefully.

Payable Turnover Ratio

Take your total purchases and divide them by your current accounts payable. Assuming that your total purchases are $500,000 and your payables are $100,000, that number is 5. If you divide this into 365, you get 73, which is the number of days that it takes your company to pay a bill on average.

Your suppliers are important to the success of your company and a source of low-cost financing as well. This is an important tracking number because you will see the trend of deteriorating payments, which may be the first sign of working capital problems. Vendor pressure may slow down your ability to meet customer needs and undermine your entire operation.

> This is an important tracking number because you will see the trend of deteriorating payments.

Taking Your Temperature

These ratios will take you only minutes to do, but they are benchmarks you must check on a regular basis. You can establish the norm for your own business, but you must track the trends to spot potential difficulty before it becomes trouble.

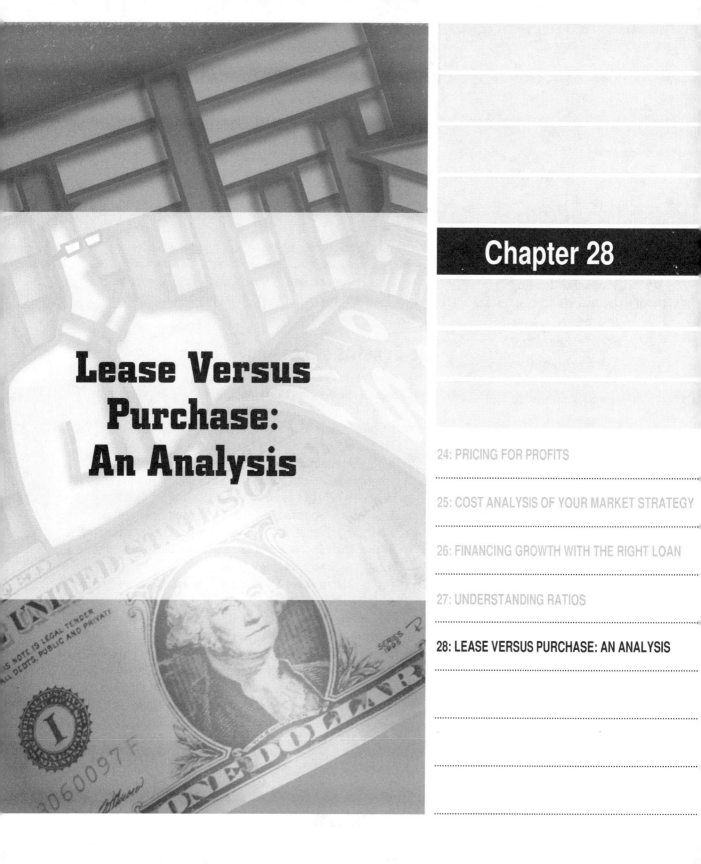

Lease Versus Purchase: An Analysis

Chapter 28

One of the other alternatives to financing growth through the use of loans is to lease equipment rather than buy it outright. For many newer businesses, this may be the only alternative since it is very often easier to lease equipment than to finance it. Suppliers of machinery, equipment, and particularly cars and trucks may have separate but associated leasing organizations to use as an incentive in sales.

If you are in a position that either choice is available to you, you should consider the advantages (and the disadvantages) of each before making your decision. A lease is likely more expensive over the long haul, but that may not be your only consideration.

> Suppliers may have separate leasing organizations to use as an incentive in sales.

The Benefits of Leasing

There are some obvious benefits to leasing, and they are as follows:

1. One of the benefits to leasing is a lower down payment. Although most lenders expect a borrower to finance up to 20 percent of new equipment purchases (particularly when you are talking about big-ticket capital equipment), leasing will normally require only a few payments (first, last, and one security). When cash is short, this can allow you to conserve capital to be spent in other areas of your operation.

2. Leasing is a secondary source of financing and does not show as additional lending to your balance at your primary lender. Therefore, other funds may be available from that lender for use as working capital.

3. Credit is often easier to obtain from a leasing company than a bank because many of them have buyback agreements with the equipment manufacturer. If they must repossess on any lease, the disposal process has been prearranged. This allows for a lower level of risk.

4. You may not have all the burdens of ownership such as taxes, maintenances, and insurance. Many leases will differ on these items, so you must have the agreement read thoroughly.

5. You may not want to own and use the equipment for the entirety of its useful life. A piece of equipment that has a use-

ful life of ten years will be depreciated over the entire period if you own it, but a five-year lease, if that is all you need, will save you the expense.

If you want to upgrade this equipment, you will be able to do so at the end of the lease because you will be able to return it to your leasing company. There is a cost for this privilege, but the convenience may be worth it.

6. There are some tax advantages to leasing. A loan for equipment will allow you to deduct only the interest payable on the loan. On a true operating lease (which will be described later in this chapter) all the costs of the lease payments are deductible.

7. The full burden of the lease will not appear as a liability on your balance sheet, as will the full unpaid amount of any loan. For newer companies, this makes your balance sheet look stronger. Some leases may require footnoted disclosure of the obligation, so ask your accountant to review yours.

The Drawbacks of Leasing

There are several downside considerations to leasing, and you should consider these as well when making your decision.

1. The ownership of the property stays in the name of the leasing company, and though you have purchased the rights to use the equipment, you cannot treat it as if it were your own. Normally, you cannot alter the equipment in any way without explicit permission. So if there are upgrades and modifications you would like to install, you must ask for permission. Any permanent changes, whatever the cost, will be the property of the leasing company, and you will not have any economic benefit beyond your own usage.

2. You are likely to pay more for a lease than for traditional bank financing of equipment. The smaller the lease, the more labor intensive it is to the leasing company and the higher

The ownership of the property stays in the name of the leasing company.

their cost, which is passed on to you. Further, many leasing companies (small ones) borrow their money from banks, so they have the cost of money to pass on as well.

3. Although inflation has been under control for a number of years, there are still circumstances (though they are fewer) when equipment actually appreciates. This increase in value accrues to the leasing company and not to you, the lessee.

4. At the end of the agreed-to payment period, you will not have a piece of equipment free and clear of loans that you can use without charge for the balance of the life of that piece of equipment.

Not All Leases Are Created Equal

There are two basic types of leases, and each has its own particular characteristics.

The Operating Lease

The ownership of the item being leased never passes from the lessor to the lessee. The total monthly charges are fully deductible. The asset will not appear on your balance sheet, and the balance due on your lease will not be listed as a liability. You will not have to charge off depreciation as an expense.

It may be possible to purchase the item at the end of the lease for its "fair market value." This value will not be established at the inception of the lease.

At the end, there is a nominal buyout of normally $1.00.

The Capital Lease

This type of lease is virtually a lease–purchase agreement with the payments throughout the life of the lease covering the full cost of the equipment. At the end, there is a nominal buyout of normally $1.00.

This type of lease does have balance sheet implications. The value of the equipment will be listed under your assets and depreciated under normal schedules. The current (12-month) portion of the lease will become a current liability, as will the balance over the long term. From purely financial record-keeping purposes, this will be treated the same as a purchase.

Where to Get the Best Leasing Deal

A number of financial institutions have leasing departments, including your bank, commercial leasing companies, and captive leasing companies such as Ford Motor Credit or GMAC. Don't take the first deal offered; shop for the best interest rates and terms. You may find them at your bank, but consider that this will count as part of their exposure to your company and may limit other borrowings.

There are several creative ways to finance a business, and leasing is certainly one of them. Keep it as an option for your business.

> A number of financial institutions have leasing departments, including your bank.

Problem Solving by the Numbers

Summary of Part VI

- **How to see the signs of trouble before they get too serious**
- **Setting up an effective cash flow system by aggressive collections**
- **Raising cash by selling assets**
- **Re-engineering a troubled firm**
- **Lowering debt by restructuring it**

Signs of Trouble: Seven Problems That Can Threaten the Life of a Business

Chapter 29

If you have learned how to read your own financials and you make it a habit to review them regularly, you will learn to spot trouble in its early stages. A number of trends will appear as minor annoyances in the beginning, but if left unchecked, they can begin to threaten the very existence of your business. The following are seven problems that, if left unattended, may grow into life-threatening problems, some over time and some very quickly. Learn to look out for the signs.

Long Periods of Flat Growth: Margin Creep

There is the startup phase when your product or service is just beginning to catch on in the market. Then, you hope, with planning, a period of more rapid growth will take place. After that, revenues tend to plateau. The question is for how long and what do you do to adjust to the circumstance.

Growth is desired for any business, and the only way to achieve that is to be very diligent about your marketing efforts. However, it is natural to take some time, catch your breath, and try to enjoy the effort you have put into getting to your current level. A year or perhaps even two of flat growth will not jeopardize the business if you keep watch on gross profit margins as well as overhead costs.

> Flat growth in terms of revenue is actually lost volume in real terms.

Flat growth in terms of revenue is actually lost volume in real terms. Either you are selling fewer units or you are deriving less gross profit from each unit. Over a period of even a few years, direct costs are bound to go up, and if you have passed the increases on in the form of higher prices, you are selling fewer units. If you have absorbed the increase internally, your gross profit margin has gone down. This can easily become a serious problem.

Flat growth periods that go past a second year (and there are times when this is true even in that second year) become critical because there are fewer dollars to pay overhead expense. Even if you can hold direct material costs at current levels, eventually the inevitable labor cost increases will take their toll, and gross profit will erode.

Even well-controlled overhead expense goes up a bit on a year-to-year basis. Items such as rent, insurance (particularly health insurance), and utilities have few if any prolonged periods of no increases. You will see these items become a bigger percentage of costs over a period of a few years, and the bottom line (net profit) will shrink or disappear. If you are paying any debt service, the principal payments will deplete your cash, and the dreaded cash crunch follows. The direction here is downward, and the only solution is to monitor early warnings and take immediate corrective action. You will need to:

1. Build up current volume with aggressive marketing tactics (not the time to cut prices to generate sales).
2. Be absolutely diligent about cost control conserving every possible dollar.

Productivity: Employee Indifference

If all is going well and your gross profit margins remain steady or rise and your net profit is healthy, you will likely assume that all work is being accomplished in an efficient way. But when there are signs that this is no longer the case, you must take action as soon as you see these indications.

The most likely place that you will need to troubleshoot is in your direct costs, particularly if you are in a labor-intensive manufacturing or service business. You want to check the direct labor percentage, and if it rises over one-quarter or more, it is time to look for the cause. A single month rise can be due to unbilled work in process that has already been expensed for labor but has shown no revenue as yet.

There are three major reasons that labor costs will rise.

> The most likely place that you will need to troubleshoot is in your direct costs.

Overstaffing

When sales remain flat or even fall off a bit and you don't take the appropriate reduction in staffing, your cost will go up. The decisions around this issue are difficult because you may have skilled workers that you don't want to lose, or you may have to meet fast turnarounds when work does come in so full staff is required.

Businesses such as restaurants and mechanical repair services (plumbing, electrical, heating) have particularly tricky balancing requirements. If a rush happens and customers become dissatisfied with the way they were handled or treated, you could lose their business permanently. The cost of replacing these customers could be higher than the labor cost. Use your experienced judgment, but set cost targets and keep to them.

Mechanical Failures or Out-of-Date Technology

A small business with limited capital often tries to operate equipment beyond its useful life in order to save money or because no cash is available to replace or upgrade equipment. But there are times when it is far more expensive to try to use the borderline equipment because downtime and slow productivity will destroy your profit margins and impact your cash flow.

This is the time when knowing how to do a pro-forma statement is a critical skill. Determine how much labor you will save and put that into the equation; then figure the cost to purchase or lease the equipment you need and factor that in as well. Now run your statement and determine if you can recapture the expense of an upgrade by increased efficiency. You might be surprised at the result and many lenders will respect and respond to such an analysis.

If your business depends on ever-changing technology, this must be a central focus of all of your capital planning. Leasing equipment over a shorter term or keeping available credit for new equipment will be central to your success.

> If your business depends on ever-changing technology, this must be a central focus of all of your capital planning.

Personnel Problems

Unlike large corporations that have human resource departments, small business owners try to do it all. You seldom have the luxury of job evaluations and formal productivity reviews. The smaller your company is, the more difficult to take the time and make the effort to replace borderline employees. Often these are in the administrative side of the business. The indifferent employee shortens his or her day by coming in late, leaving early, and taking long lunches. They are often found on the phone on nonbusiness-related calls and doing other nonproductive tasks instead of necessary work. During times of increased workload, new people may have to be hired to get the work out and when the pressure is over, they stay on to complete jobs that should have been done by the existing staff.

This will eventually show up in your profit and loss statement as overhead labor costs become an increasing number in real dollars as well as percentage cost. If you feel this might be a problem, check your numbers, and if you see the trend, take action. Set goals for work output and perhaps write or rewrite job descriptions. Be prepared for personnel changes if these strategies don't work. It isn't an easy step, but it may be necessary.

The other area of concern may be the productivity of your salesforce. You may have salespeople on commission and believe that they aren't costing you anything if they don't produce. But there is a cost to every employee—the cost of benefits, the cost of support staff, and even the administrative cost of keeping someone on the payroll. Add it all up and make tough decisions about borderline sales personnel. Replacing them may even result in increased sales by bringing in a more aggressive individual.

> Set goals for work output and perhaps write or rewrite job descriptions.

Deteriorating Capital Base:
Not Able to Retire Current Obligations

Periods of flat growth and negative cash flow (due to debt service) as well as periods of losses will eventually sap all the working capital out of the company. The day may come when you don't have enough cash flow from current sales and receivable collections to make the necessary payments to employees, vendors and lenders, and taxing bodies.

It is important to know that you cannot grow out of a situation like this, nor can you borrow your way out. The only way to cure a problem of capital shortage is to find a new source such as outside investment or additional owner equity. Both may be risky because outside investors may want too much control for their money, and you may be tying up too much of your personal capital in your company. Look at these two solutions only after you have reviewed your future strategy and run a pro-forma statement, and know that there will be enough profitability ahead to bring a return on these investments.

The other alternative is to liquidate some assets that will help with liquidity but may have balance sheet implications. Any assets sold below book value will show as a loss. However, in some cases, the depreciation has outpaced the loss of value, and you can come up with a gain instead. But moving assets from the long-term category of tangible assets to current assets such as cash looks better, and the increased liquidity certainly makes the company easier to run.

> Be cautious about becoming dependent on one or just a few customers.

Failure or Loss of a Major Customer

There have long been warnings about becoming too dependent on one major customer, and that makes good sense in theory. But in practice, when a customer becomes active and begins buying more from you or using your services at a higher level, it is difficult to turn him or her down. If the customer pays well, depending solely on them may become a really attractive proposition.

But as business cycles go up and down and purchasing habits change, it is possible to have a major change in status due to the loss of a major account and a substantial drop in volume or a large unpaid debt. The first step to preventing enormous damage is to keep in touch with customers on a regular basis even if everything seems to be going smoothly. Any warning must be taken seriously, and you should act to ensure no damage is done.

If payments start to slow down, be cautious. Worry more about your exposure than about stepping on people's toes. If what is happening is a sign of serious financial trouble, the more money you can collect before it happens, the better off you are.

If orders start to slow down and it appears as if you are losing business, don't wait around until the other shoe drops. Get in touch with someone in the know, arrange a meeting or lunch, and have an open discussion if possible. If competition has moved in, you might want to ask for the chance to sell off any special inventory before you stop being the supplier. Perhaps you might have a chance to review your own pricing and rebid the contract, being cautious not to accept work at profit levels you can't live with. Bottom line, ignoring problems won't make them go away. Any advance notice can give you a chance to make plans.

Your profit and loss statement and pro-forma cash flow statement are the tools you will need to help you determine the financial effect of the loss of any volume and the gross profit dollars. You will be able to tell how much of your overhead expense you will need to slash to get back to a break-even or stable position so that you can focus on rebuilding volume. No doubt, any loss of business has a serious effect on your cash flow, but you have a better chance of meeting your goals if you know what they must be.

> Ask for the chance to sell off any special inventory before you stop being the supplier.

New Competitor or New Technology Creating Pricing Pressure

When a new company opens, it often will be aggressive in order to generate business, and that may take the form of price cutting or heavy discounting. Many customers (some might say all) are price conscious and at least would try a product that appears to be a bargain. The question you must ask is, should you cut your own prices as well? In an earlier chapter, we looked at the effect of price cuts and how much your volume would have to go up before gross profit goals would be returned to where they began. Cutting prices just to *keep* sales volume can be very dangerous. Your loss of profit dollars that are needed to adequately fund your overhead expense may cause a serious cash shortage and undermine your capital base. Instead of getting into the price cut game, you should at least stay on the sidelines for a while to see if your competition will get back to real-world pricing.

You may also want to consider repositioning your products and adding a new twist such as delivery, alterations, design service, or special financing (which you can arrange through your bank) that will create enhanced value and justify your current pricing structure.

Use some of your own creativity before tossing in the towel and getting into a price war—no one wins.

Older companies have invested in the technology that was available to them at the time they began or at the time they were able to upgrade. It is almost impossible to be on the cutting edge of technology all the time. But not investing in improved and more productive equipment can be very self-defeating. What happens when technology allows others in your industry to do what you do, only faster and cheaper? Their direct costs will be lower, and they can cut prices and still make money. You must decide how to compete.

The best way is to find the capital either through loans or leases to bring your own company into the modern era. You will get lost in the pack if you can't deliver quickly and at a price that meets current competition. If what you are up against is a technological advantage rather than predatory pricing, you will have to find a way to become efficient and productive as well. If you can show via your pro-forma profit and loss statement that the expense you will incur to upgrade current capabilities will return a profit, then by all means you should take the necessary next steps to do it.

> You will get lost in the pack if you can't deliver quickly.

Lack of Future Focus or Strategic Planning

All businesses go through cycles from the startup phase through the growth phase and then experience periods of stagnant growth as well as times when volume begins to drop off. It may be seasonal, a result of expected economic cycles, or perhaps the outcome of new competition coming into a market that you helped create. Whatever the case, the facts are there: Business is not static; it is an ever-changing landscape.

The job of the CEO or top manager goes beyond day-to-day custodial management of the company. It involves continual review of current circumstances and the research and consideration of future possibilities. A company that does not do midrange or long-range planning is a company that seldom gets where it wants to go. If you simply stand in place, things will change around you, and you will have to respond to them rather than be proactive about what you would like to accomplish.

There may come a time when you have reached as high a saturation of possible customers in your market as you can. That is your plateau, and to grow and prosper from there, you must decide whether to sell more to each customer by increasing your products or services or to expand your market and find new prospects.

As with most other decisions, using sound financial analysis on this one is critical. You must analyze the cost versus the outcome of your strategy. The best and easiest way is to create a fresh business plan for the new direction under consideration.

Develop cost models of the new product under consideration from the standpoint of both startup costs and direct costs to produce. The benefit here is that you have a market established, so you may not have to spend a large amount on developing a new customer base. Determine the sales by using the historical records you have on your current customers to see how much new business you might be able to expect. In your review, determine if there would be sufficient increases in profits to provide payback for the investment required to bring new products or services into being.

The other growth alternative is to market your current product or services to a wider customer base. In this scenario, you will not have the cost of developing additional products or services, but you will have the cost of marketing. Going back to the model of what each new customer is worth to you, set a budget to pay for an aggressive marketing campaign and do a pro-forma using that additional cost. Be realistic in your estimation of what new revenue you can generate, paying close attention to the demographics in your enlarged target area and the competition you will find there. If you run the numbers and they make sense, this may be the next strategy you should pursue.

You must continue to pay attention to both the current operation of your business and explore future opportunities. Your lack of attention to what's ahead could cause you to stagger forward unprepared to face and solve the business challenges of the future.

> The other growth alternative is to market your current product or services to a wider customer base.

Unpaid Taxes

It is a rule, *never* borrow money from any taxing body. In short, this means that taxes collected should be paid to the taxing body and not to an insistent vendor or even a threatening banker. If you find yourself in a situation where you have some taxes due and not paid, you need to get to a professional quickly and work out a repayment plan. The interest will continue to build and the debt will grow.

> *Never* borrow money from any taxing body.

Some taxing bodies have other penalties that can make the amount double in a short time. The IRS assesses a failure to file and failure to pay penalty as well as charging interest. Your head will spin when you see how fast the actual tax can grow.

You may be held personally liable for unpaid taxes. And the IRS could take action against your assets as well as the company's. The Internal Revenue Service has some serious collection actions available to them, including leving your bank account and going directly to your customers to collect what is owed to you. An active IRS agent can choke off all the cash from your operation.

And finally, you may be subject to criminal sanctions as well. Employment taxes are trust taxes and should not be misappropriated. And in some states, should you fail to pay collected sales tax, you may even be criminally charged with theft. Even if you are tempted, don't give in to that temptation. Find another source of capital.

Most business owners get to know the rhythm of their own companies. When yours hits a sour note, pay attention and take action. These are signs of trouble and it just could get worse if left untreated.

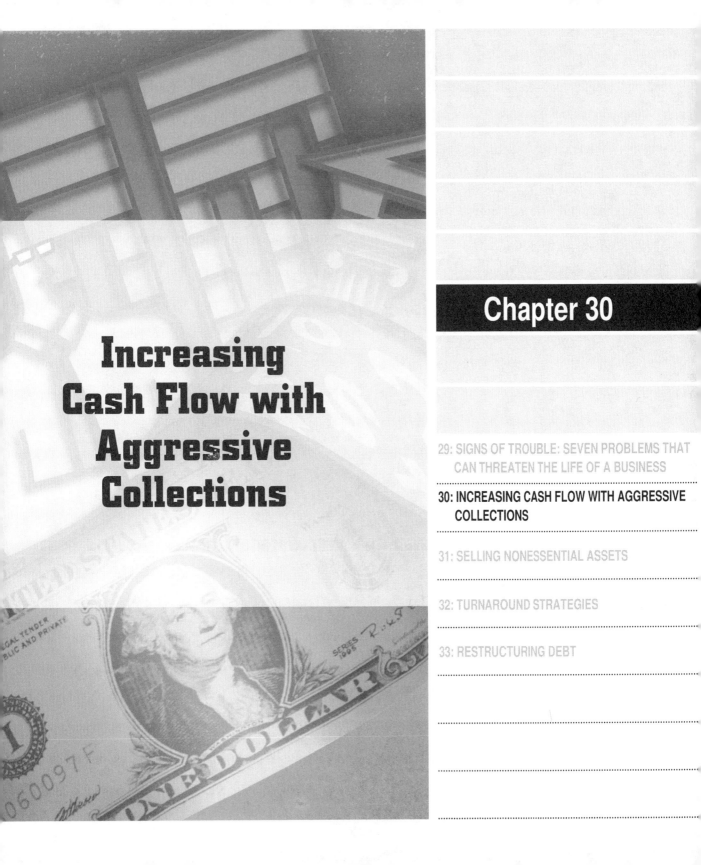

Increasing Cash Flow with Aggressive Collections

Chapter 30

For many businesses, the largest portion of their cash is housed in their accounts receivable, and that money is available only as these invoices are collected. If this is your situation and you remain constantly frustrated over your cash flow, you must take a look at your collection procedures and make sure you have a policy and its implementation in place. There are some steps you can take along the way that will increase your cash flow and lower the risk of not being paid.

> Make sure that your invoices are billed as soon as the work is complete and the amount is due.

Invoice Promptly

Make sure that your invoices are billed as soon as the work is complete and the amount is due. Letting paperwork back up means that it will take more time to generate the cash from the products you sold or work you performed. Many of your customers may cycle invoices in for payment based on either the date of the invoice or the date it was received. Any slowness on your part will give your customers reasonable excuses to delay payment.

Take care, as well, in the accuracy of your invoices. Mistakes in descriptions or, worse yet, in math may also delay payments until disputes are settled.

Establish a Procedure for Granting Credit

The first step of an effective collection process begins when you extend credit to a customer. If you are very casual about it, two things can happen, and neither is good. First you may grant an open account to an uncreditworthy individual who will never pay you at all. Or second, you may inadvertently send a message to your charge customers that you are not careful about your credit procedures, and they will begin to think it's all right for them to handle their account casually in return. Don't ever send that message.

Even if you don't have a credit manager, you can have an established procedure beginning with a formal written credit application. Get it filled in and get it signed. Make sure that your customer accepts responsibility. And check the references if you can. Chances are your customers will give you the best names, but you may be able to learn at least how long their accounts have been established. See what their high credit amount has been. Ask as many questions as you can and use your best instincts. Also get a bank reference and check that as well.

Set Limits

New customers shouldn't get the keys to your vault. Set reasonable credit limits that allow them to buy what they need yet not take you out too far. Take each case on its own merit and work with the customer on the decision so they know you are trying to meet their needs but protect yourself as well.

Perhaps you can get some cash upfront as a deposit. That will protect a good bit of your own out-of-pocket expense (your direct costs) yet allow sufficient open terms that meet the customer's needs. You can set up a number of other creative deals such as one-third upfront, one-third on delivery, and one-third in 30 days. Be flexible but be careful. Don't risk what you can't afford to lose.

Keep Track and Keep on Top

Your receivable aging is the tool you will need to see how your credit terms are being met. Have one created at the end of each month and review it carefully. Make sure that you or someone in the organization pays careful attention to the age as well as the amount outstanding on new accounts so that limits are being enforced.

Use account statements to establish both the amount and the timing and send them on a regular basis to your customers. Most computer-generated statements will automatically age the account and perhaps put extra notes on as well. You might also circle any past due invoices or send a handwritten note asking for attention and payment.

> Establish credit limits for new customers.

Don't Let Accounts Get Past Due Unnoticed

Once you see that an invoice has remained unpaid, don't become shy about asking for the money that is due. Start by sending your statement again in midmonth with a more insistent reminder and give it a week for results. If you still haven't been paid, it is time to get on the phone and find out why. It may be a simple oversight or a question about something on the invoice that caused it to be set aside. Or it may be more serious, but you won't know unless you ask.

If you haven't been paid because your customer is having a cash flow problem, don't let it go without trying to work out a solution. Perhaps a payment plan will work for your customer, and even though it isn't what you want, you will at least be bringing in some cash and the debt will be going down. Keep in touch and keep encouraging your customers to pay as much and as often as they can.

If you can't reach the person or company that owes you money, you should pay close attention and try other methods. Send a certified letter requesting payment, and if convenient, drop in for a chat. Many people are embarrassed by not being able to pay their bills but that isn't an excuse for not making an attempt or at least communicating.

> Once you see that an invoice has remained unpaid, don't become shy about asking for the money.

Turn an Account into Collections

If all of your efforts at contact have failed or you have made contact with little result, it may be time to turn the account over to a professional collection agency. If they collect, they will charge you a portion of the recovery, normally 25 to 33 percent, but you won't pay unless they are successful. Realize that you have probably lost this customer, and if you aren't going to be paid, what's the point in having the business, so you shouldn't worry about stepping on their toes by this action. The issue now is to get your money.

There are a number of different agencies to choose from, some national, very well known and effective, and some local and smaller who may also be effective. Seek recommendations from others, and if your industry has a central collection, use them because they often know the delinquent debtor from other collection actions.

Take Legal Action

The time may come when you have no choice but to take legal action either yourself in small claims court or by hiring an attorney to sue. The value of the outstanding bill is the determining factor. If it is over a certain amount, often $3,000, it is out of small claims; if it is less than $1,000, it isn't worth the time of a lawyer. If your source documents are in order, there should be no problem securing a judgment.

The difficulty may lie in collecting on that judgment after you get it. You must locate assets and execute the judgment against those assets. The easiest is to find a bank account and serve the bank. If not, you will likely have to get a sheriff to sell off company property for your benefit. It will take time.

You must exercise caution and good judgment along with a positive attitude from the beginning of the sale to the collection of your invoice. You want your customer to be satisfied, but your company needs to be paid for its effort. An order is complete only after it is paid for and not before.

> You must exercise caution and good judgment along with a positive attitude.

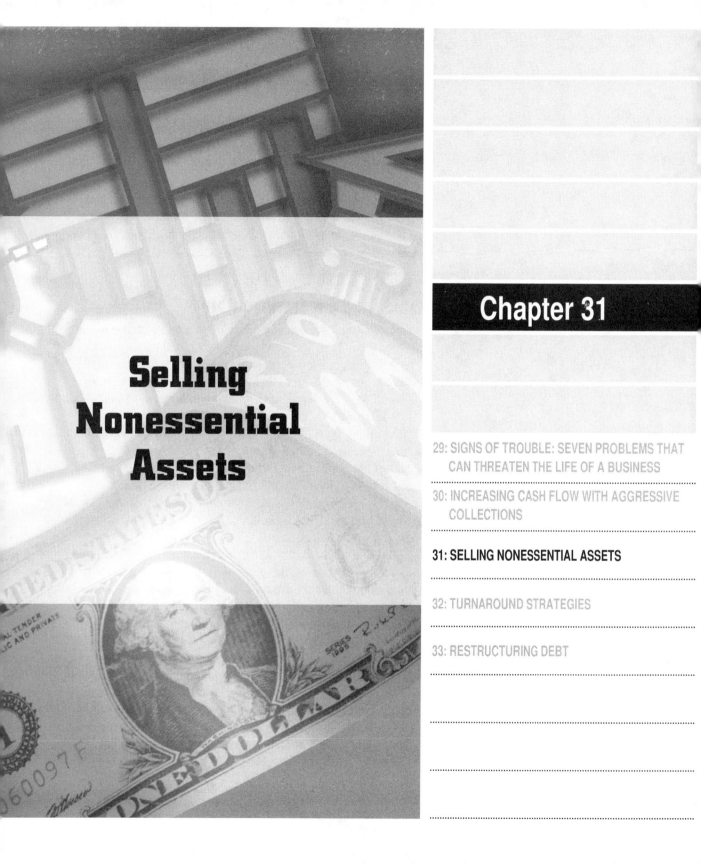

Chapter 31

Selling Nonessential Assets

There are a number of occasions when the need to sell assets to raise cash and increase liquidity not only makes sense but may be critical: when capital is stretched and borrowing not feasible, or when you've experienced a period of losses and expenses, including debt service that has drained cash reserves. But you must be careful what you sell, how you sell it, and when you sell it. You want to avoid having your business look as if it were in distress and making decisions that have seriously negative effects on your balance sheet.

Liquidating Excess Inventory

For some companies, the major source of tangible assets are in the inventory. If you have been monitoring your inventory turns and they are slowing, or even if you have just looked at the same merchandise boxes month after month, now may be the time to convert it to cash. Consider the implications before making any moves because there are a number of consequences of your decision.

The inventory will have to be written off your profit and loss statement sheet as a bottom line loss if you sell it below cost; virtually all real liquidations go for prices under cost. If you know that a certain amount of inventory will become "leftovers," you should write it down periodically to lessen the effect. Doing that at a time of profits will also reduce your taxes, and after all, it is a cost of your goods that should be considered.

Consider selling to a broker or a liquidator rather than having a massive sale at your regular place of business. Any aggressive "bottom dollar" sale may draw a different clientele from whom you normally see because serious bargain hunters usually have radar. They will take time to service even if they are only lookers, and that effort will take away from the care you can give to your regular customers who buy your product at a profit; these are the types of clients you want and need. Yes, you will net more from a sale on your own, but it will take longer, incur overhead costs, and may distract your ongoing business.

Most businesses have access to merchandise brokers—they may be general resale companies or specialized industry operations. Ask

> Consider selling to a broker or a liquidator.

around, look in the phone book under liquidators or brokers, or try the Web. Buying and selling goes on all the time there. You may even be able to list and sell your merchandise on someone's Website.

One last suggestion: You might also want to take a look at barter groups. If you value your product low enough, a buyer may want it, and you can use the barter credit you receive for something else you really need, thereby saving your cash.

If the sale will affect your profit and loss statement, you may want to footnote the document explaining a "one-time charge" for inventory liquidation. As long as it doesn't mean a major change such as a loss large enough to mean you have wiped out all of your equity, you should be in good shape. After all, your increase in current assets (the cash you will generate) will make your current ratios look better and your operations run smoother.

Selling Machinery and Equipment

Perhaps some of your equipment has become out of date and cannot be upgraded or sold, or perhaps you no longer manufacture or sell the product it was originally acquired to produce. Or you may have upgraded technology and are able to handle your needs fully with your new acquisitions. This may be the time to sell your nonessential equipment and turn a nonproductive asset into cash.

Before you begin, you must make two determinations. First, what is the current book value of the equipment you wish to sell? If it is old enough, it may have been fully depreciated and no longer have a book value. And second, do you have free and clear title, or is it secured to the bank? Most business loans will have a financing statement filed with your state taking a secured interest in all of your business assets. However, if what you are looking to sell is now "off the books," you are likely free to do what you want. If you have any questions, talk to your banker or lender.

If you want to sell something that is still on the books and secured to the bank, it may still be possible to do so, although technically all the proceeds should be used to pay down your current debt. If enough security remains after the sale, many bankers will

> This may be the time to sell your nonessential equipment and turn a nonproductive asset into cash.

accept a deal where you split the money, part to your debt and part for the company's use.

There will be profit and loss and balance sheet implications as well depending on the book value of the equipment and the selling price. If it has no value, any amount you receive from the sale will be a gain, and if the value is low, any price above that value is also a gain. On the other hand, if you sell off any asset below its book value, you will have to show the loss. Usually, either of these items will be shown on your income statement (profit and loss) as a separate line item on the income side, titled "gain (loss) from sale of asset." The amount will be added or subtracted from your other income, which is normally revenues from sales.

The book value I have been referring to may be found on a depreciation schedule that is likely kept by your accountant. It lists the purchase price and date of purchase of each piece of equipment along with its "useful life," the number of years over which it will be depreciated. Each year the value will be lowered by that amount, and the depreciation amount is expensed on your profit and loss statement. Sometimes, the equipment becomes worthless before it has been fully depreciated. This often happens with computers. For the sturdier production-type equipment, tangible value will exceed book value.

> Sometimes, the equipment becomes worthless before it has been fully depreciated.

How to Sell Equipment

You will have two primary choices in selling your equipment, and they will be either to a broker or to an individual (or company) end user. Needless to say, you will net more from the latter, but it will take more time and attention. You must decide what is more critical at this point, your time or the need for cash.

There are industry-specific brokers as well as general equipment brokers. Some brokers will buy your equipment outright and pay you immediately, whereas others will sell on consignment, meaning you won't get paid until the deal is made and paid for. Ask about shipping as well; if the buyer doesn't pick up or pay for it, you might find yourself with a major shipping expense that eats up a substantial portion of your proceeds.

Private sales may be made to new companies with limited resources to buy the most current equipment or to competitors who may be expanding in areas that you are moving away from. Local newspaper ads seldom bring results for anything but the most common equipment. Trade papers cost more, but since they reach a specific audience, outcome is better.

Make sure you specify the sale is in "as is" condition so that the buyer understands, and get the whole or a large portion of your selling price *before* you ship. Later disputes can be messy, particularly if they are over the condition of the equipment; they can be uncomfortable as well if they are with another business owner you know. Litigation takes time and costs money.

Selling Real Estate

Why would you want to sell off real estate—isn't it a great investment? In recent years, inflation has been slowed, and real estate appreciation has slowed as well. For some companies, their real property is where most of their equity is, and the return (the value of the usage) has gone down over the years. You may have more room than you need, or you may be in an area where values are higher because the visibility is more than you need. You could easily operate out of smaller and cheaper space. This is the time you should consider a sale. The capital may be very necessary as well.

Perhaps you have a mortgage on the building and think that all you have to do is satisfy this loan at closing. This may not be the case since some business loans are cross-collateralized with real estate, and the equity balance serves as additional security on your other business loan. Talk to your banker about this. Even if it is the case, you may be able to make a deal to share proceeds, so not only will you benefit from the cash, your loan balance (and interest) will be reduced. It's worth the exploration if you have given this step serious consideration.

Your decision to sell should be based on the analysis of how much your current building is worth as it is being used (the expected value of investing the same number of dollars) versus how much

> Their real property is where most equity is.

renting or buying a different space will cost you. The critical need for the cash that a sale may provide will of course figure in the mix. But if you will see a higher cost of occupancy over the long term, perhaps you are only delaying the inevitable by seeking a short-term fix.

Consider the possibility of leasing out some of the unused space in lieu of an out-and-out sale. Perhaps you could bring in a company that would have good synergy with your existing business; if so, not only will you have the income, you may be able to develop additional sales opportunities as well.

> Consider the possibility of leasing out some of the unused space.

Consider Your Intangible Assets as Well

Over the years, a business develops a number of assets that are intangible rather than hard assets such as your inventory, equipment, and real property. These intangible assets could include things such as a name, a proprietary product, a customer list, and perhaps even some of your expertise. These are things you seldom think about, but they have value to your company as well as to others in business. A name is more than clever words, it becomes public identification that has meaning and recognition. Do you have a product with a very recognizable name that no longer fits with your future direction? Large corporations divest of products all the time, why not a small company as well?

You may put together a package whose assets are part tangible and part intangible, for example, a product line with a customer list packaged with the equipment or inventory, and that includes your services as an advisor. You can set a value for this package that goes far beyond the value of the equipment and inventory but is based primarily on the profit potential to the buyer just as a sale of a business is often based. Determine the gross profit to be derived over the first few years, and base your price on some multiple of that number. For another company, there would be little added costs to its overhead, so most of the gross would drop to the bottom line.

Consider your financial reports when determining how to structure the sale. If your tangible assets still have book value, you may want to record the sale at a premium price for those assets. This will lessen the tax impact from the sale because a portion of the price will be treated as a cost of sale as the asset will be reduced. If there is no book value of any of the assets, it doesn't matter how you record the sale; the price will fall into your gross profit and ultimately increase your taxable bottom line.

If you have a good customer database, you could sell or rent it to other companies for them to market their own products. Be careful that you are not indiscriminate about these transactions; you don't want your customers to be used.

In any transaction, you want to consider the needs of your customer. Those who have bought a product from you that you are now discontinuing and perhaps selling or licensing to another company should be notified. You don't want to send them elsewhere in search of something and lose them as a customer for your other product lines at the same time. Customer service always counts.

> If you have a good customer database, you could sell or rent it to other companies.

Don't Get Too Enthusiastic

The title of this chapter is "Selling Nonessential Assets." This is an important point to remember; don't get so caught up in the drive to raise cash that you sell off assets you will need in the future. When you go to replace them, they will likely cost more, so make sure you don't begin an internal liquidation in the quest of fresh capital.

Also be discreet about your need to raise cash so that you don't start to look like a distressed business. If too much is for sale at the same time, associates and competitors alike may get the wrong impression, and customers may feel compelled to look for new sources of supply to protect themselves. Make your inquiries and your deals in confidence if possible.

Look around your business location. Where do you have assets that are not performing, not being used, and not earning any income? Consider putting them up for sale.

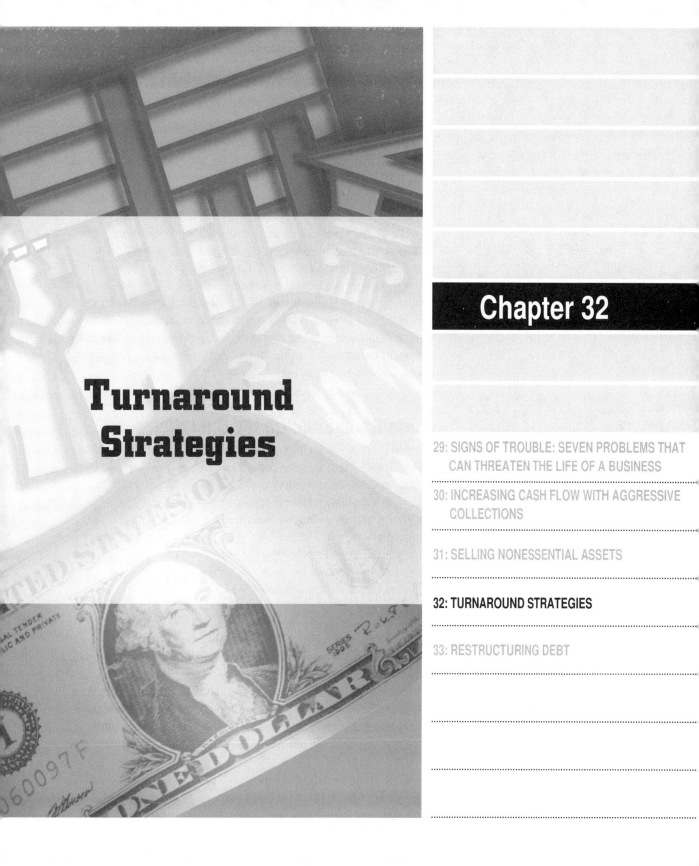

Turnaround Strategies

Chapter 32

All businesses go through cycles, some profitable and some very tough. The difficult times may pass on their own with a bit of patience and minor adjustments, but there will be times that require some real action in the form of a turnaround strategy. Normally not required to solve a single or even a few annoying business problems, turnarounds are the only way to save a company in full systems failure. The symptoms are obvious: cash crunch, delinquent loans and vendor accounts, dissatisfied customers, and disgruntled employees. And sometimes even worse.

Perhaps you think that a situation like this is hopeless, but the fact is, it is not. If the basics are intact, most companies can successfully be turned around. It takes commitment and a good bit of hard work and, of course, cooperation that will likely follow the leadership of current ownership. Turning around a business is a bit like starting a new one, and you must take a step-by-step approach.

Acute Care: Stabilize the Operation

You will require a strategic plan to be effective, and any plan requires that you have a firm starting point. One of the indications of a business in trouble is that it is in free fall, so you must take steps to stop the spiral and stabilize the operation.

Early in this process, you will need to conserve as much cash as you can; it is a critical element. There's a good chance you have been living with a cash shortage for a long time, and that remains one of the problems. However, now you will need some resources to deal with creditors and fund new projects down the road.

In part, you may be able to squeeze out some of the cash by aggressive collections of your receivables and making slower or partial payments to payable creditors. Pay only what is necessary. You may also sell unnecessary assets to increase liquidity. Don't run out of cash—your emotional comfort level will suffer if you do.

All new projects that are less than one-half complete should be halted or slowed until a full review can be done. Your total resource dollars may well be strained, and decision making must be much more cautious. When a business begins to go into a down cycle, a

> You will need to conserve as much cash as you can.

number of new ideas and concepts are considered, and often they begin as a quick fix. In the best of times, this may be too much of a scattered approach to problem solving, but in tough times, you absolutely must be more focused because of capital concerns as well as human resource availability. Everyone, including you yourself, may be stressed, and too many things going on will keep your attention from the core issues of a long-term business fix.

Now is the time for a line-by-line review of all overhead expenses with an eye to cutting any unnecessary items to save your capital resources. Many of these cuts may be short term, but you must have the will to make the tough calls. If you are to get over the current crisis, everyone will have to make some sacrifices.

Are executive salaries too high, and can they be cut for a few months? Is all the travel and entertainment spending really necessary? Can office staff watch their use of supplies and monitor phone and other utility usage? Can you lay off some staff or perhaps cut hours? This is a joint effort of everyone, and all should be asked for ideas and assistance.

Form a Support Team and Communicate

You will need the advice of a number of people from both inside and outside the organization, and now is the time to bring them together. If your accountant and attorney do not know each other, you should bring them together for a strategy session. Make sure you have the right attorney for this job—he or she should have a commercial law practice with experience in credit and collection work. You may face some lawsuits for money. If you have a few valued inside employees, they should be included in this brainstorming team as well. You must take a look at the entire picture and determine the full reality of the problems before you can create a recovery plan.

A goal of your first stage will be to open up lines of communication with all the stakeholders in your company. Your employees know more than you think; they may see inventory go down because vendors won't ship, see many packages coming in COD, or know that

Make sure you have the right attorney for this job.

customer traffic has been down and understand the implication of this. Give them enough official information to reassure them that action is being taken, leadership is in place, and their jobs are secure. Losing good people during tough times creates even more problems.

You will want to present a united and proactive impression to your vendors (if they have been waiting for money), your banker (if payments are slow or your income statement a bit weak), and perhaps even customers (if they have experienced any disruption in service). Let everyone know that some "business reengineering" is going on that will result in a stronger company better able to meet obligations or service their needs. Your spin on the situation will lead the way.

Nature abhors a vacuum, and if no information is forthcoming from you, the silences will be filled by gossip and innuendo. This could end up making small signs of trouble look like signals of great distress. You must be present and available for any questions that arise. This is a critical element of your job, leadership.

> Conduct an operational analysis comparing year-to-year trends.

The Next Step Is Operational Analysis

You should now be looking at a company that has come out of the initial stages of a crisis and is now somewhat more stable. The next step in this process is to conduct an operational analysis comparing year-to-year trends and targeting the areas that need attention and improvement. There are six areas that you should review to give yourself a comprehensive picture of what steps to take.

Analyze Sales Volume

Look at your year-to-year trend as well as period to period (third quarter 1997 versus third quarter 1998). Have sales gone up, been flat, or actually dropped? If your sales have not gone up in excess of current inflation plus at least 10 percent, you must begin to analyze where the sales have been lost and what direction your company is going. Analyze your sales by unit volume as well as dollar so that you can pinpoint the exact quantity sale in each product line.

You may be surprised to learn that there are real increases in some unexpected items that are being offset by serious decreases in others. Customer tastes change, and if you don't monitor it, you will be putting your money and effort into the wrong areas.

Have you analyzed your customer base recently? Are the same people (or companies) coming back, or are you attracting new customers all the time? If so, who are they? If you want to find additional customers, you must know who your current ones are so that you will know where to focus your efforts.

Review Gross Profit Margins

The first step to profit is getting above your break-even, which involves improvement in both volume and direct costs. You must have sufficient operating profits to cover your overhead and drop to the bottom line. If volume has stayed about the same and gross profits are down, you must look at your pricing to make sure that you are recovering all of your costs. You don't want to ship dollars out the back door with your goods.

Analyze Specific Overhead Items

Several areas in your overhead expense might be the likely culprit in any financial problems. The cost of occupancy, either rent or mortgage (plus real estate tax, insurance, and so on) may have grown too high as a percentage of your revenue—a serious problem for a business such as a restaurant.

Look at your personnel benefits. Over the recent years, healthcare costs have continued to soar, and many companies have been forced to pass on some of these costs to employees. General insurance is another area that should be scrutinized: When was the last time you had competitors bidding for your business?

Travel and entertainment, the catch-all category, may be draining cash and must be brought under control. Another place to look is in repair and maintenance; are you patching old equipment far beyond its useful life instead of looking to lease (or buy) new models and reduce that unproductive cost?

> General insurance is another area that should be scrutinized.

Look at Debt Service

Review both the interest payment as a percentage of sales as well as the principal payment that will affect cash flow and cash reserves. If interest rates have gone down, perhaps you can renegotiate (if you have a fixed rate term) or restructure the whole loan to lower the monthly total costs. This will be discussed further in the next section.

> If interest rates have gone down, perhaps you can renegotiate.

Review Your Market

The analysis you must do of your market is one of future potential within the demographics you are serving or have the prospect of serving. Will there be future growth in the product or service you currently provide? Are more people (or companies) beginning to use what you offer, or is there growth in the number of possible new customers in the future? Selling products to a maturing baby boomer group has great prospect for growth because the sheer numbers are so large that as they move from one age to another, the sales in that bracket go up significantly. Is that your business, or are you operating in a shrinking market?

Along with the question of what the market potential is, you must be honest with yourself about whether you still possess the financial capabilities to meet future demands. There will be costs of development and production or inventory and selling expense to absorb. You will need capital resources to fund these. Do you have them or can you get them? There also may be other alternatives such as partnering with another company in order to develop future projects.

Analyze Your Attitude

Undergoing the process of turning around a company may likely be a difficult and time-consuming task. It isn't for everyone— only for those who still have the energy, optimism, and commitment to accomplish the challenge at hand. You must honestly ask yourself if this is you. Do you still have the burning desire to continue even if the cost is high in terms of your time and perhaps finances? You may well find yourself working harder for less money.

If the task ahead of you seems overwhelming and you are wondering whether it is worth it, perhaps now is the time to consider an exit strategy or the possibility of succession. If you have offspring in the business, they may have the energy and the interest to do the job of reinventing the company, and you can take a back seat. If there is no succession in place, the possibility of an outright sell or merger into another company may be the most viable solution.

Make no mistake, a turnaround is time-consuming and difficult, but it can be very satisfying as well; it is the ultimate challenge. Be aware before you begin that this phase of your business life will call on all of your skills and require new knowledge.

> Perhaps now is the time to consider an exit strategy.

New Steps for New Success

If you have done your analysis, identified the areas of concern, and are sure you have the fortitude to continue, you will want to start by creating an operational strategy. Look at all the areas, internal and external, that require correction, and begin to prioritize the steps needed to make changes. Develop a team approach to problem solving, and make use of all the resources, human and capital, that you can access. Begin with the internal structural problems such as reducing inventory, correcting pricing miscalculations, and controlling costs and receivable collections. These few items alone, assuming that they have been areas of difficulty, can turn a negative cash flow into a positive one. For example, an aggressive collection program may increase cash flow sufficiently to ease your credit problems. Virtually all of a price increase will drop to the bottom line if volume remains steady. These are the critical areas of internal financial management.

Consider all the previously discussed considerations of selling off unnecessary assets, particularly product lines that may be draining resources and not creating profit. Cash you will receive will ease your liquidity. You also may want to contract out some of your borderline work to others who will pay you a fee or commission for the referral. Get back to your core business; do what you do best.

Accentuate the Positive

If you haven't given much attention to your marketing to date, chances are you have seen little or no growth. You must correct this omission, but before you make decisions of what type of marketing you should attempt, consider all the information you have learned from your analysis of current sales. What are your most profitable products, and who are your most profitable clients? These are the people or companies that you want to reach with your message. For a small business, target marketing is almost always more effective than a shotgun approach. Tailor both your message and how it is delivered to get the biggest bang for your dollar. Reach the specific people who will respond to what you are saying.

> For a small business, target marketing is almost always more effective than a shotgun approach.

Create and Utilize a Budget

Few small businesses use a budget as a form of financial control, but once you have gone through hard times, perhaps you will understand the value of this discipline. If you establish specific goals for each line item on an annual, quarterly, or monthly basis, you will be able to know when costs are getting out of control early enough to prevent any real damage. The decision on how you will measure (by month, quarter, or year) will be company specific. If your sales and the accompanying expenses are spread evenly over 12 months, you may be able to do this as an equal monthly installment. If you are more seasonal, you will want to set goals that reflect the expected ups and downs. Review your progress at the end of each period and make adjustments as required. If one area begins to trend out of control, stronger analysis and action is indicated.

Develop a System of Controls

Perhaps you only skimmed the sections on inventory control or collection procedures, or maybe you skipped these altogether. Nevertheless, you will need to institute a program that controls all these financial functions and utilizes incentives and accountability to those who are assigned to manage these areas. The CEO may have the ultimate authority, but others will have to accomplish the day-to-day tasks of a well-managed operation. Delegate authority, require regular reporting, and show that you value any change that improves the operation. Collection activity should be assigned to office staff as a regular part of their daily routine. It is an important element of cash flow for many businesses.

Create an Organizational Chart

"Who's in charge" may be a source of confusion in many small businesses, and it may be exaggerated in those who are experiencing difficulties. Many entrepreneurs overexercise control over every aspect of their operation. No one will make a decision without the approval of the CEO, and work doesn't get finished for want of that final word. You can't be everywhere, and the time comes when you must loosen the reins.

Begin by listing all the functions required to operate the company from purchasing to production to sales to administrative. Determine who in the organization is basically responsible for each of these functions and how much authority he or she should be given. Consider assigning a budget to these functions as well. For example, how about giving the office manager an operating budget from which all supplies and services must be paid? He or she can make decisions about many of the purchases or the use of outside help. When the budget runs out, no more spending. Could the sales staff manage their own marketing or advertising budget? Should production be responsible for equipment maintenance and repair? Consider the possibilities. Set clear parameters for the

> Many entrepreneurs overexercise control over every aspect of their operation.

decision criteria and be willing to reward those who get the job done effectively and under budget as well.

The Chart Begins With You

Have you ever thought of creating a job description for yourself? What are the critical areas that demand your attention, and are you so bogged down in the small stuff that you are neglecting them? Some of your areas likely will be strategic planning, financial review, dealing with outside financial people, dealing with customers, and developing a public presence for your company. Aren't these areas important enough that you should focus on them and not on the office budget?

Perhaps an answer is to appoint an overall manager who would take care of the day-to-day operation and report to you about those issues that demand your attention. The manager would deal with all other matters not requiring your personal attention. This is not an easy structure for most entrepreneurs, but it does make organizational sense.

> Consider a general manager to deal with common day-to-day problems.

Sample Chart of Organization

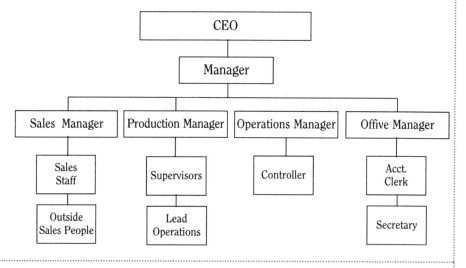

If you have a special area of expertise, you might create a modified chart such as this one.

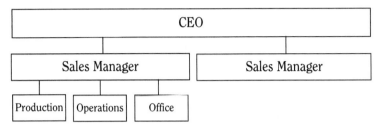

You must create the version that best meets your needs, but if you truly want an operation that is organized and under control, this is one way to get there.

If you began your turnaround early in the game, slowing down the operation to get an accurate analysis of the situation and then beginning corrective action will likely work. The longer you have let the situation fester, the more out of control it most likely has become. If you cannot make corrections within the operation that will create sufficient additional profits and cash flow to meet debt obligations, you will have to take stronger measures.

Look at Other Alternatives

You may have gotten so deeply in debt that even these preceding recommended changes will only lessen the pressure, not create a long-term solution. The only other place to look is to your creditors for some accommodation on restructuring your debt. The following chapter will cover this topic in greater depth.

> The longer you wait to deal with problem situations, the more out of control they become.

Restructuring Debt

Chapter 33

A large part of a turnaround strategy will include some minor and some major restructuring of debt—not just bank debt but obligations to a variety of creditors. This may have been precipitated by a turn-down in revenue that lowers cash flow or ongoing operating losses that drain liquidity from the capital base. Some guidelines for creating and implementing a debt restructuring plan include the following:

1. You should do a cash flow projection *first* to determine what you can reasonably offer and successfully complete.
2. You are likely to get one chance at voluntary restructuring; if you are unable to meet new obligations, creditors are not usually willing to renegotiate and will likely begin enforcement action (for instance, lawsuits).
3. You can also choose to file a Chapter 11 reorganization and force a restructure plan on creditors, assuming a sufficient number of them vote in favor. We will discuss this in greater detail later in this chapter.

You will begin this process with a pro-forma operating cash flow statement with the assumption that the only cash resource you will have will be from operating revenue less your expenses. If you *know* you will be receiving some outside cash from the sale of an asset, you may plug that number in, but don't use any speculative numbers. Always remember the admonition that you will likely get one shot to meet the new plan, so being overly ambitious will not benefit you. If you can't meet current obligations at projected cash flow, your best bet is to offer a creative plan that back loads (pays more at the end than at the beginning) as much as you can. As your business improves (you are taking a number of steps in that direction, aren't you?), you will be able to increase payments.

> Your best bet is to offer a creative plan that back loads as much as you can.

Begin with the Most Critical Debt

You may have had some legal action threatened or taken against you, and you must address this issue quickly so it doesn't get out of control. Some creditors have more clout than others. Your bank likely has a secured interest in your business assets, so they could foreclose on all of them and put you out of business. The Internal Revenue Service has the power to levy your bank account as well as your customers to collect your receivables, which will quickly dry up all of your cash. Other taxing bodies may have powers of enforcement as well.

Your landlord has the ability to remove you from the premises and perhaps even padlock your possessions for nonpayment. If the assets are secured to the bank, the landlord and the lender will fight it out in court, but the effect is the same, you are out of business.

The least dangerous of all creditors are your vendors, who are usually totally unsecured and must take long and costly legal action before they can even begin to try to enforce any collection activity. If they do sue, you have the right to answer any suit, and you may be able to keep it tied up in court for years. If you have personally guaranteed the account, action may be started against you personally.

You do not want any outstanding debts to get to these various stages of collection if at all possible. Angry creditors are never easy to deal with. Communication is critical during tough times; answer the phone, accept your responsibilities, and try to arrange a mutually satisfactory arrangement.

> The Internal Revenue Service has the power to levy your bank account as well as your customers to collect your receivables.

Talk to Your Banker

Some creditors have very strict rules on collection procedures, and your bank is normally one of them; they are required to do so under federal and state banking laws. Any loan that is delinquent must be disclosed and written off their books.

What you need to do is to negotiate with your banker before you miss any payments. Make an appointment as soon as you know a problem is going to occur. If the loan is still current, your banker can normally make some accommodations. Once a month or two have passed, it is out of his or her hands and into what is often called a workout department. They are the collectors; in the larger banks, they are inhouse, and in the smaller banks, they are usually contracted out to attorneys. Once this action has been taken, you will find little interest in the circumstance or well-being of your company; their only concern is in collecting what is due.

Your lender may be able to do a number of things before a loan gets to this point. Perhaps a few months of interest-only payments will be enough to get you through the rough times. If more drastic restructuring is required, bring your financials and a proposed new payment plan to your meeting. You won't know what is possible until you ask. It often depends on the lender individually. Many bank employees who at one time had these decisions within their authority, no longer have them. But if you have a relationship with a manager, by all means call him or her.

It is in the bank's best interest to have you pay back the loan even if the terms have to be changed, but these days, it might be your job to convince them of this reality. And to start, you will have to find the right person to talk to.

> Perhaps a few months of interest-only payments will be enough to get you through the rough times.

Be Careful with the Taxing Bodies

The state, federal, and local taxing bodies are not lenders, they are collectors. You are holding money that does not belong to you, and to use it in many cases is a criminal act although if complete restitution is made, you will usually not be prosecuted. The primary exception is sales tax, which is collected and not withheld and must be remitted to the state. You may be charged with theft or fraud if you fail to do so.

Earlier, I established how quickly taxes can add up when penalty and interest is charged. Because of that and the potential for other legal ramifications, it is best to face your problem and determine a mutually agreeable solution as quickly as you can. For the most part, a taxpayer who comes in voluntarily and offers a payment plan will be met with cooperation.

It is always best to offer a down payment if you are able. That puts money into the hands of the agent, which makes their success rate look good, and they will often work harder to get approval of those in authority. A down payment of 20 percent almost always will get the positive attention you want, and in some cases, it may take only 10 percent. You can also work out a 24-month payout plan in most cases, which seems to be the limit for how long a government agency will wait to be paid back. If you need more time, you will need a tax professional to make your case and then possibly appeal a negative decision.

You may want to be creative while technically sticking to the 24-month deal by offering the lowest payments for the first 12 months and a higher payment for the last 12. This will allow you to get on your feet a bit. You may also try a balloon payment at the end; this is tricky, but I have seen it work. Keep that final payment to under 20 percent of the total; 10 percent is even better.

Keeping the Roof over Your Head

You should pay your rent (or mortgage) with some of the first dollars coming in, but sometimes the demands from others become so intense that it isn't possible. If you get behind, your landlord has recourse, namely, evicting your business from the premises. It takes formal legal action to accomplish this, but in many jurisdictions this can be accomplished in fewer than 60 days unless there is a real dispute to be settled.

Before your delinquency gets too substantial, you must face this creditor and work out some agreeable solution. Unless you are in very desirable accommodations and you are paying far less rent than the current market, agreements are usually possible.

Consider this: There are legal fees to evict someone, and there are almost always cleaning and improvements necessary to make the space ready for a new tenant. Depending on how extensive these are, they could add up to thousands of dollars, even tens of thousands. The more personalized your space, the greater your leverage.

> Why not try to renegotiate your entire lease and back load the rent to the end of the lease.

Why not try to renegotiate your entire lease and back load the rent to the end of the lease, thereby giving yourself temporary current relief? Or why not amortize the arrearage over the next year or two along with making current rent payments? Could you give back space to be rented to others? Would you be permitted to sublet some of the space yourself? Can you barter some of your products or services for a credit against the rent?

There are an infinite number of possibilities to explore, but it's up to you to begin the negotiation. Assume that you are a needed tenant and your landlord wants to find a way to keep you if your payments can be improved. That is likely the case.

Try to Cooperate with Vendors

> Creditors' rights, particularly those who are unsecured, are fairly limited.

No one likes a barrage of collection calls; they are demeaning and very stressful. You know how you feel when you are not being paid, so you understand how your trade creditor is feeling. You should try to take the calls and explain your situation (cash flow shortage) and ask for some patience until you can work out a plan. If the animosity grows, stop talking. Refer it to your attorney or some other outside professional. Don't get involved in rancorous dialogue.

Creditors' rights, particularly those who are unsecured, are fairly limited. They can take legal action to take the debt to judgment, but that is only a first step. In most instances, you have a right to answer the charge with your own accounting of what is owed, and even if you lose, you can still appeal the decision and get even more time. The process grinds slowly, and at the end, a judgment must be executed against assets. If you have little or no tangible assets, you are fairly safe from being forced to pay. Remember that a bank account can be attached by a judgment and the money confiscated to satisfy it.

You know that your intention is to meet your obligations, but sometimes your business situation prevents you from doing that successfully. In the short term, you should try to cooperate, but when you are threatened, you must defend yourself. It is in everyone's best interest that your business becomes revitalized so that must be your priority.

If you find vendors who are willing to negotiate a payment schedule, by all means do so. Just as with your landlord, it may take many forms—from monthly payout of old debt to a short-term forbearance to be repaid in 90 to 120 days with interest. Your vendors want to keep a customer along with getting paid. Try to work with them.

You cannot overobligate yourself in trying to satisfy everyone. If you have past due obligations in one or two of these areas, you may be able to negotiate something, but if you have gotten behind in all areas, a more drastic solution may be required.

Reorganizing Under Chapter 11

There was a time that any form of bankruptcy was an embarrassment and signified the end of most businesses. That is no longer the case since over the past decade or so, a number of large businesses have gone through successful reorganizations. Macy's is still a premier department store, and Continental and TWA are still flying planes. A number of steel companies and virtually thousands of other businesses have made it through this process to once again thrive.

There are a number of things you should know before you get into the bankruptcy process, and one of the most critical elements of success is selecting the right attorney to handle the case. He or she should have a practice that has included this type of work and some track record of successful outcomes.

What Is a Chapter 11 and What Happens

A Chapter 11 reorganization gives a debtor a chance to submit a plan to all creditors detailing the amount and terms of the payback offered to them on outstanding debt. The minute a petition is filed, all creditor activities, including pending lawsuits and tax levies, are stayed (stopped) by the court. For the next 120 days, you (the debtor) have the right to file a plan exclusively, meaning that no one else can file a competing plan during that time.

While the case is ongoing, you will incur a certain amount of extra expense for your attorney and likely more work for your accountant as well. Trustee fees, which are based on your total amount of disbursement revenues, will be incurred. You will also be required to make timely court filings of your financial statements and keep all taxes paid and returns filed timely. Past due taxes will be paid under the plan.

> The minute a petition is filed, all creditor activities are stayed (stopped) by the court.

Your debt will be categorized under the following headings:

Administrative debt—Professional fees, new taxes, and all vendor debt incurred subsequent to the filing.

Secured debt—Bank loans that are secured to collateral assuming that the value of the collateral exceeds the debt. Any other debts that have been litigated through the filing of a judgment assuming that the collateral is sufficient.

Priority unsecured debt—All debt owed to taxing bodies, including interest.

Unsecured debt—Vendor debt, any secured debt that is undercollateralized, and tax penalties not liened and secured.

At the end of 120 days, you will be required to file two documents with the court, the first is the Disclosure Statement, and the second is the Plan of Reorganization.

In the Disclosure Statement, you will discuss the current financial circumstance of your business. You will also list all the debts, both the past due ones and any current ones that have been incurred, such as legal and accounting fees and perhaps ongoing vendor credit. And then you will disclose your future income projections that will show how you expect to be able to generate the capital needed to pay the amount you are offering. Another very important feature of this statement is the liquidation analysis; this is the essence of what bankruptcy is about.

The debtor must give all of his creditors an analysis of what the business would be worth if it were liquidated. You will list all assets and their potential selling price. And you will account for any costs of this liquidation. That will give you the net amount of dollars that will be returned to the creditors.

This will be contrasted with the creditors' return from the ongoing company. The question is whether more benefit would be derived from an asset sale than from future profits. In almost all cases, the best deal for creditors is an ongoing business. And this is why there is a law that allows this type of reorganization. If it works, it is in everybody's best interest—yours as well because you will be working to repay obligations, which is likely what you want to do.

> The best deal for creditors is an ongoing business.

The Plan will describe how each creditor will be treated and how he or she will be paid back. Under the law, you have the following amount of time to make payments under a plan:

Administrative debt—Payment must be made upon confirmation of the Plan or by agreement with the creditor.

Secured debt—Must be paid in full as per the terms over 72 months or by new established terms.

Priority unsecured debt—In full over 72 months.

Unsecured debt—A portion will be paid over 72 months. Many Plans offer from 20 to 50 percent, and some offer as low as 5 percent. Many judges require a payment of over 10 percent or they won't confirm a Plan, even one that has enough votes to pass.

For a company that has accumulated a good bit of debt, this is one way of making it manageable again. Everyone but the unsecured creditors get paid back in full although the time is stretched. For the unsecured vendor, they get only a portion, and they will have to wait, but at least they will get a return. A collapsed company pays nothing.

And if the unsecured vendors have been willing to continue the business relationship with you either on credit or for cash, they will still have a customer. That means profits. Many vendors will still want to do business with your company contrary to what you may expect.

Filing a Chapter 11 is a very tough business decision; it is not to be made lightly. But there are times when it is the only viable decision. It takes work to come out of the bankruptcy, but a smarter, healthier company will likely result.

> Everyone but the unsecured creditors get paid back in full.

Keeping What You Earned

Summary of Part VII

- **How to make profits from your excess cash**
- **Preparing family members to take over**
- **Setting a value for the business**
- **Selling the company**
- **Understanding personal financial needs v. corporate responsibility**

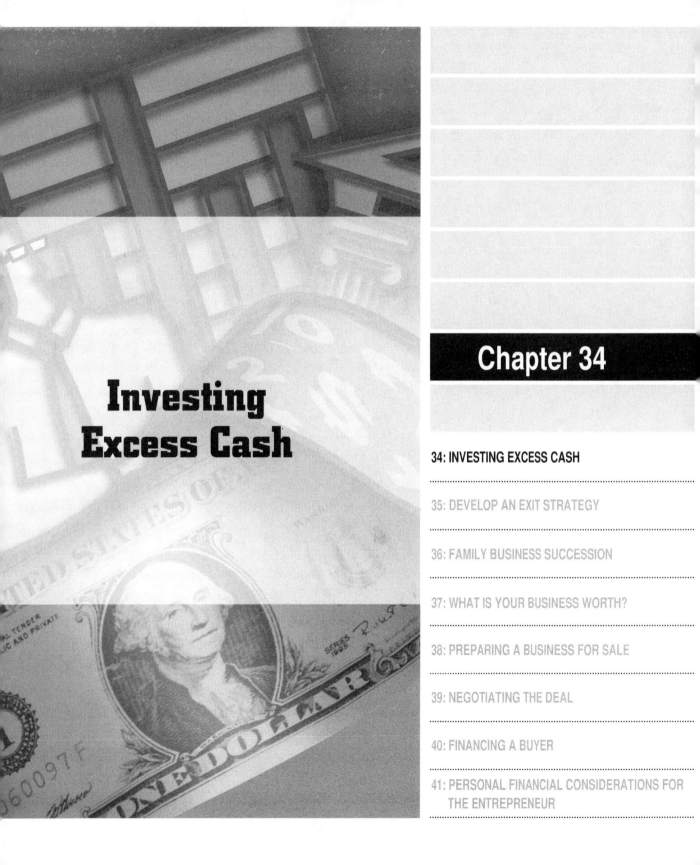

Investing Excess Cash

Chapter 34

Almost every business has times when cash received is in excess of what is needed. Perhaps your business is seasonal and, after the busy time, you are holding money needed to get through the slow times. Or better yet, perhaps profits have been good over a period, and you are retaining these excess earnings in your bank. Now you want to put that money to work for you, and there are a number of ways to do it.

Consider Opportunistic Buying

In many businesses, prices at the source go up and down according to demand. There may also be discounts available for a number of reasons such as fast payment (often 2 percent, 10 days), higher quantities, or early shipment (preseason). What this will mean to you is that you will lower your cost of product, increase your margin, and drop profits directly to your bottom line.

If you are in this position, start to make inquiries of your vendors of what "special offers" they may have. Some manufacturers and distributors have an overstock list that they will circulate on a regular basis, and some will need to be called. Don't feel shy about making an offer for even better terms—unsold product won't do them any good in their own warehouse, and you never know what incentive may be possible.

Sometimes it is your competitors who have the excess inventory that they would like to liquidate. Particularly those out of your area and not in direct competition. Make some calls or send out a generic letter asking if there is any excess available.

Last but not least are the close-out brokers. They buy from manufacturers as well as distributors and retailers offering low prices but offering needed cash. There are a few major players, and they can come up with tremendous bargains. Find out who they are and stay in contact.

A word of warning: Don't buy anything if you aren't sure that you can merchandise it well. You don't want to end up having to sell it off at a later date and at an even cheaper price.

> Don't buy anything if you aren't sure that you can merchandise it well.

Use Liquid Investments

You may want to buy a short-term certificate of deposit that will pay interest and be fairly accessible if absolutely necessary, although you will incur a penalty for cashing in early. However, the shortest term you can get would be 30 days, and surely you can project your needs for the next 30 days. A better rate can be found in six-month instruments.

As an alternative, you can keep your excess cash in a money market account that also earns interest. This is not a typical checking account because you are allowed no more than three checks per month, so it requires some planning.

For large amounts of excess cash, over $100,000, the bank will do the investment work for you, but they will charge you a fee, which is why a balance large enough to earn substantial income is necessary. Referred to as a sweep account, the bank will automatically transfer excess cash into the interest bearing account and back when needed to honor checks. These transfers may be made as often as daily.

You can do a version of this by yourself by depositing most of your money in your interest bearing account and making transfers as needed in person at the bank. These transactions are allowed on an unlimited basis.

Although currently only three checks are permitted on a money market account because of banking regulations, that number is going up over the next few years and will eventually be the equivalent of one check each business day. You will still have to make the transfer, but this will make it easier.

> You can keep your excess cash in a money market account. For large amounts of excess cash, the bank will do the investment work for you.

Buy Real Estate

It is always good to see your name on the side of a building, and this can be a very good way to invest the money you are making. It meets a number of long-term financial goals:

1. It gives you control over your space.
2. It fixes the costs over a number of years, and you won't have the problem of a substantial increase in rent.

3. As you pay your mortgage, you are building equity and also seeing some appreciation in your investment.

There are a few downsides to consider as well. One would be room for expansion, particularly if you cannot buy a large enough piece of property now and think you may need one in the future. You will have to sell your current building in order to move, and that will take time. You also will have a maintenance responsibility, and this could drain cash and human resource from your operating company. But on the whole, the benefits normally outweigh the problems. You can begin building equity now.

The money you put down on the building may not end up being unencumbered equity if you choose to finance it through the bank where you have your business loans. They are likely to want to cross-collateralize the property as secondary security on other outstanding business loans. This won't matter unless you decide to sell the building and need the equity back in cash.

> The trickiest maneuver to manage is the purchase of a portion or all of another company.

Purchase Other Businesses

Perhaps the trickiest maneuver to manage is the purchase of a portion or all of another company. You must determine what the other company is worth, whether you can afford it, and if the combination with your company makes any sense.

Perhaps the last is the most important consideration. It makes no sense to buy a business that doesn't play to your strengths no matter what the price. If you can't operate it at a profit, it isn't worth anything to you but the value of the assets. There are times to buy only assets of another company, and this may be one of your alternatives.

If you are bottom fishing, looking for machinery and equipment to increase your own capacity, then compatibility is not an issue, but if you expect to merge another company into your own operation, it most assuredly is. Do you have a similar customer base? Is your pricing strategy similar, high end or low end? Do the companies have similar corporate cultures and public identities? When too many aspects about a business combination clash, both customers and employees get confused, and the outcome may be very marginal. If you keep on personnel from the old company and they have different habits and priorities, it may cause disruption for the entire organization. If customers come expecting one thing and get something else, they will be dissatisfied. A merger is like a marriage.

As to what you should pay, the answer is fairly simple: Look at the return in terms of profits you expect from this new acquisition. Is it as high as or higher than the return you can get from any other investment? And the reality is that the return should be more substantial as consideration for the risk—the higher the one, the higher the other.

And you can afford it if you will not be jeopardizing your current company by any excess borrowing or a sudden cash flow strain where it used to be easy.

You can buy equipment, you can buy market share, you can buy patents, and you can buy a skilled workforce. All these are elements that will enlarge your existing company. But buy them wisely and after serious investigation and thought.

> A merger is
> like a marriage.

Money Is an Instrument, Play it Well

The cash that flows through your business is one of the tools—you must use it wisely. Internally, you will make expenditures on the inventory, personnel, and other allocations that will keep you profitable. When there is excess cash, it must be used productively as well. The investment you choose should reflect your own level of sophistication and your own comfort zone with risk. Don't make decisions you will fret over later. Consider all the alternatives, and choose the one you feel comfortable with.

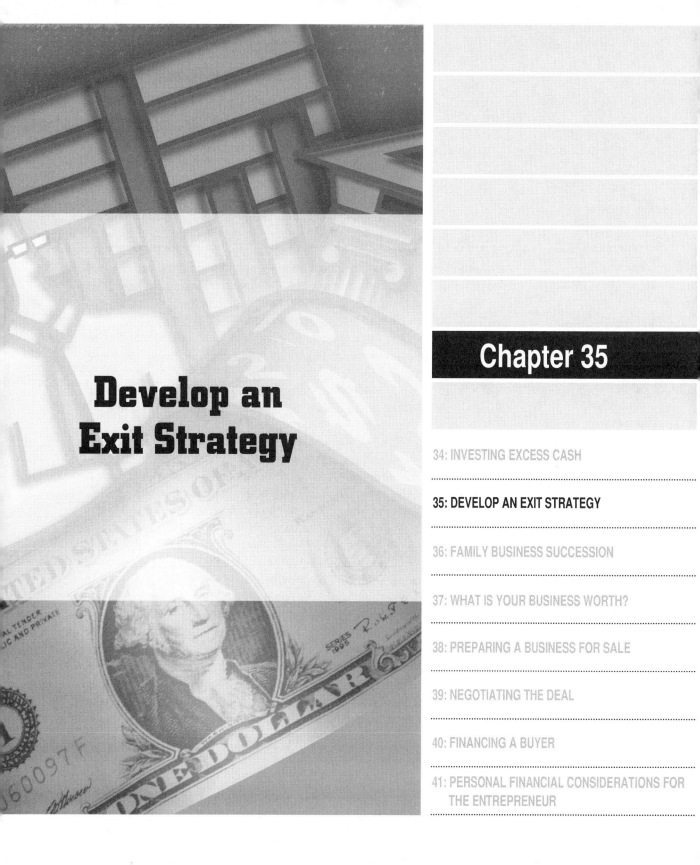

Develop an Exit Strategy

Chapter 35

If you are operating a closely held company, you should have a plan to exit the business and withdraw your equity just as you had a plan to begin the company and grow it. This is necessary both for the continuation of the business and the preservation of your personal investment. A sudden illness or worse will jeopardize both because a company without an adequate leader may not survive and may not be saleable either. So planning for the future is one of your jobs as well.

The reality is that for many entrepreneurs, the equity they have built up in their business is their primary source of retirement funds, and this equity must come out intact so that they can retire. But few plan for how to accomplish this goal.

For some owners, the business is their lifelong ambition, and they will spend most of their working lives involved in the operations. Their work is critical in the company, so if they weren't able to continue, the company may not be able to go on, and all its values would be lost. The exit strategy here is to find a buyer before this becomes a reality.

Some business owners see their current business as an investment and expect to stay only as long as they need to in order to maximize value and sell out at the high point. The plan for this is clear: Build a strong balance sheet and develop a niche with a growing customer base. Then put the entire entity up for sale.

Well, in fact, this is the model that should be used with all business owners who seek to sell their business at some point. The other major alternative is a succession plan with a child or other family member which will be discussed in the next chapter. But an outright sale must be planned for, not only from the standpoint of creating as much value as possible but also from choosing when to put it on the market. A distressed or quick sale of any company is not the way to maximize return.

Once you have come to terms with the fact that you must plan an exit, the next step is to determine what the most likely scenario will be. If you have no succession possibility in place now, is there a family member who may offer a possibility? If the answer is no, then the answer is a sale either of the business as an entity or of the assets separately.

> The reality is that for many entrepreneurs, the equity they have built up in their business is their primary source of retirement funds.

Who is the most likely buyer for your business? Would it be an inside individual, perhaps an aggressive, young manager who sees himself or herself as the owner some day? It may be to another company that would make this into a good fit with its own existing business. Or it could be an individual not yet identified who can manage and grow the company just as you have done. Your first step in developing an effective strategy is to narrow the field of candidates.

You should know whether or not your business is a possibility for another company to purchase. Sales will have to be in excess of several million dollars with a reasonable gross profit margin, particularly if it is above the industry average. The net profit may not be as critical because the purchasing company would not have your overhead. When your business could be operated by another company with little addition to its existing administrative cost, the profit potential could be substantial. If this sounds like your best bet, spend time and energy maintaining the healthy level of revenue and the best gross margin possible. Also identify candidates along the way even if it isn't time to make the move. It might be constructive as well to get to know individuals inside the targeted company.

The insider as buyer is a big challenge as well as an opportunity. You may have started out as a mentor to this person and realized over the years that he or she has the capability and the interest to succeed you. Once you identify this and are comfortable with it, you might consider a few steps preliminary to making the deal when you are ready. Would the assignment of a small block of stock to this individual make you uncomfortable? It doesn't cost anything since there would be no dividends, but there may be a good return in terms of loyalty and dedication. You might also add the opportunity for complete disclosure of the finances of the company, something you may not do for just an average employee. When the time comes to make a deal, you will begin to negotiate for the purchase of the balance of the stock in the company. Your potential buyer-employee may be willing to sacrifice short-term reward for long-term gain.

Selling to an individual outside buyer may be the most difficult challenge. Unless you know of some potential candidates, you may want to use a business broker. Brokers will charge based on the total selling price although some charge a marketing fee as

> Identify candidates along the way even if it isn't time to make the move.

> Many mature companies reach a plateau, but with more aggressive marketing and more capital for expansion, an entire new level could be reached.

well. One caution before you sign any agreement: In many sales of small businesses, the owner finances the purchase on a multiyear payout. If you use a broker, his or her fee will likely come out of the initial down payment and may, in fact, be the bulk of that payment. As an example, if the broker's fee is 10 percent of the purchase price and the down payment is 25 percent, you may come out of the closing with only 15 percent of what you assume that you sold the business for. As will be discussed later in the book, the rest of the money is at some risk, so you may never see the total cash you expected. You have sold the asset and no longer have any income. For some, this is too great a risk.

Before you take on a business broker, you might want to try to locate a buyer on your own. Are there people within your industry (salespeople are good candidates) who would understand the potential of your company? Many mature companies reach a plateau, but with more aggressive marketing and more capital for expansion, an entire new level could be reached. Who would know that better than someone working within the same industry who sees the potential on a day-to-day basis?

With a number of middle managers and, interestingly enough, bankers being laid off or retired early, the market has been brisk for the sale of businesses. Many former corporate executives don't want to go through the experience again or can't find a new slot in their field. To them, the lure of entrepreneurship is strong. Your business might be exactly what one of these executives is looking for.

Community organizations such as the Chamber of Commerce and the Rotary are places you might find potential buyers. They tend to network by attending many of these meetings. When you are ready to find someone, let some people know of your possible interest; good candidates would be your accountant, attorney, and insurance agent. Don't broadcast the desire to sell, for it could damage your existing business, but do begin to put the word out.

You can make the original contacts on your own, talking to prospective buyers and perhaps even showing them the business and discussing your thoughts about its future. But when it comes to the serious negotiation, you might do well to have someone else conduct this phase. The buyer wants to pay as little as possible and, to that end, may point out all the shortcomings of your company. You have put a good bit of yourself into your venture and may not want or need to hear this criticism. It's best, therefore, that someone else represent you.

We will cover valuing your business, preparing for a sale, and the other implications of this decision later. Your job now is to decide if this is the way you wish to exit from your company.

You Can Close and Sell Assets

The other alternative available to you is to close down the operation and sell off all of your assets. It may be more profitable in some cases if the assets have been underutilized and the return on the sale of the business is not adequate. Few buyers may want the going concern, but a number of different entities may be interested in your assets, tangible as well as intangible. You may know this now and decide to plan on this type of exit, or you may have tried the selling route for the entire company and found no takers to pay what you think it is worth. You want to get as high a return as possible, so choose the strategy that provides this even if you feel sad and sentimental.

The bottom line is that nothing goes on forever, and you must decide how and when you will phase out your business. Do it with your head, not your heart, and plan the exit far in advance. This will allow for a clean and, possibly, profitable break.

> A number of different entities may be interested in your assets, tangible as well as intangible.

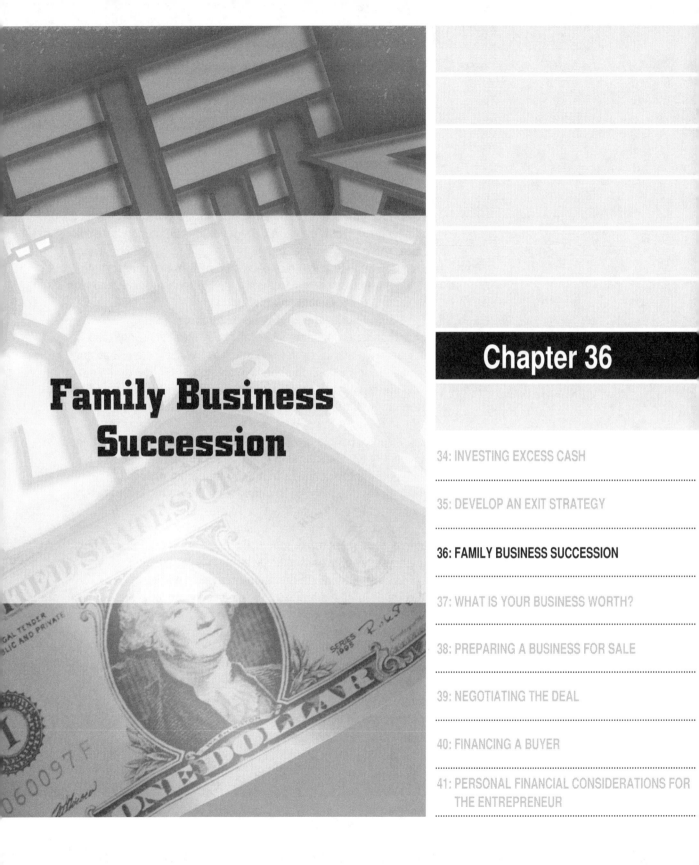

Family Business Succession

Chapter 36

Many small businesses have more than one generation of a family as employees if not owners. There is often the assumption that someday the transition in ownership will take place. However, without planning and serious consideration, the succession may take place, but it is unlikely to do so successfully. According to current statistics, only one in three businesses passed on to the second generation succeed, and only one in eight in the third generation continue as viable companies. There are a number of reasons for this, ranging from general changes in an industry to lack of commitment from the offspring, but the most common problem is the lack of a viable succession plan and the will to implement one that exists.

A family business may at times be a source of family discord rather than a rallying place where all family members can go and work toward a mutual goal. One issue may be that there will be only one successor who will take the founder's place. Sibling rivalry is one of the issues that has created monumental arguments as well as notorious lawsuits. Consider the public discord among the offspring of the founders of Harry Winston Jewelers and Koch Industries; these disputes have gone on for years and cost millions. In addition, a number of founders develop a very autocratic style and operate their companies without the input or even the knowledge of the offspring that are assumed to be taking over. Transition, in this case, may never take place completely or successfully.

A good succession must be planned and the transition strategy put into place years before it actually happens. The social as well as the financial implications must be taken into consideration.

Of course, there are the companies that have been taken over after a sudden illness or death of a parent, spouse, or sibling—some have actually worked well. But the risk is very high that the primary family asset will be lost if this transition isn't successful.

There are a number of serious issues to consider when operating a business that has a goal to be passed to members of the family for the purposes of continuation as well as conserving and growing family assets. Some of these concerns are strictly about the company, and some are about the family structure, but all are imperative to this process.

> Only one in three businesses passed on to the second generation succeed.

You Cannot Pass on a Fragile Business

If you have utilized your company to fund your personal lifestyle (which is your choice to make) and not to build equity, don't expect a sibling or anyone else for that matter to be able to take it over and nurse it back to health. There is a good chance, when this has been the history, that retained earnings are little or none and working capital is minimal. Without additional cash infusion or investment, the prognosis isn't good.

You have been the one with the vision and the savvy, and much of what you know has been learned over the years. In addition, you have a network of associates to rely on. This will not be the case with your successor. He or she will be starting out with less expertise, less experience, and no cash cushion to rely on. It's like running a race with your legs tied together.

Added to that is the reality that you will probably need some sort of a payout. Now, we have a business with less experience at the top, little or no cash cushion, and a need to make payments that hadn't been made before. This is clearly a formula for disaster.

Succession Must Be Driven by the Managerial Needs of the Company and the Financial Needs of the Owner

A company needs strong and talented leadership to survive and thrive, and putting it in the hands of someone who does not have the drive, the desire, and perhaps the ability is not productive for the company or for the individual—even if that individual is your child. Although it is difficult to be objective about your own offspring, in this case, it may be critical. If your natural successor has not taken to the business as you might have hoped, has shown few signs of entrepreneurial spirit, and doesn't seem happy, don't force the business on him or her. Sit down and have a heart to heart and find out what he or she is thinking. Help your son or daughter decide if succeeding you in the company is what he or she really wants to do. There may be great unspoken pressure to do so and little support for

> If your natural successor has not taken to the business, don't force the business on him or her.

deciding against it, but you must try to be objective when listening and contributing to the decision.

Many of the second-generation successions that fail do so because the offspring wasn't cut out for the job or never wanted it in the first place. The business was *your* dream; make sure that your son or daughter feels the same way before he or she agrees to take on the role.

Your second consideration is your own financial needs. How will you get your money out of the business? You can't give the company to a successor and then expect him or her to take care of you for life. You will no longer be a productive member of the business, so anything you are given is actually a cut from the profits. If this expense drains all the profitability away, the company will quickly lose its liquidity, and your income and your child's self-esteem will be at risk. And all this is avoidable and predictable if you exercise good judgment.

A serious purchase agreement with any successor is an absolute necessity. Set a selling price and the terms, and take your equity out as a payout of your ownership. If the company has done well, perhaps some of the money may come from a bank loan. If outside funds aren't possible, the note either will be assumed personally by your successor or may become a corporate obligation. If that is the case, the amount will go in the books as a debt, and you must consider what effect this may have on the balance sheet. After all, this document will go to bankers for possible loan continuation; or new loan consideration, and if this new debt creates a serious negative impact, the company may be handcuffed into the future with regard to borrowing.

You may be required to come to terms with the fact that the intent may be there but your need for monetary return and the individual's or the company's resources can't be reconciled. When this is the case, an outside buyer may be required, or perhaps you could find a partner willing to provide some additional capital. Your hard work built up the equity, so you have the right to cash it in.

> You can't give the company to a successor and then expect him or her to take care of you for life.

Handling Multiple Candidates

What if the circumstance is an embarrassment of riches? You have a number of family members, and all are capable and all are interested. How is succession planned in this circumstance?

Many families tend to work in birth-order sequence: The oldest assumes the top job and then on down the line. At times, this may not be in the best interest of the company, especially if the particular talent of the eldest is not the one required to do the job of CEO. An experienced financial person may be important as an officer but perhaps not the best choice for CEO where much selling and negotiating is needed. Or perhaps your company is in manufacturing and your eldest child is more production oriented than interested in administrative or management duties.

What about degrees of ownership? How do you pass on interests—in equal portions? Does the oldest get a greater share? Should the founder keep a portion, so no one has complete control?

When the founder still feels as if he or she is a part of the business, it may be more divisive than effective as a tool for succession management. The founder won't stop making decisions, but now he or she has offspring stockholders who are beginning to feel they possess ownership in name only. Over the long haul, this serves as a disincentive for the next generation to take charge and responsibility. Everything they do is overruled anyway.

If succession leading to an exit is your goal, perhaps the deal should be left to the discretion of the acquirers. Allow them to form a group and decide how much they can pay, how they expect to fund it, and who will fill what roles during and after the transition. Decisions that are made autonomously are often very empowering and often have a better chance for success. Even you may be surprised by the outcome.

Remember that when the succession takes place, formal dealings must be put into place. Not only should you have a sales contract, but you will have to remove yourself from any instrument, including loan agreements that have you as guarantor.

> If succession leading to an exit is your goal, perhaps the deal should be left to the discretion of the acquirers.

It's All in the Planning

Can you imagine going from the stockroom to the boardroom with little or no transition? The only workers who ever have that experience are the offspring of the founder. Working over holidays and summers, they may be doing grunt work, and then all of a sudden they come on board as an officer. At first glance, this may appear to be quite a good deal, but that isn't necessarily the case. Other employees may resent offspring and rather than trying to help them learn, they could be undermining their success. After all, it is human to resent someone who is younger, making more money, and getting more authority and privileges without having paid his or her dues. Offspring always have the boss's ear.

If you really want a successful succession to take place, you won't throw your offspring into the water and expect them to teach themselves to swim just because you did it. You will sit down and work out a plan to move them into various roles in the company, teach them what they need to know, and give them authority to make decisions. Most important, allow them to make mistakes and teach them how to correct them. You most likely learned more from your mistakes than from your successes. Make the effort to do this all with as much respect as you can maintain.

It is too easy to continue to think of your offspring as your child rather than your business peer. But your long-term financial well-being may be in their hands. Shouldn't that be an incentive to change the nature of the roles and work together to meet your needs and expectations as well as theirs?

> There are contracts to be drawn and payments to arrange.

Dot the I's, Cross the T's, and Remember the Tax Implications

There should be no such thing as an informal passing of the torch with a casual handshake and agreement. There are contracts to be drawn and payments to arrange. You will confuse the finances of the business if you are being paid with no formal understanding of how much or how long and for what.

You will likely want to collect your Social Security, and there will be limits on how much income you can draw. And is it income or a payout for your equity ownership? If it is a payout, what was the cost basis of your equity, and will you be paying capital gains tax? Is it part payout and perhaps a consulting fee as well?

There are ways to extract your personal capital without paying high taxes or losing benefits. This will take professional tax advice and then arriving at an acceptable agreement with your successor. Like all transactions in your business, source documents are critical. Don't neglect this part of the planning, or you might find yourself subject to painful scrutiny.

> There are ways to extract your personal capital without paying high taxes or losing benefits.

What Is Your Business Worth?

Chapter 37

There are a number of different ways to value a business, and they are used for a variety of purposes. The most obvious one is based on book values and listed on your balance sheet. There are two caveats here. One is that this *may* not reflect the actual value of your fixed assets such as buildings or equipment. These may be worth more or less than is currently listed on your books. Second, your books will not reflect the worth of your intangible assets such as the value of your name, your customer list, and your expertise, say, in the area of design or creative output. These would raise the net worth of most businesses considerably.

On the low side, there is also the liquidation value of the company, which may be determined as either an orderly sale or a distressed or quick sale of assets. In an orderly sale of assets, you may assume that you will receive the close equivalent to the current market value of all property and equipment and at least a portion of the inventory. You would be able to collect on most but perhaps not all the receivables. The worst-case scenario is the distressed sale, which brings a great deal less. Having to make a quick sale of anything means accepting much lower offers normally from buyers astute in this type of desperate selling. Your bank will often discount your assets to this level because, in a foreclosure, this is what it expects to receive. Inventory falls into this category as well, and the return may well be only 10 cents or 20 cents on the dollar. Without diligent work at collections, often less than 50 percent of the receivables would ever be voluntarily paid, and few banks work hard to pursue this effort.

The difference between the two can be substantial. A business with $200,000 in property, $100,000 in equipment, and $100,000 in inventory and receivables of $50,000 may be liquidated carefully for $360,000 or more—20 percent below the listed value. The same property at distressed liquidation may net less than $90,000—20 percent of value. This difference is $250,000!

> Having to make a quick sale of anything means accepting much lower offers normally from buyers astute in this type of desperate selling.

The Value of the Going Concern

If you were valuing your business for tax purposes, you would want it to be as conservative as legally possibly to minimize your liability. However, at this point, we are looking at the evaluation you are making for the purpose of putting a selling price on the company—one that will interest a buyer and that is reasonable enough you can justify with backup data.

You will set a general price on your business based on two factors: the value of your assets and the return (or profit) on the equity or investment. Some buyers are looking at the purchase of a business purely as an investment, and demand a return equivalent to the risk. For others, the need is to buy a job or career, so the value is not quite as rigid. A sale to another company may be for far more esoteric reasons such as the other business wanting a bigger market share or needing a product line, and they will base their value on the worth of that potential. Be astute about the motivation of your buyer in the beginning of the negotiation. Set a flexible price and be prepared to compromise. Don't be unreasonable, or you will scare away potential buyers.

> If you were valuing your business for tax purposes, you would want it to be as conservative as legally possibly.

Value to an Individual Buyer

The typical buyer is looking for what he or she can make on the money invested in the purchase of your business. That would be based on the net profit as shown on your profit and loss statement, not just for the current year but for the past two or three years so that a realistic average can be established. Even if you, like many business owners, have operated your business to fund a lifestyle, that is an accepted occurrence and will be accounted for at a later point in the form of restated earnings. The value of your liquid (current) assets such as cash, inventory, and receivables may be added to this number or may be retained by the current owner. This combination will account for the value of the intangible assets that are changing hands as well.

Your buyer will want to know what percentage return (normally referred to as the capitalization of net profits) he or she is getting for his or her invested dollar. This number is calculated by dividing the net profit (once it has been adjusted) by the desired return of investment (ROI). For example, if restated earnings were $100,000 and ROI as a percentage was .20, the value would be $100,000 ÷ (.20) = $500,000, the worth of the business based solely on earnings.

How Much of a Return Is Reasonable

Your buyer will want to achieve a rate of return that is commensurate with risk involved in the business. A number of qualifications can quantify that risk, as follows:

> If selling a mature business, a solid description of how it changed with the times may be in order.

1. The length of time the company has been in business. Fewer than five years makes it virtually a startup. On the other hand, a very old company (over 30 years) may, depending on the industry, be viewed as beyond its prime. Here is one area where you must package your company with its strengths being showcased. If you are selling a mature business, a solid description of how it has changed with the times may be in order.
2. Earnings records. If they have been steady and consistent, you've got a safe bet. If they have been erratic, some years high and some nonexistent, you have a lot of explaining to do. And if they have been minimal, there is far less value and far greater risk for the buyer. Here is where the adjustments to earnings will play a big part.
3. The current and future prospects of the market to be served. If you have been milking a mature market, any astute buyer will realize that he or she will have to invest substantial money into, perhaps, new product development and, certainly, advertising and marketing communication. This will be taken into consideration.
4. The tangible assets and what they are worth. The more the purchase is secured by solid assets, the lower the risk. If equipment could be sold off to raise capital, that may make the new business owner more at ease.

The range of return is based on the current rate of return of very safe investment, which is approximately 6 percent, so expectations of the investment return from a business purchase might range from a low of twice that, or 12 percent, to a high of 30 percent. There is no hard-and-fast rule; each party, the buyer and the seller, may see the strengths and the weaknesses very differently. You may also translate these numbers into a multiple of earnings with 12 percent return being 8 times the restated profits, 20 percent being 5 times, and 30 percent being 3.3 times.

Therefore, the same $100,000 net earnings would bring a purchase price of $800,000 as a good risk, $500,000 as a medium risk, and $330,000 as a high risk. There are things you can do to increase the value of your company using these formulas, and they will be covered in the next chapter. They require planning, which is always recommended for achieving the highest level of return.

> The range of return is based on the current rate of return of very safe investment.

Making Adjustments to the Earnings

There are items that will be used to increase your gross earnings and items that will be used to decrease them. Some of these items that may have been expensed through the business involve a liberal interpretation of the tax laws, but you are not creating an official document here; you are reconstructing events for valuation without comment on how they were or would be treated from a taxable standpoint.

Items that will reduce your earnings might be one or more of the following:

1. Expected increases in rent or other fixed costs such as insurance. A new owner may expect less earnings than you—the benefit of lower rent was yours.
2. The need to replace vehicles or equipment because of their obvious age and condition. Your deferral of these purchases enhanced earnings and now must be discounted.
3. Required new product development and marketing expense to open new markets. Modernizing any company is expensive.

4. The owner's salary is below what a professional manager would be paid for that job. The new CEO expects to be paid at current market.

On the other hand, you will increase the stated earnings based on the following:

> The private use of a car, even if the car is titled to the company, is not expensable, nor is it a tax deduction.

1. Owner's excess draw that is above the going rate for a professional manager. In essence, this has been one way the owner has been getting an additional return on his or her equity.
2. Any excess benefits paid for the owner or members of his or her family, such as life insurance and private club membership dues.
3. Auto expense unless it is limited to the amount needed for business use. The private use of a car, even if the car is titled to the company, is not expensable, nor is it a tax deduction. But it is often paid, including parking fees.
4. Any nonrecurring expense such as a lawsuit or insurance claim (only partially covered) that has not happened before and is unlikely to happen again.
5. Excess travel and entertainment (assume personal use).
6. Salaries for other family members or nonessential employees (wife or children on payroll).
7. Advertising expense that is excess and may not have to be continued.
8. Other expenses associated with current management that will not continue.

Let's take an example of the ABC Distribution Company. The net before tax income that they averaged for the past three years was $80,000. The owner was taking a salary of $104,000 per year. His wife, the corporate secretary, helped out when she was needed, and her salary was $20,000 per year. Their youngest son worked on his college breaks and throughout the summer, and he earned $14,000 last year.

Both family cars were registered to the business although only the owner's car was ever used for business purposes (he had a van that was used during the days to run errands). Total cost of his car expense was

$12,000 with a 50 percent use factor, and the wife's car cost the company $10,000 per year, so the excess expense was $16,000.

Regarding travel and entertainment, over 50 percent of the $38,000 expenditure was for travel for both the owner and his wife to annual conventions and for tickets used primarily by family members. This value has been placed at $21,000. The adjustment for this company would look something like this:

Owner's salary	$114,000	
Equivalent manager	60,000	
Excess	54,000	
Plus wife and son	34,000	
	88,000	
Personal auto expense	16,000	
Excess travel and ent.	21,000	
	$101,000	total to add to earnings

On the other hand, the current owner was also the landlord of the business property that he had been renting for $18,000 per year. That rent will go to $30,000 for the new business owner. The $12,000 difference will be deducted from the earnings. The net addition to reported earnings is $89,000, making the newly restated earnings $169,000 per year.

The next adjustment you will make will be for corporate taxes. For the purpose of this example, we will use .40, or 40 percent. So we have earnings of $169,000 x .40 = $101,400 earnings.

Using the example of various expected returns, this business could be worth from a low of $304,000 to a high of $810,000.

Much of this is very subjective although you must use formulas to establish specific numbers. From the assumptions of how high the risk to the adjustments to earnings, a case can be made at many junctures as to why one number has been set higher or lower. This is what the negotiation will be about, and this is why you must do your homework and be prepared. The sale price of virtually everything is the confluence of what the buyer is willing to pay and the seller is willing to sell for. Your job is to spend time

> The sale price of virtually everything is the confluence of what the buyer is willing to pay and the seller is willing to sell for.

and effort increasing the value and then selling the concept of that value to your prospective buyer.

The Value of Net Assets

Some businesses, particularly mature ones that have acquired tangible assets, including real estate, over the years, may have a far greater value in their assets than they do as a going concern—particularly if the company has not been operated aggressively. There is absolutely no reason to discount these assets due to a poor profit performance.

You begin the sale valuation of this type of company with the current market value of its assets, not the book value. You are using what is called "replacement value," which is what it would cost this day to go out into the marketplace and purchase comparable equipment, inventory, and real estate. Added to that, you must determine the value for the intangible assets you are selling as well, which would include the name, customer base, product identification, and so forth. This value may be expressed as a pro-forma profit and loss statement that would be used to project the result of some other company that would maximize its use of your company assets.

In this pro-forma, you are not just adjusting your profit and loss for your current costs that may be in excess, but you are recasting revenues and projecting an entirely different business scenario. You are projecting the result of a new owner through his or her hard work combined with the opportunity he or she had by buying your business. What if the new owner were able to increase sales 15 percent and maintain a lid on costs? Try that scenario out and see what the new owner's profit would look like. What would it take to show a healthy bottom line? Not as much as you think, and this is often very feasible with new energetic management. However, your selling point is the reality that this would not be possible without the established business that you are selling. Your company is the key ingredient.

For all new startups, there is a painful and expensive stage as they work to enter their new market. Customers need to discover the business and begin using it with regularity. The cost of this comes in

> You are recasting revenues and projecting an entirely different business scenario.

the form of a minimum of a year or two of losses. It happens to virtually all new companies.

Buying an existing business means that a revenue stream (cash flow) is already online and if the business is at or slightly above break-even, profits should follow early on. You deserve to get paid above the net asset value for the going concern value of your company as well. After all, those ongoing sales are the continuum of your business.

There are many ways to calculate this, but at a baseline, determine the average expected profits for the next three years. Then divide that profit by 50 percent—half is allocated for the effort of the new owner. Your half of the profits should then be calculated in a multiple depending on the risk. Perhaps three times the earnings for higher risks, and six to eight times for lower risks.

For example, you have created a plausible case that a new operator could earn $60,000 in year one, $100,000 in year two, and $140,000 in year three, giving the new owner an average $100,000 earnings. Fifty percent of that is $50,000, and if your company is in a fairly stable business environment, you might be able to multiply that by 5 for a value of $250,000 to be *added* to the net current asset value of the company. That would be your asking price.

A Single Asset That Has Strong Value

The most challenging valuation is the one where a unique asset of the company has great value, far in excess of the rest of the assets, and likely, more substantial than the company's total value along the more traditional methods. For example, the airlines hold landing slots at airports that are very valuable but often hard to quantify. For a small business, it may be a patent or a trademark with excellent potential even if not fully realized. What about a lease in a desirable place for a favorable rent? If you are holding something that would be desirable to another, by all means use it as a focal point of your valuation for selling—particularly, if what you have is at all scarce.

Your job will be to determine what this asset would mean in the hands of someone who could put it to its maximum use. What profits

> The buyer of an existing business will have an ongoing revenue stream which has real value.

Determine what this asset would mean in the hands of someone who could put it to its maximum use.

could he or she generate with your patent or your trademark? Or how much money or increased visibility would be generated by having a great location at a below market rent? You can quantify these advantages in dollars, and then the next step is to determine what percentage of that potential is yours for making the opportunity available. Being the pivotal factor for another company to earn an extra $100,000 per year for the next five years is worth a substantial finder's fee to you. The more important the asset is to the company's business strategy, the higher your asking price.

The Value Is in the Eyes of the Beholders

Long and expensive battles have been fought in tax court over the valuation of a business. There are a number of standard ways to assess the value but an even greater number of creative ways. Even within the tax code there are interpretations, so in a selling situation, you can use many variations.

It should not surprise you that you will find a great range in the area of valuing a business for sale. Your challenge will be to keep your price attractive and reasonable. Setting an exorbitant price is not a good idea because you may scare off potential buyers, and then if you must lower the price, it sets a bad tone. But you don't want to leave money on the table either. Cast your company in a number of ways so as to identify your greatest value to a buyer. Then set your price and establish the backup documentation you will need.

It is always a good idea to create a marketing package establishing the value of your company. Focus on its history, list of accomplishments, number of satisfied customers, product information, and position for future growth. If you can illustrate your numbers with a convincing scenario, you may even add to the value.

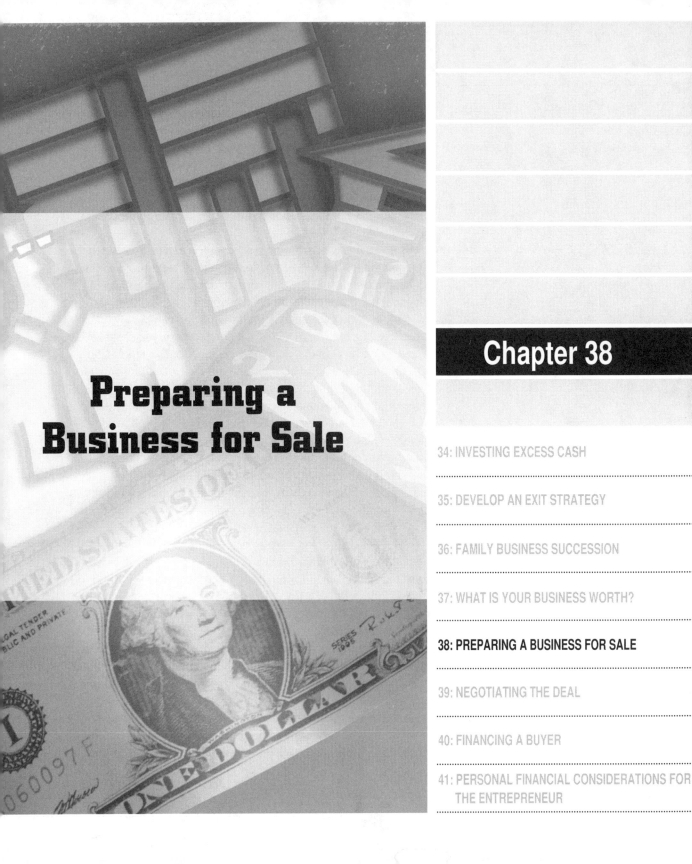

Preparing a Business for Sale

Chapter 38

If you were going to sell a car, you would clean it up before showing it to potential buyers. With an asset of greater value such as a house, you would likely do more than just clean. Painting, landscaping, and mechanical repair would all be considered. After all, when a buyer feels that he or she is purchasing good value, he or she is likely to pay a higher price and make the negotiations and the closing go smoother.

Your company may be your single largest asset, so all the time and effort you spend in maximizing its value by preparing to sell it will be worthwhile by increasing your return. The process may take a few years, but in the end, you will be glad that you did it. On the other hand, if you don't make the effort and you can't easily find a buyer, it will be too late to go back and replay what you could have done the first time. And you are now sailing in unchartered waters.

Once a business has been put into play, meaning that an effort is being made to sell it, subtle changes occur that make the management a bit difficult. You may try to keep the process confidential in the beginning, but you will not be successful forever. The word will eventually filter out by some means—the mention to associates of a casual looker or even the awareness of your employees that people have been looking and asking questions. You must expect others who depend on your company for supplies, for business, and for work to wonder what impact a change will have on them and to take steps to minimize any potential negative effect.

> Many businesses do change a number of policies and perhaps even pricing after ownership changes.

Your customers may begin to make shifts in their purchasing habits. If you have been an exclusive or major supplier, they will be motivated by the need to assure themselves that there will be no interruptions in the delivery of the goods or services that they need should you no longer be there. Many businesses do change a number of policies and perhaps even pricing after ownership changes, and an astute customer would do well to protect himself or herself. The overall effect on you may be only minimal, but if you should happen to have an aggressive competitor out there, you could see a serious erosion in sales with little ability to counter it.

Suppliers may also take a new view with regard to your relationship. Credit may become a bit tighter as they become concerned whether the terms of your business sale will include all debts and whether they will be paid in full. Special deals and advantageous pricing may not be offered as consistently as your potential as a future customer becomes limited. Offers may be saved for others, including your competition.

So, consider what you may be looking at when a business is actively for sale: Sales becoming soft and costs becoming higher are real possibilities. If your company was weak when you began this process, these changes could seriously affect day-to-day operations.

Also a possibility in this mix is the defection of some employees. When that happens, it isn't the borderline performers that leave; they can't do so easily. Your more talented performers have options and may even be recruited by others in the same industry. Until they know for sure who the buyer may be and what the strategic plan is, they may feel that their jobs are in jeopardy one can't blame them for wanting to protect their own interests.

The bottom line is that you will have one chance before you put your company up for sale to take the steps to exhibit the business in its best light. Trying to do so without any planning and preparation is possible but extraordinarily difficult.

> A possibility in this mix is the defection of some employees.

Start with the Cosmetics

Look around your offices, your warehouse, or your factory—whatever constitutes your business home. How would it look to a casual visitor? Clean, modern, and efficient or disorganized, antiquated, and hard to manage? If you have inventory that is unsold and perhaps even written off your books, having it lay around not only looks cluttered, it sends a poor message—that is, your business accumulates hard-to-move goods. Even if the problem is minimal, you may know that what is remaining in your building took five years to get there, but your potential buyer won't know that without a detailed explanation, which may or may not convince him or her.

Look at the equipment: Is it clean and free of rust or other dirt? Can you repaint some of the surfaces to make them look fresher? Are there tools or machines no longer used that are still out on the floor? They may give the entire factory a look of inefficiency and being out of date. Get rid of them; perhaps you would be able to sell them. Walk through your own space as an efficiency expert would and decide for yourself whether it looks productive to the outside observer. Your employees may even become more productive in a clean, clear environment.

Your office must be scrutinized as well. Are your files in order and your papers put away, not strewn all over desktops? After all, most of the documents used to substantiate your selling price and the underlying financials are coming from this office. The perception of their accuracy is important, and it is easier to trust information that originates in an orderly environment.

> Walk through your own space and decide whether it looks productive to the outside observer.

Preadjust Your Earnings Now

Once you have come to the point that you are turning over your financials, you will also be turning over a list of items that should be used as adjustments against those earnings for the purpose of raising the profit to be considered as the basis of the purchase price. The primary items here will be excess money paid to and expenses paid for the owner, as well as the wages of nonessential employees such as family members.

A few years of controlled expenses and maximized profits can do wonders to your bottom line and make a substantial increase on the price you get for the company.

It doesn't make sense to cut your salary and put a strain on your personal finances. But it may be very prudent to remove unnecessary family members from the payroll. The sale will eventually end their extra income within a few years, and if they do not perform any real duties, their salaries may be returned far more in the purchase price.

Cut back travel and entertainment to only the essential level; skip a show or convention one year if it isn't necessary. Auto expense may be expected, but if there is a second family car on the company books, now may be the time to remove it. Insurance is also a reasonable benefit; you may leave it in place but list it as a separate line item.

The toughest item to list and substantiate is that of cash that may flow through to you in various ways. Sometimes, it is for a cash sale kept off the books, and at times, it is an expense that is reimbursed that may not be totally business related. I won't delve further into this issue, but for those who use this side benefit, you understand the concept. If you are looking to sell the business, stop the practice. Ten thousand dollars left in the company may bring $50,000 at closing. Good return for the effort, and it is a necessary effort because you will never be able to completely explain and document this adjustment to a buyer's satisfaction.

Consider the fact that you are no longer in the mode of operating the company on a day-to-day basis for the purpose of earning a living. Now you are making a short-term sacrifice in order to achieve a better return when the company is put for sale.

Lower the Risk: Raise the Return

The other significant issue in the computation of the selling price of your business is the level of return expected by the buyer based on the risk of the investment. An older company with a mature market is a substantially greater risk than a younger, more vibrant one. Recently, you may not have reinvested profits in developing new products or creating and implementing marketing campaigns because you were considering a sale. Now that you have realized how much difference these efforts could make in the price you receive, you may want to reconsider and make the effort. Remember, the multiples based on the risk–return factor are a range of approximately 3.3 times to 8 times earnings, a substantial difference. If you are reporting $100,000 in net profit, the difference could exceed $400,000.

> Now is the time to create and fund a strategic plan for growth.

Take a look at the future potential of your business—have you seen growth in volume and gross profits? Are you still selling the same products or services as you were ten years ago, and have you been seeing competitors erode your market? Are there things you could have been doing to move the company to meet new business challenges that you have neglected to pursue? Now is the time to create and fund a strategic plan for growth so that the company is moving in a direction for the future that shows potential and convinces a buyer that there are real, new profits ahead. You don't have to fund the entire project now either; create a five-year strategic plan and simply begin to implement the first few years. If it shows early success, you will be rewarded for the effort.

> Create a new balance sheet showing the actual tangible net worth of the company.

Prepare to Analyze Your Balance Sheet

If you know that you have assets on your balance sheet that have a depreciated book value below their actual value, you will need to develop the documentation of that fact before you deal with possible buyers. Call in an industrial appraiser and have him or her set a value of your assets at their current market value. Use a sophisticated professional to get the most accurate data. Create a new balance sheet with these values—one that is notated properly as a restated balance sheet, showing the actual tangible net worth of the company as opposed to current book value. It is a good document to have readily available during negotiations.

Finding the Best Possible Buyers

Informing some of the people associated with your business that you will be looking for an interested buyer will allow you to find candidates over a long period, a technique that will enlarge the field. Your attorney and accountant should be part of the process from the beginning because they may have other interested clients, and they regularly work with other professionals who also may have referrals. Buyers looking for businesses often make inquiries in the professional community to find good opportunities. Over a period of a few years, a number of possibilities may surface. A perfect match brings the highest dollar.

Your banker may also be a good source of referrals but this is a judgment call based on the stability of your banking relationship. If your borrowing has been satisfactory and you don't think that you will be sending up red flags, by all means mention your intention to "begin" looking for a buyer. Referrals coming from a banker are normally financially capable candidates who would be able to finance such a purchase.

Within your industry may be another field to sow. Any long-term associates that you know well and trust could be a good resource for candidates. Discuss it casually—don't start a groundswell rumor, but discreet comments may get good results. The right time will be when the right person comes along. The longer the time you have to find him or her, the more likely the best candidate will surface.

Make a Decision About a Business Broker

Give full consideration to whether or not you want to handle the sale on your own or give it to a professional business broker. Finding the right broker may take some time, so you should begin well in advance of the day you expect to put the company up for sale.

> The right time will be when the right person comes along.

There are a number of good reasons to engage a broker such as:

- They help in properly evaluating the business and setting an asking price.
- They can make confidential inquiries of potential buyers without disclosing your identity.
- They prequalify potential buyers.
- They handle all inquiries and all paperwork.

The cost for these services may be substantial, as high as 15 percent of the selling price. But a good broker may be able to recoup that by bringing in a much higher offer than you would see individually. You know if you have potential candidates—if not, a broker may be a necessity.

Selling an asset that you have created over a period of 20 to 30 years or more is an important and complicated project. Take time to plan it out well, and work through that plan from beginning to end.

Negotiating
the Deal

Chapter 39

Once you have prepared for a sale and set your asking price, the next step is working with any prospective buyers and, then, beginning the negotiation process. If you are using a broker, you will most likely not be engaged in the early steps, but you should understand the entire process so that you can monitor the progress. A good broker keeps in touch frequently.

Be Prepared for a Slow Process

From beginning to end—that is, from finding a buyer to making a deal and bringing it to the closing—it would not be unusual to see a time lapse of six months. Most business owners are caught by surprise by this length of time, and the fact that the way the business operates during the interim can be critical to the closing and the final price. Often a business sale is motivated by the desire of current ownership to get out, and once a buyer has been found, lack of commitment of current management increases. This is not only a mistake, it can also be very costly.

Most deals have benchmarks such as levels of receivables and payables and inventory at closing. Any variances will result in adjustments to pricing. If you are not vigorously operating the company while the sale process continues, you may experience losses, and the resulting changes in your balance sheet and profit and loss statement will affect the price you get at that closing. For example, an asset sale will be reduced by the amount that your tangible net worth goes down. And for the ongoing business sale (a stock purchase) based on earnings, losses will reduce that price not only dollar for dollar but perhaps by a multiple of dollars if you are in transition at the end of the accounting period.

As an example, a sale price of five times earnings based on yearend results will be reduced by five times the losses you experience in the transition period. So every $5,000 of loss will cost you $25,000.

This should be sufficient incentive for you to maintain the same level of activity and energy in operating the business during the negotiation and the preclosing work. And if for any reason, the sale does not close, you will have to continue as owner until a new

> From beginning to end it would not be unusual to see a time lapse of six months.

buyer is found. The business may still be yours for longer than you anticipate.

Who Should Handle the Negotiations?

Whether you use a broker or not, the actual negotiation between buyer and seller should not go on between the principals, face to face. If you have found a buyer on your own, try to arrange that he or she designates a representative such as an attorney, accountant, or consultant to represent him or her in all aspects of the negotiation. And then you find a representative as well.

A buyer and seller are natural adversaries once the deal-making time has come. The seller wants as much money as he or she can get, and the buyer wants the best deal he or she can achieve. One wouldn't expect it to be any other way. Deals can be made that will benefit both, but it will take objectivity to achieve this result, and this is more easily accomplished by professionals.

As the seller, you are understandably proud of what you have created and built. The buyer wants to establish the reasons that the price should be lower. Some may be real concerns, others positioning, but no one wants to be in a defensive position about something he or she has put so much time and energy into. In the hands of outsiders, there will be almost no chance for you to become offended and undermine the deal.

> The actual negotiation between buyer and seller should not go on between the principals, face to face.

Qualifying Buyers and Seeking Confidentiality

A number of lookers never do buy a business although they may spend a good deal of time looking for the perfect situation. These individuals don't have the money or the vision to really take on a venture, but it remains a dream. Since potential buyers take a good bit of your time and may even disrupt your ongoing operation, you want to dissuade anyone who doesn't have serious intentions. There are several ways to accomplish this.

One is to require a financial statement as a prequalifier before you begin to disclose any pertinent financial data from the company. If the candidate doesn't have the qualifications to make the purchase, you should not be wasting your time on the discussion. A minimum net worth should be set for any real candidate. Most "lookers" will not provide this personal data.

The next step is to secure a confidentiality agreement. There are very simple one-page statements that bind a potential buyer to hold all information disclosed as a part of the negotiations as confidential information not to be shared with outsiders. This may be a difficult agreement to enforce in the long run but worth the effort to put your buyer on notice that you expect him or her to keep all inside information private. Your attorney can draw up a simple agreement for both buyer and seller to sign. Then, and only then, should you give out financial documents such as profit and loss statement, balance sheet, and tax returns.

First, Sell the Sizzle

If you are working with a broker, chances are the buyer will be given the financials first before looking at the business operation. Any candidates you may find will likely drop by to see your business operation and discuss it with you. Don't greet them empty handed. Your company brochures, catalogs, and any good marketing or public relations material you have should be waiting along with information about the general industry or area you operate in. Also show them any data on changes that are likely to have a positive effect on the future of the industry, geographic area, or the market that you serve. This is your chance to put a spin on the future. Use it.

If you have made your business environment look efficient and appealing, show it off with pride. Prepare yourself to showcase all the special features and capabilities of the business. If there are others you can enlist into this dog-and-pony show, by all means do so. If you need to keep the sale absolutely confidential, let others know that an important potential customer is going to be inhouse—just don't say that it is the business that he or she is interested in buying. For most potential owners, buying a business is a lifelong dream, a

> If the candidate doesn't have the qualifications to make the purchase, you should not be wasting your time on the discussion.

decision made with the heart as well as the head. You must help them see themselves in the role of owner.

Determine What They Want to Purchase

There are basically two ways to buy a business. The first is a corporate stock purchase that includes the entire operation, including all assets and liabilities with the possible exception of some unknown contingent liabilities. The other way is an asset-only purchase where some but not all of the assets are part of the deal and few if any liabilities are assumed. The latter may be beneficial to both buyer and seller because the deal can close fairly quickly and will cost less money in fees to professionals.

A full sale of the business provides the new ownership an immediate and ongoing cash flow from the receivables as they are collected as well as from new sales, but immediate and ongoing obligations from the outstanding payables and loans. The business operations go on as usual with a new owner. Because of this fact, all aspects of the business that are represented by the seller must be verified, including the following:

- The amount and collectibility of the receivables
- The complete outstanding balance of the payables
- All past, current, and future tax obligations
- Any possible future liabilities such as pending lawsuits or claims
- Actual value and useability of any listed inventory
- All contracts, leases, and purchase orders in effect
- Any patents, trademarks, or copyrights listed as assets
- Any employment contracts that will remain in effect
- All supplier contracts or purchase orders
- Current value of all machinery, equipment, furniture, and vehicles listed
- Verification of any other material representation

The process of checking these items is done in a period known as due diligence and requires major audits of all these categories. This will take weeks and sometimes even months and cost a substantial

> For most potential owners, buying a business is a lifelong dream, a decision made with the heart as well as the head.

> Your books and records will be audited completely, and all backup documentation will be verified.

amount of money that will be paid by the buyer. Your books and records will be audited completely, and all backup documentation will be verified. Physical inventory will be taken and checked. A spot check may be made on receivables by sending statements to customers to establish accuracy. Public records will be reviewed to see if any outstanding liens or lawsuits are pending. Tax records will also be checked. This is the business equivalent of kicking the tires and checking under the hood. Once the sale is complete, the new owner will have total responsibility for all aspects of the business, so he or she wants to take as much time as possible to acquire a full awareness of everything outstanding on the company.

The financial arrangement on a stock purchase almost always has contingencies for adjustments up or down based on a due diligence. If the actual inventory is more at closing than was anticipated, the price may go up. Less, and it will go down. If some receivables are deemed uncollectible, there will be a downward adjustment. As to any open but unknown liability such as a pending tax audit or lawsuit, this may be handled in one of two ways. An escrow may be held to cover any ultimate liability and released to the seller if it is not needed. Or the seller may assume the liability and handle it personally once a final determination is made. Providing your potential buyer with accurate, up-to-date information is vital to making sure that the deal will close, and it makes good sense as well. You won't be able to slide anything past an effective due diligence, and if your buyer thinks that you are being less than candid, he or she may pull out of the deal midstream. It's hard to recoup from that, attract a new buyer, and begin a new round of negotiation.

An asset-only sale is quicker because everything is disclosed and no liabilities have to be taken into consideration. The inventory, vehicles, machinery, equipment, and perhaps real estate are purchased. Their value is easy to establish either on the book basis, current market value, or replacement cost, which would likely be the highest. You can also sell the intangible assets such as name and customer data and what is commonly known as good will, the company's reputation and market position. This may be paid for as a premium for the hard assets so that the new owner will be able to depreciate his or her purchase for tax purposes. Or it may come in the form of a consulting contract.

You will retain the responsibilities for most or all of the liabilities, so you must consider that when determining what sort of financial deal this is for you. Once you have made the deal, few changes can be made. Are all assets being purchased, or will there be others to sell separately? Any secured liabilities must be paid by you, but nonsecured liabilities (meaning primarily vendor credit) may be negotiated.

As the seller in an asset-only purchase, the deal should be for all or almost all cash because once the transfer takes place, you will be left with at least some liabilities and no control of any assets. If payments aren't made as agreed to you, it will be almost impossible to regain any value from those assets.

In addition, you must see what outstanding leases and contracts you are still obligated to before making final agreements. The end of the corporate life may end some of these obligations, but not the ones you have personally guaranteed.

Under the "Bulk Transfer" provision of the Uniform Commercial Code, when you sell or transfer a large portion (over 50 percent) of business assets, you must notify creditors in advance. There are also state regulations that govern the sale and transfer of assets. Your attorney will be involved in your sale and can advise you about your own state.

> If you make an asset-only sale, the deal should be for mostly cash to lessen your risk.

Get the Offer in Writing

Any one of a number of steps may happen next as part of the sale process. Different brokers may have differing styles, but at some point fairly early in the serious negotiation phase, you will want to see an offer in writing. This will allow you to determine exactly what is on the table and what still needs to be negotiated. The offer must include:

- What exactly is being purchased and what is not
- What dollars are being offered

- How the deal will be structured (the payout, including any benefits to current ownership)
- What contingencies will change the structure of the deal

An offer is not a binding contract, but you must begin to commit to writing some of the agreements and refine the other areas so that the deal can be finalized. Read any offers carefully because many differences must be considered besides just the price. How quickly will you get paid? What security will you have as guarantee for the payment? Will you have any other benefits from the sale such as employment continuation or a consulting contract? Must you sign a noncompete contract, and will you be compensated for that?

> An offer is not a binding contract. What security will you have as guarantee for the payment?

The Agreement and Earnest Money

Once there has been a meeting of the minds, the offer is converted to a general agreement, which should be accompanied by a deposit that is held in escrow pending a closing of the deal. This agreement may still not be the final one since there will likely be a full-blown contract that will include a number of collateral agreements, such as the following:

- Property lease (if you own the property)
- Employment contract
- Consulting contract
- Noncompete agreement

The lease will likely be very standard—the term and the agreed-to rental charge. The main feature may be a "right of just refusal" clause, which will allow the lessee to meet any offer you may have for the sale of the building. It wouldn't be unusual if the clause prevented you from selling the property for a certain number of years so that the new business owner would not be forced to move soon after purchasing your business.

Employment or Consulting Contract

It is usually a good idea for previous ownership to stay on for a certain time to smooth the transition. That period can run as little as three months and as long as a few years. The compensation for this work will be in the form of actual payroll as an employee or a consultant fee. The payroll wage cost is a bit higher to the buyer because the company will have to pay employment (FICA and unemployment compensation) taxes on the wages. There is also some consideration for the seller when it is in the form of a consulting contract because payments will be reported as self-employment income. The portion of FICA normally paid by the employer is now paid by the employee. Depending on how long this contract is and the total dollars paid, the difference could be several thousand dollars each way.

There is a clear benefit to the buyer to use employment or consulting fees as a way to pay some of the purchase price. These will be totally paid for and deductible to the company, so it is far less out-of-pocket money—the traditional "buying the company with its own money." The risk, as much as there is one, is there for the seller. When there is a longer-term contract, it must be guaranteed in writing for the full term of the agreement in language often referred to as "pay or play." The fees are due even if the work portion gets terminated. In addition, depending on the term, the seller is dependent on the success and perhaps even the survival of the company. Any sort of long-term payout might be interrupted if the business gets into trouble, so remember that this is still money at risk.

> It is usually a good idea for previous ownership to stay on for a certain time to smooth the transition.

Covenant Not to Compete

The last thing any buyer wants to see is the former owner sell his or her company assets or the entire business and then open up down the block or even across town doing the same type of work. The seller, on the other hand, may not want to be permanently prevented from having options down the road to work within an industry or business that he or she has developed experience and expertise in. However, an agreement of this nature may be critical to the deal and should be fair and reasonable to both parties. There should be time limitations established and a self-extinguishing clause so that if any other terms of the sale fail, such as nonpayment, the covenant would no longer be in force.

Removal of Your Guarantees

Make sure, if you sell your business on a corporate stock transfer, that the signature of the new owner replaces yours where you have personally guaranteed any loans, leases, or vendor credit. Either your bank loans will need to be satisfied or they will be secured by the new owner, but car, truck, and equipment loans and leases will not automatically transfer unless you cause them to do so. In addition, over the years, you may have signed credit applications for your vendors that personally obligated you to pay any company debts that go into default. Have your attorney notify these vendors that you are withdrawing that guarantee and get an acknowledgment in writing. Or have the new owner notify these vendors that he or she is assuming these obligations in lieu of you.

> Have your attorney notify these vendors that you are withdrawing that guarantee and get an acknowledgment in writing.

Look Carefully at the Deal

The selling price is only the beginning of your review of any offer to purchase your business. How and when the money is paid is critical to how likely you are to get it all and, in times of inflation, what it will be worth when you do get it.

What adjustments are being required based on any due diligence, and what other subsidiary agreements (for example, employment) are being offered? Read all the subparagraphs and discuss it fully with your professionals. A smooth transition is important to the future success of the company, and you have many reasons to want that success. It is satisfying to see something you have created and nurtured go on. And since you may continue to have a financial stake, the success means full and timely payments to you.

Financing
a Buyer

Chapter 40

> You must realize that anything not collected at closing is a risk.

From the moment you prequalify a potential buyer, you should be giving consideration to how the purchase of your business will be financed. There are only a few alternatives, and some are better than others from the standpoint of the seller. In all cases, you want your money as soon as it is possible as well as prudent from a tax-planning standpoint. A lump sum payment, all in the form of sale price, may represent a tax burden to you depending on the basis from which you will have to pay capital gains tax. Good advice from your accountant is critical.

But you must realize that anything not collected at closing is a risk and tied to the future success of the company. You can set up some protections for yourself, which will be discussed later in this chapter but the business is likely to be leveraged enough that you are not completely secured, if at all.

Financing a New Business Purchase

There are several ways that a new business acquisition is financed. Primarily they are as follows:

- Stock in the acquiring company, usually only if it is publicly traded
- Buyer's personal capital
- Bank financing
- Venture capital
- Seller financing

Let's look at all these options.

Stock in Acquiring Company

If you sell to a publicly traded company, you will likely be paid in part or in whole on the equivalent shares of stock in the buyer's company. Since their value can be easily assessed by looking up the stock price, this may seem like a straightforward deal without any downside. But that isn't always true. Most times, the stock must be held for a certain period before it can be liquidated, and the *real* price of the transaction turns out to be the value of your stock on the day you turn it into cash.

For this reason, you must do your homework about the company–its history over the past few years and its strategy for the future. If they are on an acquisition binge with companies that may be too much for them to absorb and manage well, this may negatively affect their entire operation and drive the stock price down. You may be getting far less than you originally thought. It may be flattering to be courted by a publicly traded entity, but don't get your head turned past the realities you must consider.

Buyer's Personal Capital

Your buyer should be required to put some of his or her own money into the deal. It shows commitment to the business and means the buyer will work harder because his or her own capital is at risk. If all the buyer has on the table is bank financing and seller financing, he or she may be more inclined to walk away if the going gets tough, assuming that the debts will never be fully collected. And the bank has first lien, so your former business assets may be used to pay off the new bank loans.

On the other hand, you don't want your buyer to use his or her last dollar either. Over the next months and years (while you may still be getting paid), there may be the need for a capital infusion. If the buyer is totally out of resources, that may be impossible and put everything at risk.

> Your buyer should be required to put some of his or her own money into the deal.

Bank Financing

Few banks, even with an SBA guarantee, would be willing to loan 100 percent of the purchase price of any business. At least some owner equity must be involved. They may accept some cash from the buyer and some seller financing as equity also. This makes them more fully secured on the assets of the company. They will be in the first lien position on all business assets.

Your consideration here is to determine what this company's pro-forma cash flow looks like with this new bank loan to pay. If the new debt service has strained their ability to pay you, the financing you are holding is at risk, and the bank will be the only one to get paid.

Venture Capital

Few business purchases present the opportunity for the high level of return that is required by venture capitalists. They do not loan money to a business buyer; instead, they would put up money to take an equity position themselves. If your company is in a position to earn those kinds of profits, you should be in a position to hire experienced help with these types of negotiations. Venture investors are very sophisticated and deal directly with the seller even if there is a specific buyer dealing as well. They strike creative deals, and only a knowledgeable lawyer or business consultant would be up to representing your interests.

Seller Financing

The likely scenario in most business sales is that a portion of the purchase price is paid as a down payment and the balance is held by the seller as a promissory note. The buyer hopes to pay off this note out of the proceeds of the business. This can be beneficial to the seller for tax-planning purposes but clearly represents a risk as well. If the business is successful, the note gets paid; if the business falters, payments may slow down or cease. Caution is a key word in seller financing.

You know better than anyone else about the reality of operating your company. Are you selling it on the basis of current operating results or on future prospects? If the company has consistently been profitable, there is no reason to expect that to change. If you have been struggling yourself for years, that won't likely be changed easily either. You should accept a note that seems reasonable from your own knowledge base and not expect a new owner to accomplish miracles.

If you need to receive a fixed amount of money, it is safer to get that as the first lump sum payment. And remember that you will have a tax share to pay and perhaps a broker and some professional fees. Your net may be far less than you anticipated.

Venture investors are very sophisticated and deal directly with the seller.

Structuring the Promissory Note

There are three things to consider when drawing up a note between seller and buyer: the amount of the note, the time and interest rate, and how it will be secured. The amount will be the difference in the purchase price and the amount paid as a down payment, and may also be reduced by any amounts scheduled to be paid as compensation such as consulting fees. The time and the interest is a negotiation based on the needs of the seller and the cash flow realities facing the buyer. If you are retiring and selling a fairly stable business, a very long-term payout may be what you need. But you may be wanting to cash out soon so that you can begin a new venture. The decisions here are very subjective and highly negotiable.

The most difficult issue is how this note will be secured. Buyers often want the business assets alone to act as security, and sellers want more. A personal guarantee is not out of line, and you should ask for the signature of the spouse as well. A signature not backed by any personally held assets is worthless, and most couples hold their property jointly.

You will be holding a note signed and secured by an individual, so assessing his or her personal credit is a very prudent step to take. Along with a personal financial statement, which you should have received early on, you should have gotten or should now ask for tax returns for at least the past two years. Asking for a personal credit report would not be out of line. You are becoming perhaps the major personal creditor, and you have the right to determine the financial condition of your buyer. In many cases, the critical issue for a new business owner is how well he or she can monitor and control his or her own financial needs until the business has paid off the debt owed to the seller and grown both in revenue and profits. If your buyer has an expensive lifestyle and high personal debts, this will prove far more difficult.

A personal guarantee is not out of line.

Getting the Best Price and Getting Paid

You will receive a higher price with easier terms, and a more modest price for a quicker cashout. Be reasonable about what you expect and what you accept. A buyer offering far more than you know the business is worth but asking for generous owner financing may be too great a risk. Be cautious and be fair. In the end, you will benefit.

> The terms of the sale may be as important as the price.

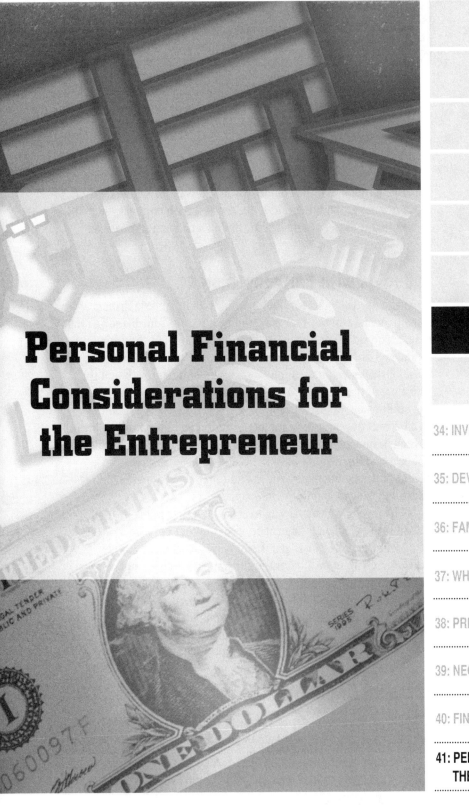

Personal Financial Considerations for the Entrepreneur

Chapter 41

No other career choice you can make will have a more complete or more profound affect on your personal financial well-being than going into business for yourself. The company will be the source of your income, your major investment, and likely a focal point of your life, as well as those of your family members. From the beginning and during the life of the company, you will want to understand the affect of one on the other and strive to keep both entities, you and the company, as financially healthy and independent as possible.

> The company will be the source of your income, your major investment, and likely a focal point of your life.

It Begins with Early Investments

From the day you start (or buy) a business, you are establishing some financial realities that may well be a part of your life for a long time. If you set off on the wrong foot by either being seriously under-capitalized or highly personally leveraged, the problems created by those obstacles will have a long-term affect on the growth and the cash flow of the business. Your available capital to fund early losses and still be able to take advantage of opportunities is critical to getting beyond the early-stage fragile condition and into a robust business environment. The longer it takes, the less robust the business will become. If you don't have the cash you need, perhaps you should postpone your start and spend time saving more or finding investors who will join in the new venture.

The most problematic way to acquire this capital is by leveraging yourself personally. All debt service, whether corporate or personal, will have to be met, and the principal repayments will be available only from profits. In the startup days before you cross your break-even point, there will be no profits to use for this purpose. Any excess money that you must take either in personal income to meet debts personally or with company payments directly will drain off liquidity and make ongoing operations more difficult.

Personal Credit Matters

If the loans are personal and you can't find the cash from the business, they will become delinquent and affect your personal credit rating. That will ultimately influence the company's ability to borrow down the line. Most small business loans below $250,000 are determined on the basis of credit scoring, and a large influence on that rating is your personal credit history. Indiscriminate borrowing with only the hope that the company will catch on and be able to pay back the loans may result in your finding yourself in a double bind: Neither you nor the company will have a good enough credit rating to borrow again.

Setting a Fair Compensation

You are the one in charge, and you can set your salary level anywhere you want. You can establish any benefits you want or require and include club memberships and sports tickets if you wish. The issue of what is deductible is up to your accountant, but the issue of what is paid from company funds is your decision. So, what is reasonable?

You should be receiving in salary and benefits (although you do *not* have to take it all), the equivalent of the fair market value of the work you perform and a return on your investment. The former is quantified by determining what a general manager or CEO (in a small business the CEO is the general manager) of businesses of your size and from your industry sector would be paid. Sometimes this is available through industry groups, or you may need to conduct some informal research. But you probably know what the job is worth, and your salary can be adjusted up or down based on the profitability of the company.

Next you determine the net equity value and decide what would be a current fair rate of return given the risk factor. If you have a business net worth of $300,000 and your risk is in the fair range, a return of 7 to 8 percent might be reasonable, so you would add an additional $20,000 to $25,000 to your salary to come up with your total package.

No one will stop you from taking an exorbitant amount in compensation. But this money isn't self-renewing, and eventually the company will face a liquidity problem. Short-term satisfaction may beget long-term discomfort.

> Most small business loans below $250,000 are determined on the basis of credit scoring.

Understand Fully Your Liabilities

You will be asked to personally sign for all loans, and though you can refuse, you will likely have to in the end. Most leases, including car and property, will require personal signatures, and some vendors will have credit applications that have you signing personally as well as corporately. Try not to sign these if you can avoid it, but most new business owners will be required to do so. You will realize that you have a great deal of financial exposure as a business owner.

Don't increase this risk by adding any unpaid taxes to your personal liabilities, and make no mistake, unpaid taxes *will* be assessed to the company owner individually. Even if you are not the one who prepared and sent the tax reports and payments to the various government entities (or failed to do so), you will be held as a responsible party. So make sure the right thing is being done. Check on this administrative task on a regular basis.

> You will be asked to personally sign for all loans.

Protect Your Personal Assets

All of your guarantees with the exception of the bank will be in your name alone. The bank may request that of your spouse as well. With two-earner families and more independent finances between couples, fewer spouses these days are willing to go along, and that requirement is sometimes being waived. Therefore, all the liability that you acquire will attach only to property you own alone. All jointly held assets may be kept safe from any business claims. Check this out with your attorney and plan your personal finances to give you the greatest amount of protection.

Don't Put Your Eggs in One Basket

When you plan for your financial future, which includes your retirement, don't just assume that someday you will be able to sell the business and cash in big for your life's work. You must make other provisions as well.

One provision to look at is a 401k established by the company. This will allow you to contribute part of your earnings to a retirement plan and have the company add to the fund as well. These funds will be kept separate and safe from the company money, and no claim can be made on them by any creditor.

Outside your business, you should be a saver and an investor to the degree it is possible. Establish an IRA if you can, and certainly set money aside as investment and protection.

If you have the opportunity to buy property with the idea of renting it to the business, this may be something to consider. The company will have to pay rent to someone, so why shouldn't it go to building equity for you instead of another landlord? Make sure that you write a formal lease between yourself as the owner and the company, and stick to the terms.

Do Not Comingle Funds

Most business owners put money in and take it out on a fairly regular basis, particularly when it comes to making a payroll. But it isn't necessarily a great idea to do this casually.

If you have bank borrowings, the bank will request that you subordinate any money due to yourself to their secured position. This means that you can't get paid back unless they are either paid or give you special permission. This can create a technical problem for you if you need to put in short-term capital.

And finally, if things begin to get very tough and cash dries up, many owners will follow their instincts to shore up the operation with personal funds. This clearly may not be a good idea, particularly if the future looks to be tough over the long term. You could find yourself still in business trouble with a personal financial crisis staring you in the face. Be a smart investor, particularly when it comes to your own (or, worse yet, personally borrowed) funds. Don't put up money you may never be able to recover. And don't ask others close to you if you are not confident about being able to pay it back.

> The bank will request that you subordinate any money due to yourself to their secured position.

Your Business Is a Valuable Asset: Treat It Well

Treat your company with financial respect and the payoff will follow.

The company you build will become your source of pride, your source of income, and your source of future assets as well. Treat it with financial respect as you build it, and the payoff will be there. You will go through easy times when cash flow is positive, but no business avoids the tough times when business gets soft or receivables don't turn a profit. Learn to temper your spending during the good times and limit your panic during the down times, and you will build and operate a solid company that will provide for your needs and create economic activity that will benefit others as well. Being in business is not a "get rich quick" scheme, but it is a creative and satisfying way to work and build your own financial stability.

Epilogue

What motivates most entrepreneurs into business is a spirit of adventure, a desire for freedom, and a healthy dose of creativity. Your belief in yourself and the product or service that you provide gave you the confidence to develop your business venture.

For many of us, it is the sales and marketing side of business that we feel most comfortable about, and we learn the operation angle because it provides the goods and services to sell. Some, with a more technical background, come in through the operations door driven by a product of their own creation. Few, however, come from the world of accounting and finance.

Instead of tackling the challenge to learn what we need to know in that area, the tendency is to hire outsiders and treat the numbers as if they were a foreign language. It is a serious mistake.

You're in this game to win, and you cannot do so unless you know how the points are scored. You must track the performance of your company through your profit and loss statement, and measure your stability by reviewing your balance. These numbers indicate what has happened in the recent past and what is likely to happen in the near term.

You don't have to have math aptitude to understand accounting, and you don't have to do all the transactions yourself. But you should want to be familiar enough with how they are done to understand the meaning of the reports that are generated by whoever does the record keeping for your company.

There are financial pressures and financial decisions to be made from the first day you begin in business. The profit that you need and deserve may become elusive if you can't make your choices based on the knowledge you require. You will make purchases, pay employees, and quote prices—all these numbers will have an implication on your bottom line. And all the people you deal with have needs of their own to meet.

Your employees want to earn as much as they can and feel they've earned it. Your customers want as good a value as they can find and believe that their business warrants that. And your suppliers want fair and full prices for their products and think they deserve this as well. It is virtually impossible to meet all these requests and still have a healthy bottom line for your own business.

Part of your contribution to the ultimate success of your business is to translate these various needs and requests into numbers to determine what impact a change in costs or prices will have on your business operation. If your employees want a 10 percent raise, what will that do to your prices? If a customer asks for a 5 percent discount, how much will that hurt your bottom line? What if the offer accompanies a big order? Will the volume make up for the price cut?

Ask yourself how well you really understand how to reach the answers to these questions. Ask further if it isn't worth the effort to learn more and make better decisions.

Do you begin to worry as soon as this week's payroll is met whether the next one will be covered? Are you unsure when a vendor calls about payment information what to tell him? Do you know how long it normally takes you to pay your bills? Once you master more of the financial management of your company, you will understand how to find the payable turnaround ratio, and you will know that it tells you in days how long the average vendor waits to get paid.

Do you have the sense that the business is improving but you can't explain why it's happened much less make an effort to continue the trend? Do you feel as if situations are deteriorating but you don't know how to stop them?

All this information is found in the books, records, and reports generated by your company or your accountant. This is powerful knowledge if you learn it and use it.

This book was written to give you that information in language most business owners can understand. If something has you confused, go back and reread the section or sit down with your financial professionals. Work with them until you are comfortable with the concepts.

Your banker will be impressed perhaps enough to give you the loan you need when cash flow is tight. And you will know exactly how much you need and for how long. Take some of the risk out of the experience.

All businesses go through cycles. You will begin with the startup and early-stage struggles to get a sufficient revenue stream and reach your break-even point. You must know where that level is and how to lower it by cutting costs or raising prices.

Next is a period of more rapid growth when sufficient capital becomes the major focus. Understanding how much capital and how long you will need it is the critical financial skill required to triumph over this challenge.

You will likely reach a plateau when growth slows and profits and cash flow stabilize. How to monitor progress and spot areas of difficulties are now your focus as well as creating and implementing the strategic plan for future development.

Your business will never remain static—it will be on the rise or on the decline. The first steps in either direction are not giant ones, just small trends and nuances that must be caught early and corrected. The period-to-period comparisons of ratios will provide great insights into the financial direction the company is taking. Learn them and watch them.

I was the CEO of a small manufacturing company for 21 years, and I know how easy it is to get caught up in the day-to-day demands of your own company. The "big picture" items like financial management do not seem urgent unless there is a cash flow problem. But I also have seen firsthand how much easier it is to operate a company smoothly and effectively if you become more financially sophisticated and use your knowledge. And believe it or not, it can be fun as well.

I dedicate this book to your learning. You may not understand it all at the first reading, but I urge you to use it as a reference guide. It was written to make your entrepreneurial experience much more fun and far more profitable.

SUZANNE CAPLAN

A Winning Loan Proposal

Appendix I

There are a number of reasons that the books and records of a company must be kept timely and accurately. The main one is to provide management information on how the company is performing and indicate the most effective way to improve that performance. There are external needs for accurate financial records as well, to submit to the taxing bodies for instance. And when bank financing is required, a loan request accompanied by complete financial documents that show the use of the loan and the ability to meet debt services is more likely to be successful. The following is a good example.

The Company

Ajax Printers is a small offset printing company with sales of just under two million dollars. Competing primarily with the franchise print shops, Ajax had staked out a successful niche for their high quality work and fast turnarounds. Complicated and interesting catalogs and mail order pieces were their main type of work that required a high level of pre-press equipment as well as complete bindery facilities. Keeping up with technology as well as demand was a challenge and required new bank financing somewhat regularly. Using the 4 P's of a good loan proposal as a basis (purpose, payment, protection, and people) the following is how their document might be constructed.

Purpose

Ajax Printers is requesting a loan in the amount of $150,000 in order to purchase additional equipment for both their pre-press department as well as the bindery. The pre-press equipment will allow for more rapid preparation of in-house work for print as well as offer state of the art facilities that will help in attracting new business. A volume increase of 5 percent is expected as new graphic designers will want access to this type of service.

The bindery equipment is a fully automated folder that not only will increase speed but will also allow for reduction of one full-time employee in that department. This will result in a savings of $17,000 annually. The specific quotes for the new equipment are attached to this proposal. They have been provided by our likely suppliers and cover the following equipment:

Pre-press scanner and digital
equipment including two new
computers with customized software: $52,000

Automated folder with collater
and stapler, includes shipping
and set-up: $149,000

Payment

We proposed to pay this loan on a five-year term based on a 10 percent interst rate. The source of increased cash flow will be from additional sales volume and the savings from increased productivity. Our current profit and loss statement (attached) shows a nominal bottom line, but our projected three-year profit and loss and cash flow statements (attached) will demonstrate how the use of these loan proceeds will improve the business and provide cash flow for debt service.

Apex Printing - 1998 Profit and Loss

Sales	$1,900,000	
Less returns	175,000	
Net sales	$1,725,000	

Direct costs

Material	$430,000	
Labor pre-press	138,000	
Labor printing	345,000	
Labor bindery	120,000	
Total costs of goods sold	$1,033,000	
Gross profits	$692,000	40%

General and administrative expenses

Rent	$36,000
Telephone	15,000
Utilities	30,000
Office wages	75,000
Office expense	15,000
Sales salaries	120,000
Officers wages	104,000
Marketing expense	24,000
Depreciation	102,000
Interest	48,000
Payroll taxes	39,000
Miscellaneous	15,000
Total expense	$623,000
Net (before taxes)	$69,000

Apex Printing - Projected Cash Flow

	2000	2001	2002
Projected net sales	$2,100,000	2,200,000	300,000
less direct	1,218,000	1,276,000	1,334,000
gross profits	882,000	924,000	966,000
less G&A	706,000	706,000	706,000
Net (before tax)	176,000	218,000	260,000
Beginning cash	100,000	61,000	164,000
+ collections	1,900,000	2,000,000	2,100,000
less direct	1,218,000	1,276,000	1,334,000
less G&A (w/o depreciation)	589,000	589,000	589,000
Available cash	93,000	196,000	341,000
Available for debt serivce	32,000	32,000	32,000
Ending cash	$61,000	164,000	309,000

Protection

We have attached the following documents to detail business assets available as collateral for this loan:

- 1998 Balance Sheet
- 2000 Projected Balance Sheet
- A list of current machinery and equipment with values based on current resale
- Accounts receivable aging

In addition, the personal financial statement of the principal is attached. Principal expects to serve as co-guarantor.

Apex Printing - Balance Sheet
December 1998

Cash in bank	$21,000
Accounts receivable	435,000
Inventory	210,000
Prepaid insurance	15,000
Total current assets	681,000
Machinery and equipment	2,024,000
Less depreciation	1,500,000
Net value	524,000
Total assets	$1,205,000

Liabilities

Accounts payable	$485,000
Accrued wages & vacation pay	28,000
Accrued taxes	14,000
Note payable - current	165,000
Total current liabilities	692,000
Long-term debt	330,000
Total liabilities	1,022,000
Net worth	$183,000

Apex Printing Projected Balance Sheet
December 2000

Cash in banks	$65,000
Accounts receivable	505,000
Inventory	275,000
Prepaid insurance	15,000
Total current assets	860,000
Machinery & equipment	2,174,000
Less depreciation	1,585,000
Net value	1,449,000
Total assets	

Liabilities

Accounts payable		$525,000
Accrued wages & vacation pay	25,000	
Accrued taxes		16,000
Note payable - current		175,000
Total current liabilities		741,000
Long term debt		395,000
Total liabilities		1,136,000
Net worth		$ 313,000

List of Machinery & Equipment
(Does not represent book value)

Type	At Cost	Current Value (resale)
Pre-press	$75,000	$20,000
Printing presses (5)	1,100,000	435,000
Bindery	72,000	24,000
Misc. Factory eq.	50,000	5,000
Computer system	25,000	2,500
Total	$2,024,000	$486,000

This is a projected 2002 statement to reflect changes:

Apex Printing Projected Profit and Loss Statement 2002

Sales	$2,300,000	
Less returns	190,000	
Net sales	2,110,000	

Direct costs

Material	$522,000	
Labor–pre-press	130,000	
Labor–printing	400,000	
Labor–bindery	112,000	
Total costs of goods sold	1,164,000	
Gross profits	$946,000	40.5%

General and administrative expense

Rent	$40,000
Telephone	16,000
Utilities	30,000
Office wages	88,000
Office expense	15,000
Sales salaries	140,000
Officers wages	114,000
Marketing expense	24,000
Depreciation	117,000
Interest	62,000
Payroll tax	42,000
Miscellaneous	20,000
Total expense	706,000
Net (before tax) profit	$240,000

These attached documents will show that with the loan requested, Ajax can substantially improve its profits, will have sufficient cash flow to manage debt service, and can increase its net worth as well. The greater efficiency will cut costs and increase marketing possibilities.

Personal Balance Sheet - John Smith

Assets

Cash in bank	$35,000
Certificates of deposit	20,000
401(k)	66,000
Stock portfolio	90,000
House (owned jointly)	195,000
Ajax ownership	200,000
Automobile	15,000
Personal possessions	25,000
	$646,000

Liabilities

Personal loans	$26,000
Mortgage	87,000
Auto loan	9,500
Credit cards	7,500
	130,000
Net worth	$516,000

Management Background

John Smith, owner & CEO of Apex has spent 26 years in this industry, the past 12 as owner of this company. He has an engineering degree and an MBA in marketing. His primary role is in administration and sales. He has a strong customer base and excellent operational knowledge.

The company employs an experienced accountant as CFO and a strong sales and support team.

A Loan Proposal should be very direct in its approach and be well documented by a variety of financial instruments. Balance sheet, profit and loss, and cash flow statements are required.

Trouble Shooting by the Numbers

There are a number of key ratios that will tell you how the business is doing and where the trouble spots are. You can begin to see your business in comparison with others in the field by using RMA (Robert Morris Associates) Ratios. You can find these ratios in the library or on the internet, or you can purchase a book. Your accountant can give you more information. You may also be able to ask your banker what ratios they require and then you will know in advance how you measure up.

Some of the computations are found only on your balance sheet and some only on the profit and loss statement. Others require the use of both financial reports. I have shown both where to find and how to compute these numbers in the following examples, as well as given brief explanations. Try them with your own numbers.

Profitability Analysis—Gross Margin
Profit and Loss Statement—ABC Manufacturing

Sales Income	**$1,500,000**	(1)
Direct costs		
Labor	595,000	
Material	300,000	
Cost of goods sold	895,000	
Gross operating profit	**605,000**	(2)
General and administrative expense		
Rent	25,000	
Office salaries	60,000	
Office expense	25,000	
Sales expense	50,000	
Advertising	35,000	
Travel and entertainment	40,000	
Utilities	20,000	
Depreciation	80,000	
Telephone	15,000	
Officers salaries	104,000	
Interest expense	78,000	
Miscellaneous	15,000	
Total costs	547,000	
Net before taxes	58,000	
	605,000	(2)
Sales divided by the gross profit	1,500,000	(1)

$$\frac{605,000}{\$\ 1,500,000} = .40 \text{ or } 40\%$$

What is normal is dependent on your type of business and can range from just a few percentages (high volume grocery store) to high percentages. Compare from year to year as well as with industry norms.

Profitability Analysis—Net Profit Margin
Profit and Loss Statement—ABC Manufacturing

Sales Income	**$1,500,000**	(1)
Direct costs		
Labor	595,000	
Material	300,000	
Cost of goods sold	895,000	
Gross operating profit	605,000	

General and administrative expense

Rent	25,000	
Office salaries	60,000	
Office expense	25,000	
Sales expense	50,000	
Advertising	35,000	
Travel and entertainment	40,000	
Utilities	20,000	
Depreciation	80,000	
Telephone	15,000	
Officers salaries	104,000	
Interest expense	78,000	
Miscellaneous	15,000	
Total costs	547,000	
Net before taxes	**58,000**	(2)
Sales divided by the	58,000	(2)
Net profit	1,500,000	(1)

$$\frac{58,000}{\$1,500,000} = .37 \text{ or } 3.7\%$$

The important concerns here are the trends from year to year, and for any individual company, is this sufficient to meet debt service. It is also useful to compare with industry norms.

LIQUIDITY ANALYSIS—CURRENT RATIOS
Balance Sheet—ABC Manufacturing

Cash in bank		$12,000	
Accounts receivable		400,000	
Inventory		500,000	
Prepaid expense		38,000	
Total current assets		**940,000**	(1)

Fixed assets

Building		750,000	
Less Dep.	525,000	125,000	
Machinery & equipment	800,000		
Less Dep.	200,000	600,000	
		725,000	
Total fixed assets		1,665,000	

Liabilities

Accounts payable		450,000	
Current portion–note payable		250,000	
Total current liabilities		**700,000**	(2)
Long-term balance on note		500,000	
Total liabilities		1,200,000	
Net worth		465,000	
Current assets		940,000	(1)
Current liabilities		700,000	(2)

$$\frac{940,000}{\$700,000} = 1.34$$

This is an indication of how a company can retire current debts from current operating cash flow. A ratio of 2.0 is desirable because it allows for substantial asset loss while still being solvent. The most likely way to improve this is to lower inventory.

Debt Ratio
Balance Sheet—ABC Manufacturing

Cash in bank		$12,000
Accounts receivable		400,000
Inventory		500,000
Prepaid expense		38,000
Total current assets		940,000

Fixed assets

Building	750,000		
less dep.	525,000	125,000	
Machinery & equip	800,000		
less dep.	200,000	600,000	
		725,000	
Total fixed assets		**1,665,000**	(1)

Liabilities

Accounts payable	450,000	
Current portion–note payable	250,000	
Total current liabilities	700,000	
Long-term balance on note	500,000	
Total liabilities	**1,200,000**	(2)
Net worth	465,000	
Total liabilities	1,200,000	(2)
Total assets	1,665,000	(1)

$$\frac{1,200,000}{\$1,665,000} = 70\%$$

This means that 70 percent of the company is financed by debt. A number this high makes it very difficult to acquire any new assets for growth or improvement. Focus should be on cutting costs and paying off existing debt.

Return on Investment
Requires Profit & Loss and Balance Sheet
Profit & Loss Statement—ABC Manufacturing

Sales income	$1,500,000
Direct costs	
Labor	595,000
Material	300,000
Cost of goods sold	895,000
Gross operating profit	605,000

General and administrative expense

Rent	25,000	
Office salaries	60,000	
Office expense	25,000	
Sales expense	50,000	
Advertising	35,000	
Travel and entertainment	40,000	
Utilities	20,000	
Depreciation	80,000	
Telephone	15,000	
Officers salaries	104,000	
Interest expense	78,000	
Miscellaneous	15,000	
Total costs	547,000	
Net before taxes	**$58,000**	(1)

Balance Sheet—ABC Manufacturing

Cash in bank		$12,000
Accounts receivable		400,000
Inventory		500,000
Prepaid expense		38,000
Total current assets		940,000
Fixed assets		
Building	750,000	
Less Dep.	525,000	125,000
Machinery & equipment	800,000	
Less Dep.	200,000	600,000
		725,000
Total fixed assets		**1,665,000** (2)

Liabilities

Accounts payable		450,000
Current portion–note payable		250,000
Total current liabilities		700,000
Long-term balance on note		500,000
Total liabilities		1,200,000
Net worth		465,000
Net profits		58,000 (1)
Total assets		1,665,000 (2)

$$\frac{58,000}{\$1,665,000} = .035 \text{ or } .5\%$$

This means that the money invested in these business assets are returning 3.5 percent, which is very low for the risk. The rate of return is higher on government guaranteed bank instruments. Is this a good use of the owner's capital?

Inventory Turnover Ratio—Balance Sheet & Profit & Loss
Balance Sheet—ABC Manufacturing

Cash in bank		$12,000	
Accounts receivable		400,000	
Inventory		**500,000**	(1)
Prepaid expense		38,000	
Total current assets		940,000	
Fixed assets			
Building	750,000		
Less Dep..	525,000	125,000	
Machinery & equipment	800,000		
Less Dep.	200,000	600,000	
		725,000	
Total fixed assets		1,665,000	

Liabilities

Accounts payable	450,000
Current portion–note payable	250,000
Total current liabilities	700,000
Long-term balance on note	500,000
Total liabilities	1,200,000
Net worth	$465,000

Profit & Loss Statement—ABC Manufacturing

Sales Income	1,500,000	
Direct costs		
Labor	595,000	
Material	**300,000**	(2)
Cost of goods sold	895,000	
Gross operating profit	605,000	

General and administrative expense

Rent	25,000	
Office salaries	60,000	
Office expense	25,000	
Sales expense	50,000	
Advertising	35,000	
Travel and entertainment	40,000	
Utilities	20,000	
Depreciation	80,000	
Telephone	15,000	
Officers salaries	104,000	
Interest expense	78,000	
Miscellaneous	15,000	
Total costs	547,000	
Net before taxes	58,000	
Annual inventory cost	300,000	(2)
Current level of inventory	500,000	(1)

$$\frac{300,000}{500,000} = .60$$

This means the inventory has sold less than once in the entire year. This happens when old and obsolete inventory remains on the books year after year and it is never turned over. This could represent a warehouse full of unusable goods that may be liquidated to raise capital and lower debt.

Accounts Receivable Turnover Ratio
Balance Sheet and Profit and Loss
Balance Sheet—ABC Manufacturing

Cash in bank		$12,000
Accounts receivable		**400,000** (1)
Inventory		500,000
Prepaid expense		38,000
Total current assets		940,000
Fixed assets		
Building		750,000
Less Dep.	525,000	125,000
Machinery & equipment	800,000	
Less Dep.	200,000	600,000
		725,000
total fixed assets		1,665,000

Liabilities

Accounts payable	450,000
Current portion–note payable	250,000
Total current liabilities	700,000
Long-term balance on note	500,000
Total liabilities	1,200,000
Net worth	$465,000

Profit and Loss Statement—ABC Manufacturing

Sales income	1,500,000	(2)
Direct costs		
Labor	595,000	
Material	300,000	
Cost of goods sold	895,000	
Gross operating profit	605,000	

General and administrative expense

Rent	25,000
Office salaries	60,000
Office expense	25,000
Sales expense	50,000
Advertising	35,000
Travel and entertainment	40,000
Utilities	20,000
Depreciation	80,000
Telephone	15,000
Officers salaries	104,000
Interest expense	78,000
Miscellaneous	15,000
Total costs	547,000
Net before taxes	58,000

Total Sales	1,500,000	(2)
Accounts receivable	400,000	(1)

1,500,000
$400,000 3.7 (or almost four times
per year)

This means that your receivables are turning every 90 or so days, so that an invoice sent on January 5th is not likely to be paid until April 5th. This can create cash flow problems and should be improved by aggressive collection policies. Monitor this number to see positive progress.

Accounts Payable Turnover Ratio
Balance Sheet & Profit and Loss
Balance Sheet—ABC Manufacturing

Cash in bank		$12,000
Accounts receivable		400,000
Inventory		500,000
Prepaid expense		38,000
Total current assets		940,000
Fixed assets		
Building		750,000
Less Dep.	525,000	125,000
Machinery & equipment	800,000	
Less Dep.	200,000	600,000
		725,000
Total fixed assets		1,665,000

Liabilities

Accounts payable	**450,000**	(1)
Current portion–note payable	250,000	
Total current liabilities	700,000	
Long-term balance on note	500,000	
Total liabilities	1,200,000	
Net worth	$465,000	

Profit & Loss Statement—ABC Manufacturing

Sales income	1,500,000	
Direct costs		
Labor	595,000	
Material	300,000	(2)
Cost of goods sold	895,000	
Gross operating profit	605,000	

General and administrative expense

Rent	25,000	
Office salaries	60,000	
Office expense	25,000	(2)
Sales expense	50,000	
Advertising	35,000	(2)
Travel and entertainment	40,000	
Utilities	20,000	
Depreciation	80,000	
Telephone	**15,000**	(2)
Officers salaries	104,000	
Interest expense	78,000	
Miscellaneous	15,000	(2)
Total costs	547,000	
Net before taxes	58,000	
Total purchase	390,000	(2)
Accounts payable	450,000	(1)
	390,000	
	$450,000 = .86	

This means that there are outstanding debts on this company's that are over a year old payable, and are turning less than one time a year. The possibility of legal action against a company in this circumstance is great and the future is very insecure.

There is no doubt that the company described in this appendix is in a dire circumstance. However, all of the tools for correcting the problems can be found in the ratios.

The ongoing operation is solid as seen by a profitability ratio. Debt is serious but not critical, and return on equity is low but could improve.

The problem is centered in the inventory that must be liquidated quickly and not allowed to grow to this proportion. Losses will be taken as it is written off.

Receivables must be collected more quickly, cash flow is inadequate, and payables are dangerously high. With the money received from sale of old inventory and quicker payments for current work, deals could be struck with vendors to prevent any legal action and repair business relationships. This company is also under collection pressure, which takes time and effort away from building a successful future.

Analyze your company this way and see what you find.

Glossary

Accounts Payable

This listing of outstanding debts to vendors is kept as a subledger of the general ledger and appears on the balance sheet as a liability. Normally listed alphabetically as well as by date of invoice, a well-tracked system provides information about repayment terms. A significant source of working capital used to finance inventory and receivables, some invoices may carry a penalty if not paid by due date. These rates are normally in excess of traditionally borrowed funds.

Accounts Payable Turnover Ratio

This ratio is calculated by dividing the total dollars of purchase by the total dollars of accounts payable. To quantify in days, you may divide 365 (number of days per year) by the ratio. This number is used as a comparison with similar companies as well as with previous periods within the business. When the days increase, accounts are being paid on a less timely basis. This may be an indication that working capital is being financed by trade credit that is meant as a short-term strategy, not permanent financing.

Accounts Receivable

Maintained as a subledger, this is the list of customers who have purchased goods or products from the company on a credit basis. The amount of outstanding credit is shown on the balance sheet as an asset. A receivable represents incoming cash flow, and the timing may be established by a receivable aging.

Accounts Receivable Turnover Ratio

This ratio is calculated by dividing the total dollars in purchases by the outstanding dollars of accounts receivable. It may be quantified in days by dividing by 365. This management tool is used to compare with peer companies and to highlight trends. If the number of days increase, it could mean that collection activities have not been sufficient and cash flow will be slower, possibly causing a cash crunch.

Accrual Basis Accounting

This method recognizes income at the time it is earned, and expense at the time it is incurred. This matches the revenue and expense to a fixed accounting period and allows for comparisons to be made period to period.

Accrued Expenses

These are expenses that are anticipated but not yet due such as taxes incurred during one month but payable at a later time. Other payroll expense such as vacation pay may also be stated as accrued. Accruing expenses will produce a more accurate statement of current business conditions.

Amortization

The process of allocating a portion of the total amount over a fixed period. In a long-term loan, the principal will be allocated over the life of the loan. This will show the amount of the payment applied to interest expense as well as principal reduction over the life of the loan.

On the expense side, the total cost of acquisition or development of a major long-term project will be allocated over the useful life of the project.

Assets

The total cost of any tangible property and property rights less any reserves set aside for depreciation. Hard assets may not reflect any appreciation in value that is not strictly quantifiable under current accounting principles.

Asset Purchase

When purchasing a business, buying only certain identified and specific assets, not the corporate common stock.

Bad Debts

Unpaid obligations that are deemed uncollectible for a variety of reasons. These may have been pursued through collection activities or not, but they are written off accounts receivable to give an accurate reflection of financial status.

Balance Sheet

The summary of assets, liabilities, and net worth of a business at the end of a monthly or yearly accounting period. Balance sheets include current assets such as cash, accounts receivable, and inventory, as well as long-term assets such as property and equipment. Liabilities are listed as current such as accounts payable and current loan amounts, as well as long-term portions of loans, mortgages, and notes.

Book Value

Value of an asset shown on the balance sheet listed at cost and then reduced by total accumulated depreciation. Accelerated depreciation schedules may reduce value to less than current market value.

Bulk Transfer

Article 6 under the Uniform Commercial Code (UCC), which regulates the sale and transfer of more than 50 percent of a company's assets. Under this article, notification of all creditors is required in advance of completion of such a sale and transfer. This is meant to prevent any fraud from taking place in a business sale.

Business Plan

The written document used to describe what the business does, its market strategy, sources of revenue, and projected outcomes. Written before a business begins, it should be updated annually.

Capital

The worth of a company as determined by the total amount of all assets less all outstanding liabilities.

Cash Basis Accounting

This method recognizes revenue when the money is received and expense at the time that payment is made. There is no match of revenue against expense in a fixed period, so comparison on a period-to-period basis is not possible. This system provides less financial control since unpaid expenses are not recognized.

Cash Flow

The difference between the cash at the beginning of a period to the cash at the end of a period. Cash flow may be increased by the sale of assets or the acquisition of new debt. Cash flow may be decreased by large purchases or principal debt payment.

Cash Flow Statement

There are several different types, the basic one being simply the measure of cash in and out of the business. Most important as a management tool is the operating cash flow statement that measures inflow of revenue versus the outflow of expense and does not reflect cash reserves or borrowings.

Chart of Accounts

The numerical list of all sources of revenue and expenses in the company's operating business that are used to organize and track all financial transactions.

Collateral

The tangible assets of a company or a third party or both that are pledged and encumbered for the payment of a loan. Although some collateral such as stocks, CDs, or money market accounts are under the control of the lender, most collateral such as equipment, inventory, and accounts receivable remain in the possession of the borrower. Rights, however, remain in the control of the secured lender.

Compensating Balances

These balances on deposit by the borrower are normally the operating accounts that are maintained by the lender. The lender will desire a certain average daily balance to partially compensate for a special rate of interest charged on a loan. Some loan fees may be waived by lenders to borrowers who maintain a high level of compensating balances.

Confession of Judgment

This describes a clause in many loans that permit the lender to record a lien on record against all assets of the borrower without having to bring suit against the borrower in court. This is normally exercised only when there has been a default. In the states that permit this clause, banks often use it because it saves them time and money. If the "confession of judgment" clause contains the phrase "as of any terms," the bank can record the note without any default much the same as it would record any mortgage.

Cosigner

Any signator to a note, beyond the primary signator, is a cosigner who is fully obligated to all clauses of the note until it is paid.

Covenant Not to Compete

Agreement between buyer and seller that prevents previous owner from competing in a similar business for a period or in a specified geographic area.

Credit Memo

Source document required to back up any adjustment made to customer invoice lowering its value.

Credits

Credits always appear on the right-hand side of the general ledger. A credit will increase items on the revenue side as well as on the liability side.

Current Assets

These are the assets that are in cash or expected to be turned into cash within one accounting period (one year) such as inventory and accounts receivable. They will normally not include items such as notes receivable from officers since these may not be paid to zero during a specific period.

Current Liabilities

These are the corresponding liabilities, that is, those due within one accounting period (one year). These would include all accounts payable; the current portions of any long-term loans; and any accrued but unpaid items such as taxes, insurance, or benefits. Operating lease payments will not be listed on the balance sheet.

Debit

Listed on the left side of the general ledger, a debit increases the asset account and the expense account.

Debt

The amount of money owed to others, either formally (by written agreement) or not. Some debt is secured by the pledging of assets and the filing of liens under the Uniform Commercial Code. Others such as vendor credit are considered unsecured since no asset is backing the obligation.

Depreciation

The conversion of the cost of an asset into an expense expressing the useable life of the item covered. Set up over a fixed period in a depreciation schedule according to current tax regulations. Once an item has been fully depreciated, it no longer is carried on the books of the company as having any asset value.

The depreciation can be made in equal amounts over the useful life, known as straight line depreciation, or taken more in the early years, known as accelerated depreciation.

The balance sheet will show the asset at its original cost and then the reserve for depreciation resulting in the net asset value. This number reflects book value, not necessarily actual value.

Debt-to-Equity Ratio

Banks rely heavily on this number, which is calculated by dividing debt by equity. Increasing ratios, more debt in relation to equity, means that the company is being financed by creditors rather than by its own positive cash flow.

Direct Costs

Normally the costs of material and labor that are directly attributable to the level of sales or production. May also include the costs of direct subcontractors. Also referred to as variable costs because they rise as volume increases and drop as it decreases. Total revenue less direct costs results in the gross profit from operations.

Due Diligence

The period during which a buyer under contract to purchase the business conducts an investigation into the company's financial condition and operations. Financial statements and their backup documents are scrutinized and verified, and tax and public records are checked for accuracy. Physical inventory is taken and all equipment is checked. Leases and loans are verified as well for balances.

Equity

Referred to as net worth, this is the difference between the total assets of an entity and the total liabilities. Shown on the liability side of the ledger, it may be thought of as the amount owed to owners since theoretically, this would be disbursed to them if assets were sold and liabilities paid.

Equity Financing

Raising capital through any instrument that carries equity risk and reward such as stock. Some debt instruments will carry convertible features that allow them to be redeemed for stocks. Since there is an additional risk to this type of financing, the cost is higher than more traditional ways of raising capital.

General Ledger

The central listing of all activities posted on the subledgers. This covers all financial transitions and may be used to audit activities that may have been incorrectly posted.

Gross Profit

This number is derived from the gross (total) sales revenue less any direct costs such as labor, material, and subcontracting that is directly attributable to that sale.

Also referred to as operating profits, the gross profit represents the money available to pay overhead expense and taxes, and to generate a net profit for the company to retain as working capital.

Guaranty (Guarantee)

The document that represents the agreement by a third party to pay all or part of the borrower's obligation to a specifically named creditor. The pledge is for payment of any or all of the installments not made in a timely manner or the total debt if accelerated, including principal, interest, and perhaps, collection costs. A number of different types of guarantees may hold the guarantor not only responsible for a single note but all borrowings of the company (a continuing guarantee).

Income Statement

The document generated monthly or annually that defines the earnings of a company by stating all relevant income and all expenses that have been generated by that revenue.

Indirect Costs

Expenses not directly related to sales, including items such as rent; utilities; and administrative over-

head such as office salaries, professional fees, and selling expense. Called overhead or fixed expense because this cost continues regardless of the sales level of the company.

Inventory

These are the assets held for resale, which may be finished goods, works in progress, or raw materials. When valuing work in progress, there is the added value of direct labor involved, which may increase the real worth of inventory yet not be realized until work is complete and goods are released.

Inventory Turnover

This ratio is calculated by dividing the total costs of material in costs of goods sold by the current inventory. Decreasing ratios (fewer turns per year) may indicate that there are slow-selling items in current inventory, which puts a pressure on cash since it will not turn to cash in current cycle.

Invoice

The source document required as backup to any sale that is posted as income or accounts receivable. Hard copies should be retained for at least three years.

Journal Entry

Transaction entered on a subledger and into the general ledger that includes the date of transaction, account number, and which accounts were debited and credited as a result of the transaction.

Labor Costs

There are two types of labor, direct and indirect. The first is related to production and performance of products or services, and the latter is related to the work involved in distribution, sale, and administrative duties involved in operating the business. Labor costs include any taxes and benefits that are incurred as the result of the payment of wages.

Letter of Credit

Issued by a bank, this document using very specific language is issued to suppliers or vendors as a guarantee for payment with the bank standing as guarantor rather than the customer. Often used for international transactions, a letter of credit promises payment once goods are received by the customer and may be drawn by the beneficiary. This instrument allows a company to import goods without tying up capital while they are in transit.

Line of Credit

An instrument of credit issued by a bank or other lender for short-term (one year) capital needs. Most lines are revolving; that is, they can be drawn down, repaid, and drawn on again. A nonrevolving line may be drawn only once.

A line of credit should be paid to zero at least once during the year since its purpose is short-term financing of inventory and receivables. Although they are granted for one year, they may be renewed on a regular basis.

Liquidity

The ability to pay obligations as they become due from cash or the normal turnover of inventory or receivables into cash. Long-term assets (property and equipment) are not measured since they provide no cash from which to retire current debts unless they are sold outright and become a cash item.

Loan Agreement

This document covers some short-term but all longer-term loans, and it is the basis of the agreement between the borrower and the lender. The rules that govern the borrowing are known as loan covenants, and they are used to determine if the borrower is in compliance with the credit requirements of the loan.

Even when a loan is fully current, failure to meet all the loan covenants will subject the loan to being in default. Some of the typical covenants are the timely submission of financial information; payment of all obligations, particularly taxes; and maintaining adequate insurance. Minimum equity levels may also be required.

Most loan agreements will allow the borrower to cure certain elements of a potential default before the loan is called and payments are escalated.

Note

This is the actual document of the debt of a loan, including the amount, interest rate, maturity date, and parties obligated to pay. Notes are quite simple, but there may be additional loan documents such as a security agreement and the loan agreement itself. A note may be sold or assigned to a third party, and the borrower becomes obligated to the new holder.

Overhead

The indirect or fixed costs of operating the business ranging from rent to administrative to marketing costs. The majority of these costs stay fixed regardless of sales volume although a few that are sales related may be considered semivariable.

Post

The act of entering a financial transaction on a subledger as well as the general ledger. In a dual entry system, each transaction will be credited to one account and debited from another.

Profit and Loss Statement

Prepared annually and often monthly and quarterly as well, this is the report of the income and expense, and the results as expressed in profit or loss. This report identifies by category all income whether from product sale or other activities and reports all direct and indirect costs. Operating (gross) profits are listed, as are the net (before tax) profit.

Prime Rate

The prime rate is not an official benchmark that governs the lending rate of different institutions. Each is free to set its own although that is seldom done since most banks follow the lead of the larger institutions. This rate is based on the current federal rate for funds, which goes up and down according to the Federal Reserve Board decisions.

Pro-forma

May be created in the form of both a profit and loss statement and a cash flow statement. This is a prediction of financial results in future periods based in part on historical happenings and in part on anticipated new income or expense.

Rates of Interest (Fixed and Variable)

The interest rate that is in effect at the start of a loan may not always be the interest charged during the life of the loan. Only a fixed rate loan has one rate during the entire term, but this normally is limited to five years or less. The only long-term loans that are fixed are mortgages, and these loans are sold off through Fannie Mae or Freddie Mac, which relieves the bank of the interest rate risk.

A variable rate loan has a floating rate pegged to an index such as the prime rate and goes up and down according to that rate. Some loans may have semifixed rates for one year and then they float, and they may also have a minimum floor as well as a maximum ceiling.

Retained Earnings

Profits that are not distributed through dividends but are left in the business and carried on the books as retained earnings. This number is reduced over time by any losses.

Secured Loan

A loan that has assets pledged as collateral that may be liquidated if the loan is not paid according to agreement.

Subledger

Used to record transactions of revenue and expense items to accounts payable and accounts receivable journals. Subledgers are posted to the general ledger as well to track all financial transactions.

Subordination Agreement

This agreement between creditors covers the priority of each one on all or certain assets of the borrower. This may be necessitated when one lender has filed financing statements (VCC-1) on all assets of a borrower and a second lender is asked to make a loan. The primary lender may release some assets as security for the additional capital. This also comes up when an officer has a note payable to a closely held company and the bank requires that the note be subordinated to its claim regardless of the timing.

Trade Discount

A 1 to 2 percent price reduction offered by some vendors for prompt payment usually covering ten days.

Uniform Commercial Code (UCC)

When a lender wishes to perfect his or her secured interest in certain assets, he or she may do so in a number of ways. One is to take possession as with stocks and bonds that are held as security. Another is to file an encumbrance on a title such as a vehicle. Where there is a variety of assets in the possession and control of the borrower, the lender will file a Uniform Commercial Code financing statement with the secretary of state where the borrower is located. These financing statements are normally signed by the borrower at the time the loan closes.

Unsecured Loan

A loan that has no underlying collateral pledged to the borrower to offset any losses in case of default. It normally carries a higher interest rate than those loans secured by collateral.

Venture Capital

Funds flowing into a company in the form of an investment rather than a loan. Controlled by an individual or small group known as venture capitalists, these investments require a high rate of return, and they are secured by a substantial ownership position in the business. Equity interest transfers back to original owners when all loan payments or premiums are paid.

Working Capital

The difference between current assets and current liabilities, which is an indication of liquidity and the ability of the company to meet current obligations. The assumption is that current assets will turn into cash concurrently with obligations such as payables and loans coming due.

The variable here is the collectibility of current receivables and the saleability of inventory, which may mean that a company is less liquid in reality than it appears to be on paper.

Working Capital Ratio

This number is calculated by dividing current assets by current liabilities. A decreasing ratio indicates that working capital is being reduced by losses, the purchase of long-term assets, or distribution to owners. This tool may be used to compare peer companies and to monitor trends.

Find more on this topic by visiting BusinessTown.com

Developed by Adams Media, **BusinessTown.com** is a free informational site for entrepreneurs, small business owners, and operators. It provides a comprehensive guide for planning, starting, growing, and managing a small business.

Visitors may access hundreds of articles addressing dozens of business topics, participate in forums, as well as connect to additional resources around the Web. **BusinessTown.com** is easily navigated and provides assistance to small businesses and start-ups. The material covers beginning basic issues as well as the more advanced topics.

✓ **Accounting**
Basic, Credit & Collections, Projections, Purchasing/Cost Control

✓ **Advertising**
Magazine, Newspaper, Radio, Television, Yellow Pages

✓ **Business Opportunities**
Ideas for New Businesses, Business for Sale, Franchises

✓ **Business Plans**
Creating Plans & Business Strategies

✓ **Finance**
Getting Money, Money Problem Solutions

✓ **Letters & Forms**
Looking Professional, Sample Letters & Forms

✓ **Getting Started**
Incorporating, Choosing a Legal Structure

✓ **Hiring & Firing**
Finding the Right People, Legal Issues

✓ **Home Business**
Home Business Ideas, Getting Started

✓ **Internet**
Getting Online, Put Your Catalog on the Web

✓ **Legal Issues**
Contracts, Copyrights, Patents, Trademarks

✓ **Managing a Small Business**
Growth, Boosting Profits, Mistakes to Avoid, Competing with the Giants

✓ **Managing People**
Communications, Compensation, Motivation, Reviews, Problem Employees

✓ **Marketing**
Direct Mail, Marketing Plans, Strategies, Publicity, Trade Shows

✓ **Office Setup**
Leasing, Equipment, Supplies

✓ **Presentations**
Know Your Audience, Good Impression

✓ **Sales**
Face to Face, Independent Reps, Telemarketing

✓ **Selling a Business**
Finding Buyers, Setting a Price, Legal Issues

✓ **Taxes**
Employee, Income, Sales, Property Use

✓ **Time Management**
Can You Really Manage Time?

✓ **Travel & Maps**
Making Business Travel Fun

✓ **Valuing a Business**
Simple Valuation Guidelines

http://www.businesstown.com